IF YOUR BACK'S
NOT BENT

IF YOUR BACK'S NOT BENT

THE ROLE OF THE CITIZENSHIP EDUCATION PROGRAM IN THE CIVIL RIGHTS MOVEMENT

Dorothy F. Cotton

Foreword by Andrew Young
Introduction by Vincent Harding

ATRIA BOOKS

New York • London • Toronto • Sydney • New Delhi

ATRIA BOOKS

A Division of Simon & Schuster, Inc.
1230 Avenue of the Americas
New York, NY 10020

First Atria Books hardcover edition September 2012

ATRIA BOOKS and colophon are trademarks of Simon & Schuster, Inc.

Unless otherwise noted in the caption, all photographs are courtesy of the author.

For information about special discounts for bulk purchases, please contact Simon & Schuster Special Sales at 1-866-506-1949 or business@simonandschuster.com.

The Simon & Schuster Speakers Bureau can bring authors to your live event. For more information or to book an event, contact the Simon & Schuster Speakers Bureau at 1-866-248-3049 or visit our website at www.simonspeakers.com.

Designed by Dana Sloan

Manufactured in the United States of America

10   9   8   7   6   5   4   3   2   1

Library of Congress Cataloging-in-Publication Data
Cotton, Dorothy F.
   If your back's not bent : the role of the Citizenship Education Program in the civil rights movement / Dorothy F. Cotton.
      p.   cm.
   1. Cotton, Dorothy F., 1930– 2. African American women civil rights workers—Biography. 3. African American women educators—Biography. 4. Civil rights movements—United States—History—20th century. 5. African Americans—Civil rights—History—20th century. 6. Citizenship Education Program—History. 7. Southern Christian Leadership Conference—History. 8. United States—Race relations—History—20th century. I. Title.
   E185.97.C83A3   2012
   323.092—dc23   2012004463
   [B]

ISBN 978-0-7432-9683-0
ISBN 978-1-4391-8742-5 (ebook)

TO MY FATHER, CLAUDE DANIEL FOREMAN, *who "served his country" as a navy man in the Second World War only to live through the pain of being refused entry to a restaurant in Atlanta, Georgia. He was with three of his White navy buddies; all were in uniform. They stayed at the restaurant to have their meal without him. Daddy said he would never go back to Atlanta.*

How I would love to say, "Daddy, you can go back now. My special friend Andrew Young has been the mayor for two terms. You will be welcomed."

He didn't live to see the changes in race relations that his daughter struggled to help bring about.

And to the many hundreds of people whose names are never mentioned as participants in the civil rights movement. These people were abused and some died as they struggled to change the system that did not acknowledge their rights as citizens.

THE REST OF THE WAY

I went into the silence
    to note what I could hear.
There were voices loud and clear
    yet no one was near.

Perhaps not voices but SPIRIT
There to cheer me
To cheer me on.

I calmed myself
with open mind and heart.
I felt a surge of strength.
Voices came that made things clear:
I have plotted a journey for you
Do not hold back; go!
    Onward and up.

I will light your path.
    The blocks in the road
    Will make you bold,
Will open your heart.

    Your desire to heal will
Make you strong
    Will clear your mind.
In the silence you will
be infused with a Spirit;

a Spirit—readily available to
one such as you.
One who is ready, willing, open,
Hungry for Truth!

You are anointed by my Spirit
    Know this.

As you are infused with my Spirit
    You will know love,
You will show love,
    and cause it to stir
    in all you encounter.

When you feel unclear
    just hang in there;
I will light your way.
I will give you clarity of purpose;
I will guide you to where your
    skills are needed.
Imprinting on the minds and hearts
Of those you touch
    You will gain the Spirit of love
    the ability to see those
    you touch.
An openness to great and
    healing values,
    They will be yours
    to share.
I will remove walls of hatred
and intolerance

a new era will arise
a new country will appear.
You will be called to
let your light shine
Showing others the way forward
on this journey,
this blessed journey.

—Dorothy F. Cotton

CONTENTS

Foreword by Andrew Young   xiii

Introduction by Vincent Harding   xv

Prologue   1

1. Sharing the Prize   7

2. When the Spark Was Lit   23

3. "There's Your Ready Girl"   39

4. People Get Ready, There's a "Change" A-comin'   51

5. Meeting Dr. King   73

6. Grew Like Topsy   91

7. Why Not You?   111

8. "The Cobwebs Commenced A-movin' from My Brain"   125

9. The Reason I Sing This Song   147

10. The Essence of Nonviolence Is Love   161

11. Dr. King and the Team of Wild Horses   185

12. On into the Twentieth Century via Birmingham   207

13. "The Spirit Was Movin' All Over This Land"   225

14. Growing Challenges to Our Approach in
     Working for Change   241

15. The King Is Dead! What in the World
     Do I Do Now?   255

16. After the Assassination   271

17. Legacy: Revisiting the Dorchester Center   279

     Epilogue: Going Forward in the
     Twenty-first Century   297

     Acknowledgments   307

     Appendix A: Letter to Martin   311

     Appendix B: The Dorothy Cotton Institute   319

FOREWORD

by Andrew Young

THE CIVIL RIGHTS movement had not yet discovered women's rights when Dorothy Cotton joined the Southern Christian Leadership Conference in 1960. Dorothy came with her Boston University master's, teaching credentials from Virginia State University, and a personality bubbling like fine champagne to be the only woman executive in the recently formed organization and was determined not to be intimidated by the gathering of young, self-important egomaniacs who became the staff that would ultimately change the South and impact the planet.

Dorothy was the right woman in the right place at the right time, so Wyatt Tee Walker, the newly appointed executive director, invited her to join the staff as education director. There were very few of us who had academic, administrative, and movement experience in 1960, so Dorothy was charged with developing a department that would train new leaders for this burgeoning movement and ensure that the disciplines of nonviolence and good citizenship prevailed over the anger, frustration, and bitterness that tended to dominate the Black community.

As the staff grew, Dorothy assumed a very natural role as everybody's sister. The men began to relate to one another through her. The precise enunciation and elocution of her speech demanded that her opinions earn respect. Her charm and effusive personality inspired admiration and also kept potential male admirers at bay; her quick wit crushed many egos.

The Education Department soon became the Citizenship Education Program, which originally set out to train two hundred leaders across the South. Each country or rural village had someone that everyone respected, "the Wise Elder," though they were often young people. They were people of courage and insight, the natural leaders, people with Ph.D. minds who often had never received much formal education. These were the leaders who became the foundation of the nonviolent movement.

Andrew Young and me. (Photograph courtesy of Clayborne Carson)

INTRODUCTION

by Vincent Harding

At this powerful moment in the life of our nation it is clear that Dorothy Cotton's important—and long-awaited—memoir opens a crucial opportunity for us to wrestle with several essential matters concerning our past, present, and future engagement in the continuing national experiment known as the quest for a just and compassionate multiracial democracy in America. Indeed, at the heart of Dorothy's account is the story of her crucial role as director of education for the Southern Christian Leadership Conference (SCLC), the freedom movement organization led by Martin Luther King Jr. That was the rich, challenging, and boundless context in which my friend played such a central part in developing SCLC's Citizenship Education Program (CEP) in the 1960s, leading one of the movement's most important contributions to the continuing American search for "a more perfect union."

Remembering her early years in the SCLC setting, Dorothy reminds us that "our work with SCLC was not just a job, it was a life commitment," one that took her all around the South, working with adult grassroots leaders and encouraging brave children and youth from Birmingham to St. Augustine to stand firmly against the deadly threats of Klan members and the brutal forces of "law enforcement," often accompanying the endangered children at great risk to her own life. And it is not surprising that Dorothy had no idea at first that her participation in the great struggle unfolding would completely consume her and become her life's work. Now, half a century after that beginning period, she continues to carry out her work by sharing with us in this book many lessons we need to learn as new generations (and their unrelenting elders) continue the great struggle "of creating a more perfect union."

For instance, there are the extraordinary lessons embodied in Dorothy herself. We need to explore carefully how and why it was that this southern-born motherless child of a poor, widowed, uneducated Black tobacco worker came to blossom magnificently as a deeply committed, broadly educated leader in the unending struggle to transform her segregated, White-dominated nation into the multi-racial democratic community she believed it could be.

And even as we ponder the creative possibilities her extraordinary life opens for all of us—especially the young and deeply disadvantaged, and even as we recognize the likelihood that there are Dorothy Cottons hidden everywhere (she surely saw them on the streets of Birmingham and Memphis and on the beaches of St. Augustine), waiting to be nurtured and encouraged into seeking and discovering their best selves, their magnificent capacities for leadership in the transformation of our nation—there is still much more to discover and explore in the pages of this important work.

Dorothy's work with the Citizenship Education Program and her account here of that transformative process reflect the most important challenges in our own current "great struggle" to expand, deepen, and authenticate democracy in America. This effective program of adult grassroots leadership education originally grew out of a fascinating collaboration between the European-inspired Highlander Folk School in Monteagle, Tennessee, and Esau Jenkins, a wise and courageous grassroots community organizer among the African American people of the Sea Island communities, located off the coasts of Georgia and South Carolina, in the 1950s. Over time it became the central element of SCLC's grassroots educational work, a program that would eventually serve the political, educational, and spiritual needs of thousands of Black southerners who came to occupy the heart of the freedom movement. Generally these were persons who had long been formally and informally educated to be underpaid servants and hapless victims of the White ruling classes of their communities. Instead, Dorothy and the CEP process opened very different alternatives, encouraging the participants to actively re-vision themselves and create their radically new roles in the necessary transformation of their communities, their nation, and their world.

In carrying out this crucial task, Dorothy worked closely with Andrew Young (who later became mayor of Atlanta and then U.S. ambassador to the United Nations) and with Septima Clark, one of the exemplary, wise, courageous, and compassionate mother-teachers of the freedom movement. Under Dorothy's direct leadership, and working with other SCLC staff, this trio successfully developed the powerful model for an early "pedagogy of the oppressed," a movement-shaped educational program that would help prepare "ordinary" women and men to become extraordinarily creative and courageous in the work that is meant to be the hallmark vocation of all American citizens—creating a more perfect union, often a dangerous calling in Dorothy's time of being "swept up" into the struggle.

As she tells the story of these CEP workshops, usually a five-day gathering held in settings near the coasts of Georgia or South Carolina, Dorothy is clearly still deeply moved by the remarkable transformation she saw (and felt) unfolding in the lives of the women and men who came to the sessions fresh from southern communities where they were engaged in the difficult and risky struggles for the creation of democratic, human communities of hope. She recalls the sometimes harrowing, often humorous stories they shared, the delicious home-cooked meals they ate together, and the exciting role-playing experiences they created. Significantly, she reports on the palpable excitement and determination the participants exhibited when they studied the Constitution of the United States for the first time and realized they could appropriate that ambiguous document for their own democratic uses as they fought to create a new America.

As an occasional participant in those CEP sessions of the 1960s, I was glad to be reminded here by Dorothy of the extraordinary power of the church-bred community singing that literally rocked the gathering places and provided the cohesive force for almost every workshop. It was, in addition, a beautiful experience to recall with her in these pages what it meant to see (and hear) human faces, voices, lives—and bodily stances—all literally transformed by the new visions the participants were creating for themselves and their communities, even as they boldly and loudly sang, "Ain't gonna let nobody turn me 'round."

And it was great to be reminded of how much everyone enjoyed the long and lively nighttime social dance sessions and volleyball games that often kept the CEP participants up, especially those occasional times when Dorothy's beloved friend and leader, Martin King, was able to attend the sessions and to amaze the folks with his skills and his good-humored enthusiasm on the dance floor and the volleyball court. (King's words to the participants in one of the more formal CEP sessions provided the title for the book: "Nobody can ride your back if your back's not bent.")

I confess that I was tempted to long for more details in the book concerning those powerfully transformative CEP workshops that Dorothy was so centrally involved in creating and guiding. But what I eventually realized was that the greatest teaching value of the Citizenship Education Program will never arise from even the most detailed stories Dorothy can tell us here. Rather, it is now up to those of us who claim the powerful identity of "we the people" in the twenty-first century to interrogate ourselves and our communities about the fundamental implications of such a program and such an experience for our time, our lives, and the lives of our grandchildren.

So, if Dorothy's story prompts us to recognize that it is only since the 1960s that the explicit goal of creating a just and inclusive multinational, multiracial, multicultural democratic society has begun to be a conscious moral and political commitment of our country, then we may recognize a powerful, humbling truth: in the light of such a challenging goal, we are still a developing nation, still searching, stumbling, trying to envision "a more perfect union" for our time and place, still trying to decide if we really want to join Dorothy's continuing "great struggle." (Perhaps we may begin to realize that we are not yet—and may never be—qualified to instruct a magnificently diverse world in the ways of democratic community, certainly not qualified to send our instructions via drones, "smart" bombs, or arrogant threats.)

In the light of this still developing situation in our own land, we may, we *must* ask ourselves what is the education necessary and appropriate for developing citizens who are prepared to participate fully and creatively in that great struggle for a multiracial democracy that Dorothy discovered and continues to pursue as her life's work. How do we prepare ourselves and our children for the creative task that Langston Hughes described as the necessary work "to make America again," the task Martin Luther King envisioned when he repeatedly said, "America, you must be born again"? Beginning with the youngest children and moving into the lives of our increasingly long-lived and active corps of elders, what is "a citizenship education" for our time? Where and how can it best take place? How do we insert the goal of nurturing creative, responsible, visionary, and compassionate builders of democratic communities at the heart of both our formal and informal educational agenda in America? What is the future of a living democracy in America if these questions are not at the heart of our ongoing national debate concerning the future of our nation? (Is creating the capacity "to compete with the Chinese" an adequate humanizing, democratizing purpose for the lives of our children and of ourselves?)

Because Dorothy Cotton faithfully and creatively continues to give her life to the democracy-building work that she began a half century ago, these questions for the present are not unfamiliar to her. Indeed, near the end of her book, she makes a telling connection between her work in the 1960s and the work we must do now. She quotes the contemporary words of Robert Leming of the Center for Civic Education, words that her life helped to create. Leming says, "Democracies do not just sustain themselves; they must be nurtured by engaged, knowledgeable citizens. Engaged, knowledgeable citizens are not born; they are developed through citizenship education."

Along with Leming's words, Dorothy's life and work steadily, insistently push us to recognize that we have come to this demanding moment in our nation's history not to "take our country back" (as some would say), not to resurrect a partly nostalgic but largely racist and exploitative past. Instead she points us to the exciting, life-giving task of creating the America that has not yet existed, a multiracial, just, compassionate, and ecologically responsible democracy, a nation with a creative, collaborative, and nondominating view of our role in the world.

Through her CEP story Dorothy reminds us that such a work of democratic creativity cannot be carried forward without women, men, and young people who are prepared for and committed to the great struggle for the development of democratic America. Moreover, she tells us that this is the work of many lifetimes, which neither begins nor ends with our own, but which also can never find its best democratic direction without us, "we the people," we the amazingly diverse people who carry within ourselves great gifts and resources that constantly surprise the world, beginning with ourselves. How shall we take seriously the declaration of June Jordan that "we are the ones we've been waiting for"? How shall we "occupy" every educational setting from Sunday schools to prison cells and college seminar rooms with this vision? How shall we envision and create the new settings that do not yet exist?

In the African American communities of our country we have long sung a church song that ends with the words "We'll never turn back. We'll go on and see what the end will be." Now, for all of us in all the diverse communities filled with creators of the new America, we surely need to continue the pledge to go on; but now we are planning to *create* what the end *must* be, starting now.

Fortunately, on that irreversible creative path, we are able to continue to call on the large and living wisdom of Dorothy Cotton. At the very close of her book, she opens up a generous, personal invitation to all of us who are seeking to create the education for democracy that speaks to the new realities and deep needs of our time. We should certainly do our best to read and accept Dorothy's invitation, and go on, with her—and with all the others who want to create what the end will be. In other words, let us occupy democratic hope with one of its great creators.

IF YOUR BACK'S
NOT BENT

PROLOGUE

A s I REFLECT on the journey I've been on and talk with others who were also committed to the civil rights movement, I sense that many have come to the same conclusion as I: We were open to the spirit and it was this infusion of spirit that caused us to commit to this special path for our lives. We were ready to take the steps we took. I'm not sure any one of us could say in any certain intellectual terms why we did so at that time or how we evolved. But I accept now that there is a certain spirit that permeates the very being of each of us and opens us to guidance.

I experienced a kind of alienation from some of my blood relatives when I confessed my sadness for having "left the clan." A very perceptive teacher once said to me, "Even if you had stayed you would have been weird." I laughed at his use of the word *weird*. I know there was humor in what he said, but he meant it nonetheless. I accepted the truth in what he said. As a child I had the sense that "one day I will have to leave." And without a blueprint, a clear way as to how I would leave and to where I would go. I didn't have a specific answer to where—or even how. But doors began to open for me, showing the direction.

I have come, in the words of the Negro National Anthem, "over a way that with blood and with tears has been watered." Yet the path on which I found myself has been incredibly enriching, providing opportunities to see many places around this wonderful yet challenging world, and this opportunity has helped me see and feel at a very deep level the possibility of our connectedness as human beings.

The civil rights movement was a significant milestone on the journey to a better world. Though we have much further to go, we have covered some basic steps; if we had not taken them, we would not now see the possibilities of change, of progress toward our ultimate goal—our goal of learning to live together, to relate to one another in peace and joy and celebration of our wonderful diversity. The possibility of seeing the planet as a bouquet of many flowers comes to mind.

I have been asked if I saw a connection between the recent Wall Street protests and the civil rights protests of the 1960s. Though I can feel some pleasure in the fact that many people in many cities—and perhaps especially many young people—are responding to what they determine to be grossly unfair economic practices, I don't believe they are able to articulate what the protests are about and specifically what they are demanding. I find myself struggling to determine the vision, the goal of the protesters. I reflect on the teaching, the methodology we used in the 1950s and 1960s. I sense that many of the Wall Street protesters are just angry—and for good reason. A major difference between the protest actions we are seeing now and the protests staged by SCLC and other organizations in the time in which I worked is that we could articulate very clearly what our grievances were, in no uncertain terms. Not a single African American person nor any of our White allies was unable to state or to discuss fully what our grievances were. I find that many people struggle to try to determine the goal of the Wall Street protesters today, but massive numbers of people cannot state in a focused way the goals, the program for change. I reflect on the teaching methods we used in the modern civil rights movement and I know that I and many others could discuss with anyone who wanted to listen why we were organizing, why we were protesting.

We were clear as to the goals we had set for ourselves, for our neighborhoods, cities, towns, and our country. Everyone knew them—even those who disagreed. We articulated through many forums our determination to tear down the walls of segregation and end racial oppression. Of course we can continue to go back further "over the way that with blood and tears was watered," but the part of our freedom struggle starting in the 1950s and 1960s is my reference point here.

We explained to the country, to the world, piece by piece, section by section, unjust law by unjust law, habits and practices enforced as rigidly as laws on the statute books; we explained to them all; told what those things did to us and measured their impact on us—citizens of the country. Forced by violence and other extraordinary means, we African American people often internalized a negative assessment of ourselves. It was like having to erase some erroneous tapes.

The goal of the Citizenship Education Program (CEP) was to provide a setting where these "tapes" could be erased. As the forty, fifty, sixty people studied and worked together for five days, they were transformed, and the culture was changed, relationships changed. Our country had to change because "we the people" had changed—changed our concept of ourselves. We claimed the words of our founding documents as applying to *all citizens.*

Participants in these CEP training sessions were charged with a responsibility when they returned to their homes. They were to help others understand the goals of this movement—our movement—for change, and why they felt miserable so much of the time. Participants learned to change what was wrong after making it very clear why it was wrong. Those who "got it" were supported by our organization, by our staff, and by our leaders at every level. These monthly five-day training sessions were further supported and enhanced by weekend "refresher courses."

I'm not sure one can effectively protest against Wall Street. If the intent is to ensure that people at every level—economic, educational, social, political—clearly understand the problem, success is ensured when the source of the problem and the problem itself are defined. The ability to articulate the problem so massive numbers of people can come to understand it and realize its connection to individual and group circumstances is basic.

Having a voice, a spokesperson, emerge is fundamental. Having a leader who puts it all together for the body politic is important. I highlight here the fact that Dr. King emerged—his voice was heard explaining, challenging, teaching, justifying protest actions—but he did not start the actions. The people were energized; the people acted. He did not tell Rosa Parks to keep her seat; he did not tell the four students in Greensboro, North Carolina, to take seats at the Woolworth's lunch counter where Black people were not allowed to sit (though we could shop at every other counter in the store). He did not tell Fannie Lou Hamer and Annie Devine to demand the right to vote in the Mississippi Delta. He did not tell the Reverend Fred Shuttlesworth to take his bold action in Birmingham, Alabama, which was the catalyst for a hotbed of protest action and is still talked about around the world. (Rev. Shuttlesworth declared that he would test the *Brown v. Board of Education* ruling, which clearly stated the goal of ending segregation in public schools.) These people and so many more who had taken similar actions were scattered broadly across the land—most visibly in the southern and border states. People took actions that connected with those of other people, in other places.

4

In his early essay "Pilgrimage to Nonviolence," Dr. King states very clearly that he did not start the Montgomery Bus Boycott or other protest actions. It is important to note that "the people" did it. The local people in many places caught the spirit of the times. The zeitgeist was upon us.

Dr. King's voice was heard explaining, teaching, and encouraging across the area, across the country, even across the seas. He rose from what the people were doing. People saw his leadership when he was "drafted" to lead the protest against the Montgomery, Alabama, public transportation system. We heard him explaining and connecting our actions until we realized a massive *movement* had evolved. People understood his message as explaining the rightness of our cause to anyone who was critical of our actions. We had felt and suffered abuse, the denial of our citizenship rights for generations. Dr. King's powerful oratorical skills, his ability to weave together poetic, folksy, theological, and academic language, was like a gift from God. No one was left wondering what our movement was about even if they were resisting our determination to change the unjust system.

So Dr. King is honored the world over for bringing to light the message of the rightness of our cause and describing the powerful weapon of love and nonviolence that must be used to right the wrong. He explained nonviolent struggle in a way that everyone could understand and so relate to it and become part of it.

I believe this tool, this philosophy, this spirit and way of nonviolence will successfully take us to the next leg of our journey toward wholeness. I hope the study of nonviolence will become a basic part of the curriculum in our public education system. I trust that we will discover how we might understand it deeply enough such that people here and abroad can realize the power of this tool of love and compassion. I'm convinced nonviolence can be successful in working for positive change in our relations with other countries right now. I have often pondered the question "What if we could get there first, before people, young and old, are turned into suicide bombers?" *I believe that where there is a will, there is a way.*

The election of President Barack Obama is undoubtedly a result of our journey in the last four or five decades. This includes the individual and the group transformation that occurred in the people. It includes the tool, the weapon of love, as many refer to the way of nonviolence. It includes having clear goals that are easily articulated and understood.

Yet for all we see before us needing attention, I conclude that the journey is forever. Each generation is called to lead parts of it—building on what was achieved before; building on what we learned.

Let's keep going.

Let's acknowledge what we've learned, taking the spirit of positive change in all the places where we spend our time.

See my list of "Lessons." See my vision statement. See my "Letter to Martin."

Let's talk. Let's be clear about the end we seek. Let's not worry about the time it takes or how difficult the way. "Change is gonna come" if we "Hold On"!

It always does.

Chapter 1

SHARING THE PRIZE

Going to Oslo for the Nobel Peace Prize

S ITTING ON A transatlantic jet airplane with Dr. Martin Luther King Jr. en route to Oslo, Norway, where he would receive the Nobel Prize for Peace, is an experience I can't help but juxtapose with my years growing up poor on Greenleaf Street in Goldsboro, North Carolina. How could I have come so far from that small town, one of four motherless daughters of a tobacco factory worker who made nine and sometimes twelve dollars a week? When the news came on the radio that Martin had won, I fairly danced out the front door of our Auburn Avenue office excitedly exclaiming to some of our organizers standing there, "We won! We won! Dr. King is the winner of the 1964 Nobel Peace Prize!" I shared the news with people we knew in the shops and eateries, all the little business establishments along "Sweet Auburn." I'm not sure all of them even understood the enormity of this incredible honor. But the excitement escalated. I walked

Dr. King's entourage on the trip to Oslo to accept the Nobel Peace Prize.

around in a state of high exhilaration as well as in sort of a daze. I'm aware still of having felt vindicated—even more justified in the rightness of our cause. There were smiles and there were tears of joy.

My title at the Southern Christian Leadership Conference (SCLC) was Director of Education. Though we all had rather impressive titles, most of us were fully involved in every direct action and voter education campaign. My main responsibility was directing the Citizenship Education Program (CEP). When I found out that I would be accompanying Dr. King, along with almost thirty other friends and team members, transformation truly occurred in my life. The once poor little girl from Goldsboro would be among those honored to be with Martin Luther King Jr. as he and all of us were feted in

Norway's capital by Norwegian royalty and other European dignitaries.

When the news came, Martin was in the hospital, where he was spending a few days for a thorough physical examination and much-needed rest from our hectic schedule. He was exhausted. Not surprisingly, he was now under even more stress as he bore the heaviest burden of our struggle to end segregation and the abuse that was inherent in such a system. It seemed the whole burgeoning civil rights movement structure was begging for his input, his guidance, and his opinion about what to do next and how to do it. Everyone wanted him in *their* town. They wanted to experience his powerful oratory, his guidance, and the confident spirit of hope he projected. And Martin wanted to respond even as the passage of the historic Civil Rights Act of 1964 generated even more requests for his presence.

President Lyndon Johnson had signed the historic bill, and Senator Barry Goldwater, the Republican candidate for president, had opposed it. Our choice was very clear. And there was our own organizational commitment to urge people not only to vote but to continue to work to change the unjust segregation system.

Even though he was exhausted he wanted to respond. His ability to encourage and energize people was unmatched and he had accepted the *calling* to help "set at liberty those who are oppressed."

At the same time there were the rumbling noises of a few who, I believe out of jealousy of his leadership, were beginning to criticize his nonviolent approach and strategies, and, most important, the spirit and philosophy we held on to to tear down the walls of injustice. Our organization was committed to the struggle to "redeem the soul of America."

The exhaustion and this emerging negativity from others contributed to Dr. King's need to take a break, to rest and recharge. What a propitious moment for the news of his winning the Nobel Peace Prize to come to him.

Dr. King was my best friend and I wanted to share with him this moment, of his getting the wondrous news of this prestigious prize. So I soon made my way to St. Joseph's Hospital and had a long visit with him. Though we interacted regularly, sitting alone by his bed in that hospital room as he reflected is one of my most memorable times with him. He took my hand for a moment. No words. He knew why I was there. I pulled up a chair. He began to reflect on his days as a college student, in a slow, almost sad sort of way. One observation he shared I'll never forget. He talked about seeing tall, handsome "football player type" guys around the campus. He said, "I would consciously determine that I could pursue the girlfriends of such guys until I won their girlfriends away." He spoke as though he felt great guilt for this habit and others in the context of his feeling of unworthiness for such a prize. I wondered if he was questioning whether he deserved such an honor.

Though this was not to be the first time I experienced him in such a pensive mood, it was probably the time when he was most self-reflective—on his calling, his life and work. Coupled with these deep and mixed emotions was what seemed almost a sense of sadness. I was with Dr. King at an event in New York when Rabbi Abraham Joshua Heschel introduced him for the speech he was about to give. Somewhere in that introduction Rabbi Heschel referred to him as a saint. Afterward, as we were preparing to go to dinner, I asked him, "What's the matter? You seem so dejected, sad. The response to your speech was great. What are you feeling?" His response to me: "Rabbi Heschel called me a saint, and I know I'm no saint."

I told him that I had shared this exchange with Andy Young and what Andy's reply was. I've never forgotten it. Andy said, "The saints weren't saints, either!" That pretty much captured my own sense of the matter. I had read of babies found buried under nunneries. *The saints weren't saints, either!*

Dr. King was in a mood seldom seen by most of the staff, and even few of his friends were privy to this kind of sharing—the intimacy of it, and the unvarnished, total honesty. His decision to share the prize with other organizations whose goals were the same as ours at the Southern Christian Leadership Conference may have eased this guilt somewhat.

I listened to him quietly for a long time, feeling his need to reflect. If I could talk with him now I know I would remind him of something he knew at a very deep level, and that is that the God he loved uses many who are not thought of as perfect human beings. Indeed, he knew the biblical example of Paul. After all, he was a Baptist preacher.

Of course, Dr. King not only accepted the award but rose to the occasion, delivering a magnificent, incisive speech giving generous credit to all people who were struggling for basic social change and human rights—not only workers at SCLC, but people struggling for freedom everywhere.

Since that December in 1964 in Oslo, I've spent a good deal of time observing what we do with and to our leaders, and the impact that has on them—how we respond to them, our expectations of them, and the burden sometimes laid on leaders by how we respond to them. Our expectations of them *can be* a burden.

I knew that Martin's mood during his hospital stay would pass and that he would get back to focusing on the work that was waiting for us back in Alabama, including our continuing challenge to the segregation system we were determined to dismantle.

Preparation for the Oslo trip would soon begin. It was an organizing project in itself, given the number of people traveling. My attention went to what I would wear at the ceremony. I located a woman with a reputation as an exquisite seamstress. Having seen her artistry, I commissioned her to make me a special outfit. Strolling through the fabric store, I chose a rich maroon velvet. I got fitted for a suit with a hat to match. It turned out indeed to be a strikingly beautiful outfit. Notwithstanding our minuscule SCLC salaries, never had I felt so committed to spend however much it would cost to make sure I looked smashingly good!

I had visited Caribbean islands before, but never had I traveled out of the continental United States on such a long journey. Our entourage of about thirty friends, staff, and family was divided into two groups. In those days, when air crashes were more common, Martin and his wife, Coretta Scott King, had a policy of not taking long trips on the same plane. It was a safety measure. They had four small children to care for. So Martin, his mother, and about half the group, including me, were on one plane with him; the other half, including Coretta, was on a different plane.

Something remarkable happened on our overnight flight. High above the clouds, as I was awakening, it seemed as though we were flying into the sunrise. Alberta King, Martin's mother, said, "Dorothy, look out the window." We beheld this unearthly view—seeing the sun coming up from such a height. Mrs. King started singing a song relevant to what we were witnessing. She sang, *"Oh, day; yonder come day, day done broke in 'a my soul; yonder come day. It's a glorious day, yonder come day!"* (I cry as I write this so many years after the experience.) "Mama King," as a few people called Martin's mother, stood in the aisle and invited everyone to join with her in singing that song. A call-and-response song being one of the styles prevalent in African American churches, it was very easy for everyone to join in. When Mrs. King, who sometimes played the piano at Ebenezer Baptist Church, would sing *"Oh, day,"* the rest of our group would respond, *"Yonder come day."* She would continue with *"Day done broke in 'a my soul; yonder come day . . ."* Someone would pick it up and soon there was a full chorus on that plane as we flew into the sunrise.

Amazingly, I don't even recall if there were people on that plane other than our group. I think there were a few though I can't be sure.

And yes, Dr. King would be up and energetically singing along with his mom and the rest of us. He loved to sing and always had fun doing so. He and the men on our team, Andy Young, Bernard Lafayette, Ralph Abernathy, Wyatt Tee Walker—any who were around—would often form a quartet, a popular form of singing among Black men in the South at the time. They all loved to sing. (So did I.)

In any case, though we were all tired, we were all one excited and happy group. We *welcomed the sun*—and it seemed to welcome us to a memorable experience and a new beginning in our lives.

After landing in Oslo at Gardermoen airport and settling into our rooms, our intense program for the trip began. There were receptions, orientation meetings, and schedules to be handed out. The Nobel Committee planned some social events for us and we had the opportunity to plan a few gatherings that we ourselves wanted to have. I was asked to help handle a good bit of the organizing and logistics. This task mainly involved seeing that everyone was aware of the next thing on the schedule and where in the hotel our entourage needed to be and when.

After one dinner gathering we were all relaxing and having a great time in the dining room set aside for us. Everyone who could sing—and some who couldn't—took center stage to perform his or her "show-off" piece. Usually it would be a song. I'm thinking now of what a fantastic singer Christine King Farris, Martin's sister, is. I don't remember Christine doing a solo that evening, but I wish she had! We would remember it still. Some in our group loved to recite poetry and did so that evening. Sometimes people would just emote a little, or a lot, about the event that brought us to Oslo. It was a joyous and emotional evening.

I was getting nervous because it was time for us to vacate the dining room. As I was trying rather anxiously, though diplomatically, to stop this spontaneous talent show, someone pulled my sleeve and pointed me toward Daddy King, Martin's father. Daddy King was crying.

At that moment my compulsive need to keep the group moving as scheduled seemed, and indeed was, totally unimportant.

A sort of hush came over the group as Daddy King said, "I want you all to join me in this moment of thanksgiving for this honor bestowed on my son. I want you to lift your glasses and with me share in a *toast to God.*"

I never knew Daddy King, Reverend Martin Luther King Sr., to be a drinking man, but in this moment, some Baptist teaching aside, he would engage in and indeed lead us in a toast without hesitation. In any case, I know there was no one in this very special group who was programmed against imbibing. This was certainly a spiritual, prayerful moment and could be compared to Holy Communion if one was praising God. There came a poignant moment of silence as we raised our glasses and joined Daddy King in his toast to God.

There were now other teary eyes — some because of the deep feelings surrounding the whole event and some because of the unique moment and expression invoked by Daddy King.

JUANITA ABERNATHY had a medical emergency that evening. Marian Logan went with Juanita to the hospital and stayed with her overnight there. Marian Logan was my roommate on the trip. Marian was a real singer and used to sing in supper clubs (after our journey to Oslo, Marian always called me "roomie"). So the two of them missed this very special happening. Juanita wasn't the only person who didn't feel well that evening. Her husband, Ralph, wasn't having physical pain but did express hurt feelings. Sitting in an adjacent room as Dr. King went for an interview with the press in Oslo, Ralph began to share with me the story of the Montgomery Bus Boycott and the action that catapulted Martin into national and international prominence. Ralph described that now historic event, when in 1955 Rosa Parks refused to give up her seat for a White man on the bus in Montgomery. Ralph shared with me how he had been on the scene long before Martin, how many of the people involved in the beginning of the boycott were people he had worked with for years before Martin came to Montgomery.

As he described the leadership role he had played, tears began to roll down his face. I could feel the pain he must have felt as his good friend was getting all this glory and he was hardly mentioned, actually not mentioned, at all. And of course as Ralph was pouring out his heart to me, his wife was in the hospital for emergency medical care. This may have also contributed to his sense of loss and pain that evening. I can't be sure.

The next morning, before sunrise, we were welcomed and honored by a candlelight tea service. The "service girls" would simply open a bedroom door and walk in with a lit candle, tea, and pastry. I was told this was a typical holiday welcome in hotels in Oslo, especially for honored guests. It was December, close enough to the holidays, and there was already an aura of Christmas in the air. It was rather surprising that they felt no need to knock. They would just walk in carrying the lit candles. I don't know if everyone in our group was so honored, but I was included.

The special day arrived—December 10, known as Human Rights Day to commemorate the approval of the Universal Declaration of Human Rights by the UN General Assembly in 1948. We would now spend hours dressing and otherwise getting ready for the Nobel ceremony.

We arrived at Oslo City Hall. There was a feeling of reverence and awe as we entered. As we took our seats, I was overtaken—moved to tears as the orchestra welcomed us by playing tunes from *Porgy and Bess.* But I also remember feeling confused by their selection of this popular opera. I knew the reason: the Nobel Committee wanted to play music they saw as representative of Black life in America. Even amid my tears and emotions of the moment I was just a little confused by the Norwegians' choice in trying to connect with us, to make us feel at home.

I was able to release the feelings of confusion and even hurt as I realized they probably did not know the historical reaction to that opera, supposedly based on the life of Black people on a little island off the South Carolina coast. You see, *Porgy and Bess,* with music by George Gershwin and lyrics by his brother Ira Gershwin and DuBose Heyward, was troubling to a lot of African American people, perhaps most especially African American artists. A play by the same name was written by DuBose and his wife, Dorothy, and was based on life in a fictitious Catfish Row, in turn based on the real life of Cabbage Row in Charleston, South Carolina. Septima Clark, whose home was in Charleston, told me that she used to see Porgy, who was crippled, scooting around on a cart. Still, a good number of Black people, including artists, assessed the play and the music purporting to emanate from Porgy's life as demeaning.

Yet many of the songs became extremely popular. "Summertime," which even *I* used to sing a lot, was probably the most popular song from the opera. I've read that some famous African American singers like Harry Belafonte refused to sing the songs or take a role in the opera. Many artists considered the opera and the play on which it was based to be racially demeaning in their portrayal of African Americans. But how could I expect the Norwegians to know this? I must ask Harry if his response to that opera has evolved or changed.

Nevertheless, as we entered the auditorium the feelings of love and awe and wonder at what we were about to experience were mixed with some of the old feelings aroused by the story of "Porgy." Black Americans, blessed or cursed with what W. E. B. Du Bois called "double consciousness," have always struggled with confused feelings as we reflect on life as it once was lived on these shores. Dr. King said once that it's a wonder that "Negroes aren't actually schizophrenic, based on our humanity and yet the way we are treated in this society." Some of these mixed feelings can still be identified today in African Americana.

The introduction of the honoree, Martin Luther King Jr., would soon begin. Our friend, coworker, and leader was handsome in his tuxedo and ready to accept in a gracious, profound, and memorable way the prestigious Nobel Peace Prize. While waiting for Martin to be introduced, I thought of what I had learned of the reason why Alfred Nobel created the Nobel Prizes. His brother had died but the newspaper reporting the death wrote the obituary about Alfred, not his brother. Alfred had become rich and famous for creating dynamite. Many people had been injured and even killed by his invention, since no one had discovered how to safely transport the explosive. Alfred Nobel's legacy would have been one of a careless killer if he had not found a way to correct this erroneous report of his death and especially to change people's assessment of his life and legacy. Reading the obituary, he determined to find a way to transform his legacy as a "merchant of death" to one of an honored person who made great contributions to the betterment of lives the world over. Thus from his fortune and his vision and his wish to encourage and serve humanity, we have his endowment of the Nobel Prizes in medicine, physics, chemistry, literature, economics, and, above all, peace.

Tears roll down my cheeks even now as I recall Martin being introduced on that memorable day in Oslo, Norway. The presentation speech was given by Mr. Gunnar Jahn, chairman of the Nobel Committee. Martin Luther King's acceptance speech was and still is a masterpiece, synthesizing the goals of our freedom struggle and pointedly acknowledging those who indeed made the movement, one that would ultimately rearrange the social order in our country. Dr. King acknowledged that though he became the "pilot," the "ground crew," the untold numbers of ordinary people who were now giving their lives and energy to this movement, were the ones in whose recognition he was receiving this prestigious prize.

After acknowledging the royals and officers of the Nobel Committee, Dr. King said, "I accept the Nobel Prize for Peace at a moment when twenty-two million Negroes of the United States of

America are engaged in a creative battle to end the long night of racial injustice. I accept this award on behalf of a civil rights movement which is moving with determination and a majestic scorn for risk and danger to establish a reign of freedom and a rule of justice." He then spelled out what he saw as the reason our movement was chosen for the Nobel Peace Prize: "This award which I receive on behalf of that movement is a profound recognition that nonviolence is the answer to the crucial political and moral question of our time—the need for man to overcome oppression and violence without resorting to violence and oppression. . . . Following the people of India, Negroes have demonstrated that nonviolence is not sterile passivity, but a powerful moral force which makes for social transformation. Sooner or later all the peoples of the world will have to discover a way to live together in peace, and thereby transform this pending cosmic elegy into a creative psalm of brotherhood." He affirmed his strong belief that "unarmed truth and unconditional love will have the final word in reality."

In the days and months ahead, Dr. King emphasized regularly his awareness and appreciation of the fact that though he was receiving the great honor, it was the thousands of unsung activists who were the ones in whose name and honor he was accepting the award. He truly saw himself as the caretaker of the prestigious award and confirmed that it belonged to all involved in the struggle. Out of this spirit Martin would share the $54,000 prize with other civil rights organizations, keeping none of it for his own family (despite Coretta's plea that it would help pay for their children's college education).

Soberly, after the impressive award ceremony, the banquets, the tours and visits with European notables, we headed home, with a stopover first in Paris. There Martin insisted we locate an African American woman who now had a very successful restaurant that specialized in African American "soul food." I couldn't help but point out that we could get all that kind of food back home! Why would we order American southern soul food from our culture when we were in Paris? I exclaimed. But the restaurant was contacted, the order was placed, and soul food was soon delivered to our hotel. I'm reminded of a man who called me fairly recently wanting a statement declaring that Dr. King was "totally against eating meat," because of the violence it involves to animals. I know the man was sad to hear me say that "Dr. King was happy when he had a beautiful steak on his plate." Martin loved southern soul food. In any case, we were not as conscious then about the damage this style of cooking could potentially cause. Earlier African American soul food was always cooked with fat and much of it was fried. Fortunately there is now a healthier consciousness about food abroad in the land.

During this stopover in Paris we also enjoyed an evening at a nightclub that we had been told had an array of dancers and singers and other first-class entertainers. It was a very pleasant interlude. We thoroughly enjoyed the show.

Back on our own shores we had a planned stopover in New York City, where a reception was held for Dr. King and his party. I recall recognizing Malcolm X in the gathering of people waiting to welcome Dr. King and his party home. I walked up to Malcolm, who was in an aisle seat. I touched him on the shoulder. He looked startled, even fearful. He had grown a beard on his recent trip to Africa, but I recognized him right away. I met with Malcolm when he was on a visit to Atlanta in 1964, the year after he left the Nation of Islam and made his hajj to Mecca. He came to my office at SCLC and my home. We also went to the popular African American restaurant Paschal's, on Hunter Street (now renamed Martin Luther King Jr. Boulevard).

Malcolm was a pleasant and charming fellow, and we spoke of many things. "I hear you like to sing," he said to me. Malcolm was not courting but was, I was told, looking for strong Black women to join the organization he was planning. I shared with him that I'd never had a singing lesson, but that the songs of our Black church life seemed to just fit the bill in these days of struggle. I even told him how my dad seemed to enjoy telling people, "Dorothy can be washing the dishes and while she's drying a plate she stops midway, holding the plate up until she finishes the song. Then goes on to finish drying the plate."

Back in our own hometown of Atlanta, where Martin Luther King Jr. was born and raised, there was a big debate as to whether the city would officially welcome him home and celebrate this triumph—whether they wanted to honor Dr. King in any way on his return for having received the Nobel Peace Prize. At this point in our fight for social justice not everyone was happy about the honor Martin had received, especially because of the boost this honor would give to the Black freedom movement and to him as a leader. After all, there had been protest demonstrations in Atlanta as in other cities. Atlanta's White community, most notably the elite that still ruled the city, could not be pleased with this still young African American preacher being so honored—and increasingly at a global level. There was a sense, too, that even some older Atlanta Black leaders could not bring themselves to be happy for Martin's honor. The honoring of this young preacher was somehow felt to be a threat to them. They saw a younger generation emerging and actually replacing them— they who had seen themselves as *the* Black leaders in Atlanta. These feelings were visible to many of us.

My beautiful velvet suit made especially for this notable trip was stolen after I accidentally left it in my car one day, intending to wear it in a fund-raising fashion show at the Ebenezer Baptist Church. Coming down from the heights of celebration, I and all the others on this journey with Dr. King were putting away our fancy outfits now, donning our movement clothes, preparing to continue confronting Bull Connor and other forces of violence that reacted to our nonviolent protests. Interestingly, through the years I have not thought about the loss of my fabulous maroon velvet suit. And there is an important lesson in that. Putting my full energy into our mission caused me to totally let go of any focus on material things.

We were soon back in the trenches—in Georgia, Alabama, Florida, Virginia, North and South Carolina, and Mississippi, struggling against the system of what I called our American-style apartheid—rigid separation of the races that was enforced by legal and extralegal means.

And of course the struggle wasn't just against Bull Connor. We had to envision ways to expand our movement to intensify pressure on the system and especially the holders of political and economic power, and make them see the rightness of our cause. In a sense, we were just getting started.

Chapter 2

WHEN THE SPARK WAS LIT

Tell me how did you feel when you
come out the wilderness
Come out the wilderness
Come out the wilderness
Tell me how did you feel when you
come out the wilderness
Trusting in the "change"

—AN OLD CHURCH SONG
WITH MY PARAPHRASE OF THE LAST LINE

"DOROTHY, SWEEP THE yard!" my daddy would command, in the Black rural tradition of keeping the yard nice and tidy even where neither grass nor flowers grew. Back and forth I moved the broom, evening out the dirt. My three sisters and I all did this chore, chosen by whoever Daddy saw when the yard needed sweeping. I remember sweeping the whole yard when I was no more than seven or eight years old.

We lived in what was referred to as a shotgun shack. Our house was so small one could see the outhouse in the backyard while merely standing in the front yard. Houses like these got their name because if you shot a bullet through the front door it would go straight out the back.

Me, years later, on the porch of my childhood home, 917 North Greenleaf Street, Goldsboro, North Carolina. It has since been torn down.

North Greenleaf Street was an unpaved road that went past the tobacco factory where my father worked and then around the bend and across the railroad track to reach the downtown area. There was a store on the corner of our block in a little wood-framed building. When Daddy got paid, he would give us a nickel or dime and my sisters and I would go there to buy BB Bats. I don't know if they make that candy anymore, but it was on a stick, kind of chewy and cara-mel-like. BB Bats were a good buy because they lasted a long time.

Our neighborhood was all Black, except for one elderly White woman who lived across the street and a White store owner, but he lived elsewhere. One day, a young White boy about my age, around ten, was pedaling his bike toward me. He was carefree, riding casually as he looked around and sang loudly enough for all to hear, *"Deep in the heart of Niggertown!"* He was paraphrasing a once popular tune, "Deep in the Heart of Texas." I seethed with rage as he sang. Greenleaf Street was my street, not his! Although we were close in age, our lives were worlds apart. He was free to go anywhere and shout hateful slang without any fear of retaliation. In fact, he believed it was his right to hurl insults. I don't know if anyone else heard his performance, but I certainly did and have never forgotten it. Such acts of hatred and humiliation were so common and acceptable to the general population that no Black person emerged from our collective numbness to respond. In general the entire neighborhood seemed to droop with utter helplessness and hopelessness, so many Black folk escaped to dysfunctional methods of survival, such as selling moon-shine, a type of homemade whiskey. My dad sought no particular refuge—not church or any social club outlet. Actually he seemed to hate preachers; I heard him say of a preacher once, "That's just his racket."

My daddy, Claude Daniel Foreman, reflected a lot of hopelessness. I didn't know much about his upbringing. He rarely spoke of it, but I knew he had grown up on a farm, where he worked very hard. Many years later, I learned from his sister that he had been physically abused as a child by his mother, who whipped him mercilessly. I never heard Daddy speak of a father being around. I learned that my mother's father was a "holiness preacher" who had three different wives and three sets of children. He did not like Daddy because Daddy had "stolen" his daughter, my mother. They were very young and had run off to be married; apparently Grandpa never forgave Daddy.

My father did all he could do to scrape out a meager living for us once he was left a widower with four toddlers. I was told that my mother, Maggie, died as she suffered through her fifth pregnancy. She had us very close together, having conceived three months after each of the first three was born. All four of us were born in the same little house with no indoor plumbing. Fees for even the racially segregated hospital were out of the question. They had four girls: Effie Mae, four; myself, three; Dazzelle, two; and Annie Margaret, less than a year old. I have no recollection of my mother; I was only three years old when she died. One of my mother's sisters told me that Aunt Sis (Clara Pelham, Daddy's oldest sister) was present when she died. I heard that my mother said, "Claude, I can't even see you." Aunt Sis, I'm told, said to him: "Claude, have you got your insurance paid up?" She said Daddy cried, realizing his wife was dying.

I do vaguely remember somebody holding me up to peer at her body as it lay in the casket. At that time in our community, the body of a deceased person was always brought to the family's home. There were times I've wondered why my mother was not tended to in a hospital. But this was in the 1930s, when hospital care was not readily available to Blacks and definitely not available to a Black man making nine dollars a week.

WHEN PEOPLE of our circumstance had any insurance in that neighborhood, the premium was paid to a White man who would go to houses and collect a few dollars in cash. I've often thought that poor Black folk and perhaps poor White folk as well were getting ripped off with such payments.

My mother had eight sisters. These women were my aunts, but they were also my cousins because my grandfather Seymore Pelham married my daddy's sister. Various ones of them wanted to take one of us after my mother died. Daddy would have none of that! He said, "I want to keep these young'uns together." And he did. But what a hard time it was. It is often said that it takes a village to raise a child, but the village was not there for my daddy, or perhaps Daddy didn't know how to call on the village for help and support. On the other hand, I've heard a friend and colleague at Cornell say, as he raises his children alone, that resources are not available or offered to men.

In any case, Daddy must have been bewildered by all that was going on in his life—the death of his wife, who was supposed to take care of the house and children; the prospect of raising four girls alone; the idea of feeding and clothing all of us on a wage of nine or sometimes twelve dollars a week. I can't recall him being anything other than deeply burdened. Daddy worked any job he could find, but the wreckage of the Great Depression, no education, and his ebony skin made it impossible to earn a decent living. His longest job was working in a branch of the Brown & Williamson tobacco factory a few blocks from our house. Sometimes he would hop on a truck that came into town to take day laborers to farms to work in the fields "putting in" tobacco or picking cotton. Daddy could pick a lot of cotton; a few times I was allowed to go with him and when I was a little older he would let me go to the tobacco farms alone. Still, his struggle to feed us was a difficult one. I remember once he came home with one head of cabbage, nothing else. I have always believed he took that cabbage from somebody's garden just so we could have something to eat.

When I was about six years old, I saw my daddy crying. He had taken me into town with him. I don't know why it was me, but I remember holding his hand as we walked there and went into some business office. I was puzzled and concerned and even felt sad for him but wasn't able to express my feelings or ask him why he was crying. I knew he was hurting and I wished I could have made his pain go away. I wish I knew now why he was crying. He seemed so big, and I felt so small. Just looking up and pondering the situation of this *big* person in my life with tears rolling down his face is a scene written indelibly in my consciousness. Daddy was really quite small and willowy, but not to me at six years old. I was frightened to see him crying quietly and wanted to comfort him, but I had no words for that feeling at six years old. I just clutched his hand a little tighter. I cry now as I recall and write about this.

My relationship with my father was complicated. On the one hand, I can now recognize how hard it was for him to raise us alone. On the other hand, my sisters and I feared him.

I recall nothing nurturing in my home environment. The beatings from my father's belt, a piece of stovewood, or a switch were very often the order of the day at home. When he wasn't in a mood to start striking, he would silently glare in anger and hostility, paralyzing us with fear. On a good day he would end the long stare by saying something like "Get on out of here." Other times, such as once when I was sixteen and came home one evening (it was not late), he would land a hard slap to the side of my face without saying a word. In retrospect I realize he was making assumptions about where I was and what I was doing. But in those moments of intimidation and fear, all understanding was lost. His method of intimidation was also very effective against boys who took any interest in me.

If I could talk to Daddy now, I would tell him how cruel and crazy this habit of his was. Even still, amid my feelings of compassion for him lie twinges of anger. I find minimal comfort in the thought that perhaps things would have been different had he had the language to express his thoughts or emotions instead of with the silence and

the violence. What Effie and I learned from interviewing his then re-
maining sister, Aunt Penny, about our father's childhood reaffirmed
that, unfortunately, history does often repeat itself. Violence was not
only a function of the community in which I lived, but it was passed
down like an heirloom in some segments of my family. The prevalent
"teaching" at the time was "spare the rod and spoil the child," and
though Daddy was not a churchgoing man, he was both a product
of this teaching and a purveyor. Now, over twenty-five years after
his death, I can manage a little sadness for him—even sadness that I
didn't have the chance to have him travel the world with me, or even
around our own country.

I wonder now why Daddy didn't always have someone to look
after us when he had to be at work. When I had to have my tonsils
taken out, I walked to the doctor's office where it was done. The
nurse in the office said to me, "You need to have someone with you
when you are having surgery!" I got myself back home somehow,
and when Daddy got home from work, he looked over at me in the
bed and inquired, "How you feeling, Dorothy?" "I just got a real
bad sore throat," I answered. I used to feel deeply sad, for years,
feeling sorry for myself, when I would remember having to go alone
for such a procedure. And it didn't help that the nurse would make
such a comment to me, a child not more than thirteen or fourteen
years old, too young to make such plans for myself. I wish I could
ask Daddy if he told the doctor I would be coming alone. I assume
Daddy couldn't get the day off or perhaps didn't ask to take the day
off to go with me to have surgery because he feared for his job or felt
plain intimidation, or maybe it was just plain ignorance. It was probably a combination of all of the above. Even now, I sure wish I could
ask him. So many painful and scary things happened before I reached
twelve years old.

One of those scary moments happened when I was nearly eight

years old. Daddy was making breakfast when he handed me a dime and told me to go to the corner store and get a can of Carnation milk. He liked to use this in his coffee. It was not quite full daylight and as I started to the store, I saw *something* looming very large in front of me. I didn't have any idea what it was, but it was ominous, a monstrous-looking thing, and huge. I was so frightened, I turned and started back to our house. When I was almost in front of our house I turned and looked back toward the store. Nothing was there. The "thing" had moved. It had been a heavy fog, but I didn't know that then. So I turned and ran very fast to the store, got the can of milk, and ran home. Daddy said, "What took you so long?" I said, "I don't know." He just stared at me for a moment.

Another time, I was playing across the street from my house. A White man came up to me and asked me if I would let him "do it" with me. I was around ten or eleven, and I think I said, "That might hurt." He said, "No it won't; I'll show you," at which point he pulled down his trousers and "showed me." I ran and made it safely back across the street to my house.

I know now that I am lucky that I did not become one of the statistics we hear so much about these days, children disappearing and their abused and dead bodies found much later. I am lucky that the man in the bushes across the street didn't force himself on me or even worse. I never told Daddy about this, or anyone else. I can imagine that I would have gotten one of his terrible beatings for being across the street, since he couldn't unleash his anger and frustration on the man who had offered to rape me. Then again, maybe he wouldn't have done anything. After all, the Supreme Court in 1857 declared that the Black man had "no rights which the white man was bound to respect." That pattern would have prevailed in this instance.

I've often fantasized about what my childhood would have been like if my mother had lived. Would Daddy have been gentler? I have felt a huge void for not having a mother to offer me a peanut butter sandwich as I got home from school, no mother to let me sit on her lap if I needed cuddling, no mother to talk with me about *girl things.* My father once said to me with a sort of frown on his face, "Ain't your teacher ever talked to you?" I can still laugh and cry at the same time when I think about that inquiry. Daddy had no schooling. It took me years to realize what he was referring to by the phrase "girl things."

When Effie, Annie Margaret, and I get together (Dazzelle died of lung cancer in 1981), we reminisce about so many painful memories during our childhood; now I try to recall and talk about a few happy times, when I can remember any one of them.

The satisfaction on my father's face as he proudly held our hands and walked us to the county fair is one happy memory. When he had enough money to pay for all of us to ride on the Ferris wheel, the merry-go-round, or hoppy horses, I could tell he shared in our excitement. I've often wondered what joyful experiences he had as a child, if any—then I feel sad for him.

I also recall the pride and joy at Christmastime when Daddy purchased a doll, a tea set, and a shoe box filled with fruit for each of us (raisins on the vine, apples, oranges, pecans, and walnuts). He would also make at least three cakes—pineapple, chocolate, and coconut— in addition to the famous southern sweet potato pie. He liked to have us in the kitchen with him; we begged to grate the fresh coconut and lick the spoon he had stirred the cake batter with. I don't know how he learned to cook, but he was a good cook. Of course, after all the fun and excitement, we were tortured with the angst of having to wait until Christmas Day to eat the delicious cakes. The cakes and pies would line the table, but Daddy would say, "We can't cut the cakes until Christmas Day." I remember thinking, *When I get grown, I'm going to make a cake or pie and cut it as soon as it is out of the oven!* And I have done just that. It was torture to see and smell the wonderful cakes and not be able to have any *until tomorrow*! His joy was most visible when he could provide us with a table laden with food, a symbol of his success. This was one family tradition I was willing to continue throughout my life—cooking too much, needing the food to be beautiful and bountiful.

My father, Claude Daniel Foreman, was drafted into the military when I was around twelve or thirteen years old. This is him in his navy uniform. I remember asking him many years later, "Daddy, why didn't you tell them you had four small children, and no wife or mother to care for them?" He said, "I did."

Family gathering. Left to right, standing: Aunt Penny Parks, Daddy's sister;
Daddy; Daddy's brother, James; Leslie Gibbs, Effie's husband; Betty,
their daughter; Effie (and more of their children); Dazzelle's children.
Left to right, seated: George, my husband; Dazzelle's husband, David "Pep"
Hinton; my sister Annie Margaret Barbry; Dazzelle's children; Dazzelle.
I was probably taking the photograph and we were probably in the yard of
one of my sisters, but I don't recall now.

As a young teenager Daddy let me take before- and after-school
jobs doing housekeeping and food service in the homes of some White
families. There were three such families: Mrs. Broadhurst, who ran
a boardinghouse for teachers; Captain and Mrs. Harris (he was an
army officer); and Mr. and Mrs. Gordon, who owned the Carolina
Shoe Repair shop in Goldsboro.

Housekeeping work was what most Black people I knew did then,
or they worked in the fields picking cotton or putting in tobacco. I
did some of that, too. In high school I would go to Mrs. Broadhurst's
house before school to serve breakfast and clear the tables for the
teachers boarding there. I would sometimes run most of the way to
school, either because I was late or because it was cold and I didn't
have a coat. After school I would return to Mrs. Broadhurst's to help

serve dinner. At the end of the week I would take home five or six dollars. This helped Daddy out some. I remember him letting me keep all of the money one week because my only pair of shoes had paper to cover the worn-out bottoms.

Mrs. Broadhurst also ran a summer vacation home at Wrightsville Beach, near Wilmington, North Carolina. Daddy would let me go there in the summers to "live in" and work for her. I was in charge of keeping things clean, picking up, and organizing. One day she came into a bathroom and saw a lot of sand in the bathtub. She exclaimed, "You people sure do get dirty before you take a bath!" I was furious and fairly shouted back at her, "That's not where I took a bath! Some of the children with one of the families brought their beach toys in from the beach and were playing with them in the tub! And I don't get that dirty before I take a bath." My heart was pounding. That was the first time I remember actually speaking up for myself. I had never talked back to an adult before—not Daddy and especially not a White woman.

Me with my two sisters, my dad, and his oldest sister.

Mrs. Gordon lived in the downstairs of a house that had two apartments, one up and one down. Mrs. Harris lived upstairs. Mrs. Gordon asked me one day if I could babysit sometimes for Mrs. Harris. She continued: "She had a babysitter who left her to go take care of a *little old colored baby.*" She said this to *me*! Babysitting upstairs when no one else was at home, I couldn't resist reading a letter that was lying open. It was from Mrs. Harris's sister. This sister was recounting for her how she was taking a bus trip and could hardly stand the odor on the bus. She wrote: "I thought it was the niggers on the bus, but got home and found that I had not removed a piece of cotton from my own body that should have been removed." When Captain and Mrs. Harris returned home, I remember that I couldn't look directly at them, feeling hurt and angry, wondering if they too referred to Black people that way. I resented the time I babysat for them.

As I matured and moved into the world of work, I continued to learn more about racism. Studying the strange phenomenon and later doing antiracism work, I began to ponder how deep and pervasive racism ran in the culture and psyche of many who were not even conscious that they held racist views, and who certainly would not have acknowledged it. After all, the Harrises were "nice" people.

I decided that there was something better on the horizon for me. Actively aware of my surroundings, looking for a way out of the bed of poverty on which I was born, I observed the homes of the White families in which I worked, the way they lived, served meals, furnished their homes, and entertained their guests. I surmised that this was clearly a powerful improvement over my own circumstances. It took many years before I realized that such material manifestations were no more than the trappings of affluence and could never reflect the value of one's life. Yet material prosperity was a powerful stimulant for my dream—the future toward which I was moving. I never could *romanticize* poverty, as I observed some people did.

35

My sisters and me.

There are myriad numbers of poor families whose members are motivated and encouraged to become their best selves, who are loved and cherished. But there are untold numbers in circumstances that resemble mine, and worse, where the scars seem to be deeply embedded in a painful memory. A painful memory of poverty, the lack of a nurturing environment, and high levels of violence in homes and in neighborhoods can lead to terrible scars and destroyed lives. I know the opposite is also true. There's that saying, *Scars can lead to stars.*

Another time I went to that same corner store where Daddy sent me for the can of milk—a little older now—having been given a dime to spend. I asked for a dime's worth of "nigger toes," to which the store owner responded, "You've already got ten of them." As funny as that might be now, I did not laugh. The cashier proceeded to scoop up some Brazil nuts; I paid him the dime and left. I didn't understand what I had just done, or what had just transpired. My use of that commonly spoken, derogatory term was a classic example of how internalized oppression plays out. I had never heard of Brazil nuts being called English walnuts. I had heard only the derogatory term, and in my childhood ignorance accepted the derogatory term as "correct."

I'm standing in front of what used to be the corner store,
four doors down from my childhood home.

I didn't realize that the incident was funny until I shared it with Julian Bond, Connie Curry, and some others while in a car in Memphis, looking for the church whose minister was Al Green, the soul singer. We were in Memphis for a commemorative event at the Civil Rights Museum honoring the sanitation workers whose strike was the reason Dr. King and most of us SCLC organizers and trainers were in Memphis on April 4, 1968, when Dr. King was killed. Riding along in a rather celebratory mood, I mentioned to Julian that I had been struggling with the idea of doing a book for a long time but wasn't sure how to get started. Julian said, "Begin by talking about your first neighborhood. Was there a neighborhood store? Talk about that. The people there. Find a focal point and just start writing." I then shared with everyone my trip to the store to buy the "nigger toes." Julian burst into uncontrollable laughter. Soon everyone in the car was laughing, including me.

We can find, *must find*, humor in some of the ludicrous happenings of our Black experience in America. The telling of this story reminds me again how much—amid all the pain—we could laugh, even at ourselves. We came to appreciate the importance of laughing together, as well as singing powerfully together. But I'm also reminded of how internalized oppression can manifest itself.

Chapter 3

"THERE'S YOUR READY GIRL"

I GREW UP feeling I was in the wrong place. Somehow I knew that one day I had to leave. *I had to leave.* I had no words for this feeling, but I know now I felt it deeply as a youngster growing up. One day I had to leave and move into a place that would project me onto a path of fulfillment as well as contributing toward making a better world. Sensing there were opportunities waiting made me anxious to move toward my dream for a different life, a better life. High school was the next step, and I took it at Dillard High School, an all-Black school in Goldsboro.

Miss Rosa Gray, an English teacher and a drama coach at Dillard High, was my divine intervention; we connected immediately. I felt incredibly drawn to her, and would like to think the feeling was mutual. Miss Gray took a real and constant interest in my welfare and education; our bond probably grew from my passionate excitement for learning. Whether she was making sure I had lunch or that I did well with my assignments, Miss Gray never failed to look out for me. I got the lead female role in plays she produced during all four of my high school years, including the year we did *David Copperfield.* I'm sure this was because I was an excellent student in every class I took with her. I know she saw my love for theater.

Miss Rosa Gray (second row, far left) was our English teacher at Dillard High School. This is my class: I am in the front row, fifth from the right, in my box pleat skirt and pearls.

I remember once getting upset when another teacher, the history teacher as well as athletic coach, took me to task for something, I don't remember what for. I complained to Miss Gray about what I perceived as a mean demeanor toward me. She said, "Dorothy Lee Foreman, you're still a child to be trained." I sensed that she was telling me to "cool it," not make a fuss about what he'd said. I'm glad I didn't because it probably was not that important. Miss Gray's advice was my first lesson in learning to pick my battles.

In Miss Gray's class, students were always required to speak up. Walking with confidence to the front of the class, I would have to conjugate verbs on the blackboard, and sometimes even recite a memorized poem or a passage from Shakespeare. No student performed better than I did. I excelled in every assignment. She saw it.

One day as I walked back to my seat after I had finished reciting a poem, Miss Gray said to the class, "There's your ready girl." This was a phrase often used in the forties to compliment a person who was the best in their field. As I walked back to my seat, pride electrified the never-ending smile that ran across my face. I'm convinced she is the reason I majored in English when I got into college.

To this day that compliment rings in my ears when I walk up to podiums to give speeches; I did not and do not to this day want to disappoint Miss Gray. Her compliment both motivates and challenges me. For years I still wondered, *What would Miss Gray say about my preparation today, my delivery?* My experience in Miss Gray's English class exerted the greatest influence on me, specifically regarding speech and the liberation attained through learning. It was under her tutelage that I first read and heard the lines from Shakespeare's *Hamlet.* I was so impressed, and continue to quote it now when I am trying to encourage students to project:

> *Speak the speech, I pray you, as I pronounced it to you,*
> *   trippingly on the tongue:*
> *but if you mouth it, as many of your players do,*
> *I had as lief the town-crier spoke my lines. . . .*
> *in the very torrent, tempest, and, as I may say,*
> *the whirlwind of passion, you must*
> *acquire and beget a temperance*
> *that may give it smoothness.*

I can hear, even now, Miss Rosa Gray admonishing us in her English class to "pronounce the words!" For me that also meant don't sound whiney. "Project!" she would say. "People in the back must hear you else you lose your audience." I catch myself now thinking this from time to time, so much so that one friend shyly reminded me, when I was speaking a bit too loudly, "Dorothy, you're not making a speech, I'm right here. You don't need to project here." This friend had heard my account of Miss Gray in my life.

Me as a sophomore in high school.

In high school, I wanted to be popular, so I made sure I knew the more popular folks in school. But I really was a bit of a loner, mostly because I didn't know how to join a group. I know now I wasn't sure I would "fit" given my childhood experiences. It would be a long time before I realized some of my classmates had similar childhood experiences. Even so, I had two or three good friends and enjoyed inviting them to my house. I learned how to make lemon pie and used to invite them over and serve it, setting as nice a table as I could with what we had. I'm sure I was trying to set the table like I saw it set in the White folks' houses where I worked all through high school.

The Junior-Senior Prom at Dillard was always a very special event; it was an occasion where junior and senior girls wore their first ball gowns and were most often escorted by a favorite boyfriend. Several teachers were always designated as chaperones. I wanted to go, of course, but my father wouldn't consent. I don't think Daddy even knew what a prom was; remember, he only got through the third grade. I was crushed. Teary-eyed, I told Miss Gray about his decision. What did she do but show up at my house to plead with Daddy, telling him that she would take me, be my chaperone there, and bring me back home.

Daddy put on his best shirt before meeting with Miss Gray. Teachers were almost like celebrities in my neighborhood. And Daddy, I think, was even intimidated by teachers. When she arrived, I went under the porch of the house so I could hear the conversation. (Our house was slightly improved now, with a front porch under which there was rather high space.) "I isn't ready for my girls to go to dances," he said. You see, he had to speak "proper" for the teacher. I had to stifle the sobs.

My father.

I was shocked that Daddy did not give in to her. I thought his respect for her and a teacher's influence would change his mind. This was one of the worst days of my life.

Years later I realized the real reason he said no: he had no money to buy me something appropriate to wear. Daddy was not about to tell the teacher that he had no money and he was not about to have me at a dance not looking as good as any other girl at the prom. However, poverty did not take away his pride. I can get all choked up when I think about how my dad would have been a good student had he been able to go to school. Nonetheless, his life was on the farm, where he, his mother, and siblings worked from sunup to sundown. I cry for Daddy even now.

By the time I was a high school senior, I was focusing on what would come after. Miss Gray had been asking me whether I wanted to go to college, and I certainly did. More than anything else about the White families I worked for as a young girl, I was impressed that they had all gone to college. I surmised that going to college caused one to have a richer life, a fuller life, a life that provided more interesting experiences. One day I asked my cousin Frederick Parks ("Pete," we call him) what made him want to go to college since to my knowledge nobody in our family ever did. He said that he noticed that people who went to college lived better. Making the same assessment, I also included my observation that they seemed to express themselves in more complete and interesting ways and that they knew how to speak "good English."

I was always impressed with a confident use of language. Later this would put me in good stead, as public speaking is an important tool for the work I do now and have done for many years. I grew to love beautiful, poetic language.

However, English spoken in a "White southern drawl" evoked negative emotions in me in the past, and actually still does today. *Black* southern speech is different. The White southern drawl brings to mind the horror of the experiences Black people underwent in this country in general and the humiliation suffered in my youth growing up Black in North Carolina in particular.

Guy Carawan accompanying us on guitar.

A good friend of mine, Guy Carawan, helped me moderate my reaction to White southern speech. Though Guy, a fantastic musician, was not born in the South, I used to tease him that his speech reminded me of White southern speech. He was probably the first White person I got to know as a friend to Black people, in part because I came to see that he did not have a prejudiced bone in his body. When Guy came among us, he was just a friend and wonderful musician.

"I'm on My Way"

One day Miss Gray asked me if I wanted her to call colleges for me. I happily and nervously said, "Yes!" She made calls to Shaw University, located in Raleigh, on my behalf. Shaw was about fifty miles north of Goldsboro.

As with the Junior-Senior Prom, I don't think Daddy knew what the college experience would do for me. At least this decision did not require him to put up any money. Perhaps he was starting to realize we had to leave the nest at some point, or maybe he was just plain tired of having responsibility for four girls for so long. In any case, Miss Gray arranged for me to have three jobs while at Shaw: working in the dining hall, cleaning the teachers' dormitory, and later working in the president's residence as housekeeper.

With a cardboard box that served as my suitcase, Henry Bowden loaded the trunk of his truck to take me to Shaw. Henry, a sort of boyfriend, was a very nice farmer boy who once told me that if he didn't marry me, he wouldn't marry anybody. Conversely, marriage ran far from my mind. I had hitched my wagon to a star since early childhood and I wanted out; I wanted better. He was a kind fellow, and, since he had a truck, he drove me from Goldsboro to Raleigh, where I got settled in Estey Hall, the freshman dormitory at Shaw.

How I managed three jobs and a full course load is still a mystery to me. It certainly sapped my energy and ability to study in a proper manner. I know now it was hard, though I don't recall realizing this at the time. I was just grateful to have an opportunity to begin my college education.

MANY YEARS later, when I was the director of student activities at Cornell University, an administrator in the dean's office asked me to go over to Day Hall, the main administration building, to convince students who had taken over a section of the building to leave. They were demonstrating to demand more financial aid and scholarship money. As I walked across the beautiful Cornell campus to engage with the students in their sit-in, I couldn't help but reflect on my days as a freshman at Shaw University. I did not receive a penny that did not come from my three jobs, though some costs were waived in exchange for some special extra tasks performed. The secretary in the Shaw office did give me five dollars once. I'm not sure why she did, but I was grateful. My economic situation must have been apparent, or maybe she was impressed with how diligently I applied myself to achieving my goals. This was a very long time ago, and as I walked from my office in Willard Straight Hall across the campus of this Ivy League school, I had to make an adjustment in terms of these students' experience and expectations, and my own.

At Shaw I was a dedicated college student worker with deep gratitude for having the opportunity to be there. It never occurred to me to be embarrassed that I had arrived with my things in a cardboard box, including one dress that was for special occasions. We dressed up for everything in those days—to go to required chapel and to go downtown. I still vividly remember my only "Sunday dress": it had horizontal green, yellow, and black stripes going around it. My roommate and I would exchange our dress-up outfits on alternate occasions.

I'm sure that my dedication, thoroughness, and commitment to my work impressed all who supervised me. So, when the president of the college, Dr. Robert Prentiss Daniel, and his wife, Mrs. Blanche Daniel, needed someone to work in their home, I was targeted for this "honor." I was able to give up cleaning the teachers' dormitory but kept the dining hall job.

The first time I walked into the basement of the president's home at Shaw, I saw another student. She was from Liberia and was using a big press to iron sheets. This was the kind of press used in commercial laundries, where you lift up the heavy top, straighten the sheet on the bottom rest, and pull the top down, which irons the sheet as steam oozes out all around. This student, Angie Brooks, would one day become Liberia's attorney general and later sit in the United Nations as convener of the Security Council. Visiting Liberia years later, I had a dramatic and tearful rendezvous with Angie. We both cried as we recalled our first meeting in the basement of the president's home at Shaw University—both very poor students working our way through college, mopping, scrubbing, shining floors, cooking, and cleaning.

One time my dad and one of my sisters came over from Goldsboro to Shaw University to see me. I was proud to show them where I lived. I'll never forget my dad's expression as he exclaimed, "What in the world does anybody want their floors shining like this for?" Daddy had never been in a fancy polished house. His work was in the tobacco factory and sometimes the cotton fields. I think he came to see me because I had gotten word to him that I would be moving to Petersburg, Virginia, with the Daniels and going to college there when Dr. Daniel got the job as president of Virginia State College. At this time it was the Black arm of the state university system in Virginia.

What an impact an unplanned event can have on one's life. This move with Dr. and Mrs. Daniel from Raleigh to Petersburg would open doors and present challenges and opportunities that set my life on a path I could not have imagined—for here I would meet a preacher from Montgomery, Alabama, named Martin Luther King Jr.

Chapter 4

PEOPLE GET READY, THERE'S A "CHANGE" A-COMIN'

WHILE I MAY have started out as a girl born in a shotgun shack, that little three-room house with an outhouse in the backyard, and had been reared by an impoverished single father, I now had the passport to the better life I had envisioned as a child, thanks in part to Dr. and Mrs. Daniel, as well as to Miss Rosa Gray, who first touched my heart and my life in a special way.

Dr. Daniel was offered and had accepted the presidency of Virginia State College in Petersburg, Virginia, in 1952. When they gave me the news, they also said that I was to go with them. They didn't ask me—they told me. That was okay because I had not yet "come into myself," that is, was not mature and confident enough to make my own choices. There I moved into the third floor of the president's home, an attic-like space reserved for household "help" that I would later share, at different times, with two other students, Janice McManus and Ruth Green. While they moved in and stayed for short periods to help keep the president's residence in good order, I was there for the long haul, through graduation and even my marriage.

I looked upon my new residence as plush, but it was simpler than that. My room on that third level contained a rod on which to hang a few clothes, which was enough since I didn't have much to hang anyway, and a small three-drawer chest that I would share with my roommates, Ruth and Janice. Still, living in the president's residence afforded me the opportunity to live in a fantasy, a dream I always held. Movies starring the likes of Bette Davis, Joan Crawford, and Dorothy Lamour had fueled these fantasies. I saw them during high school. We'd pay a quarter and had to walk through an alley-like space to get to the seating designated for Black people. We couldn't enter through the main entrance. No matter what I saw in the movies, the reality was that I was live-in help for the Daniels. My job was to keep surfaces dusted, the floors shiny, and the house clean. When they had company, I was to help with the cooking. Sometimes when they had special guests, I was obliged to dress up in a starched white uniform and serve even if I had also cooked the meal, which was a role I moved into quickly.

Once I was in charge of preparing the meal for the entire company visiting the house. Dr. and Mrs. Daniel often hosted guests, mostly speakers and entertainers who appeared on campus. I looked forward to it since I used to enjoy making a fancy meal back home every once in a while, inviting two or three friends over, Annie Doris Lofton and Alphena Bowen being the most regular.

However, the sense of pride I felt in having this assignment was undermined when Mrs. Daniel came into the kitchen and interrupted my process of preparing the meal for the university guests. I took so much pride in everything I presented, as I do with anything that has my name on it. That night the smell of a succulent and tender roast beef radiated throughout the house. Also, a beautiful lemon pie, one of my specialties, awaited the guests on my meticulously set table. The centerpiece was specially crafted with breathtaking tulips that resembled the color of my rose-pink lipstick and gardenias the color of white lace.

After I had labored diligently, when the meal was complete Mrs. Daniel said, "You couldn't have prepared this meal unless I helped, could you?" I reluctantly, in a soft voice, said, "No," though I was incredibly annoyed by her continuous interruptions while I cooked. Nonetheless, only because I was still lacking a sense of self did I answer her as if nothing were wrong. The whole time she was in my way in the kitchen, I wanted to yell, "Get out of my way!" I wish I had told her that she didn't help me at all; she interfered with my efforts and my pride, attempting to hinder me from producing a beautifully set table and meal that I made all by myself. At least, in the end, I was proud of the meal and thought it was special.

In hindsight, I think she needed to feel a sense of pride and accomplishment as well. I don't think, given her sense of self, she could let me have that success and get all the credit.

At another time one of my professors was invited to come to a dinner the Daniels hosted for a visiting speaker. I hated being seen by one of my teachers in that starched white uniform, strolling around the table serving. I had started to cultivate a reputation on the campus as someone who had a talent that would lift me out of the "poor student" category. My humiliation must have shown, because the professor later said to me, "You are embarrassed to be seen serving meals in the president's home, aren't you?" And I was, I think not so much because of the serving, but because at such times Mrs. Daniel would play to the hilt the role of "grand mistress of the manor." She would press her foot on the floor bell under the table to call me in to bring some food or to clear some dishes. I hated being called by that bell.

Somehow I felt it as a tremendous put-down, especially since the three of us sat together to eat when we were alone. She made me feel like I was not good enough to eat with them when company came. This bruised my already damaged psyche and impacted my ongoing struggle to erase the scars of my painful childhood, which I had viewed largely as a matter of racial prejudice.

"Tomorrow, I'll be at the table / When company comes," wrote Langston Hughes in his famous poem "I, Too, Sing America." But this was not about race—it was because Black folk typically worked in White homes. The Daniels and I were all African American. The issue at the heart of this matter was class. This eventually was manifest within Black culture as well.

Although my professor's comments hurt me, I knew that one day I would indeed "be at the table," eventually even with royalty while in Norway at the Nobel Prize ceremony. Nonetheless, the professor meant well, or at least no harm; the supersensitivity was probably mine. However, what was most upsetting about my professor's comment was that he *knew,* that he *saw,* and that he dared to tell me, having seen right through my struggle with my identity.

My work in the house was time-consuming and my responsibilities great; still, I began to explore involvement in extracurricular activities and was pleased that the Daniels did not try to stop me from doing so by giving me too many things to do when I needed to study. I often took only two classes per semester, occasionally three. I felt compelled, nonetheless, to do something on campus that would show a different dimension or aspect of who I was and how I saw myself.

I became active in the Student Christian Association (SCA), which I loved because it gave me a social and spiritual outlet from the rather oppressive and isolating life in the president's home. I met other students and made friends at Virginia State College. It was a place where I could stretch—discovering who I really was and exploring dreams of leading and singing, which I loved to do. It was a place where I could be visible, useful, and recognized for my talents and not be seen as a maid or housekeeper. Ironically, I later realized that students thought I was special for living in the president's residence, when the opposite was the case.

Once when I had the flu, Dr. Daniel said to me, "You can't just go to bed like other students because you don't feel well." Living there was a very mixed blessing. I was sure the Daniels liked having me around, despite their sometimes poor treatment of me. They had no children, and Dr. Daniel even admitted once that he and his wife had no experience in dealing with a child of their own. I think they felt guilty when they questioned me about nothing more than opening a box of cookies. When I said I would pay for them, Dr. Daniel apologized, saying they didn't mean to suggest that.

Although Mrs. Daniel did lack self-esteem and was a bit of a snob, my feeling of resentment is slightly mitigated by the realization of her own internal struggles. She did not like to be alone, especially when Dr. Daniel was out of town. Once when Dr. Daniel was traveling during her recovery from a surgery, she insisted that I sleep on the chaise longue at the foot of the bed in their room. At some point she also asked me to take my sheets and bring them onto her bed and sleep there. I really resented that. She was saying to me that I could sleep in her bed for her comfort, but was not good enough or clean enough to sleep on her sheets; I think that's what she meant. This was just one of the many little insults that I would experience as I continued to be part housekeeper, part *daughter*, part student. Mrs. Daniel was confused about how she viewed me and left me confused about my relationship with them. She spoke to me once about adopting me, but I'm not sure if she was serious. What was I to them really? Student? Maid? Daughter? I held strong feelings of resentment, especially at times when my need to study was not respected.

As a part-time student, it took me about six years to complete my bachelor's degree. I couldn't have taken more classes, though; my household duties required a great deal of time.

One of my duties was to accompany Mrs. Daniel on her shopping trips to Richmond, Virginia, to shop at larger department stores—especially Thalhimers. There she would sit in her big black Buick wearing her full-length mink coat and carrying our lunch in a brown bag. Although she was a college president's wife and bought her fur coat at Thalhimers, the most popular department store in Richmond at the time, she was not allowed in the store's dining room. We would have to go to a basement area if we needed to use a restroom or else drive until we could find a place where "colored" could go. Though I was a student at the time, I felt great shame and humiliation for both of us. I feel it still today, as I remember those years. There she was, one of the fancy ladies from "up on the hill," but she still was not treated with dignity. She was just another Black woman, subject to the same humiliation as my father, who went to the third grade, if that, and worked nailing the tops on barrels in a tobacco factory.

THERE IS something positive to be said for a dormitory experience in the early years of one's college life, because one can then really experience a sense of autonomy and important growth, though campus rules and regulations might not allow for too much freedom. Students were required to be in their dorms by a certain time each evening and the girls were obliged to, for example, wear white gloves when going downtown. At Virginia State College, I had to search for some of the experiences and feelings of autonomy that dormitory life would have naturally provided.

Dr. Samuel Gandy was the advisor to the Student Christian Association. The SCA was the student arm of the Young Women's Christian Association (YWCA). A small group of students was invited to gather in a circle every Sunday evening in a lower-level room in the library. We would have discussions and sing a lot of songs. I got to be one of the song leaders in that group. My love of singing and discussing interesting topics found a happy outlet and expression there. The love of and comfort in singing, especially leading group singing, would come in very handy years later when I went to work with Martin Luther King Jr., but I'm getting ahead of my story.

As you will recall, reciting poetry was a hobby of mine back in high school with Miss Gray, my English teacher. This Sunday-evening gathering provided another wonderful outlet for me. There was a program in the chapel earlier on Sunday afternoons called Evensong, sponsored by the campus YWCA, which consisted of poetry and music. I was chosen to be the "reader" for the Evensong, and so I read poetry behind a curtain every Sunday with a beautiful centerpiece on center stage. A spotlight would shine on the centerpiece as I read a poem that pertained to the theme for the week. How I loved doing this program! It was a marvelous outlet for the ham in me, who had a secret desire to perform. While I used to fantasize about going to drama or music school, I didn't really have the language to express the desire back then.

In the Evensong, the college organist would play some beautiful music. As the volume of the music was lowered, my voice would be heard from behind the great curtain, opening with these lines in an almost romantic tone:

> *This is your Evensong*
> *Designed for your meditation*
> *Designed for your listening pleasure*
> *Designed to bring you within the shadows of the*
> *Everlasting Hills.*

The music would come up for a brief time, then go down again and the poetic readings would begin, alternating with beautiful organ selections.

Around holiday periods I would create a decorative centerpiece focused on the theme of the particular holiday. This centerpiece would be on the stage with a spotlight focused on it. For the Thanksgiving period it was always a table draped with colorful foliage from around the campus and laden with fruits and vegetables and candles. The poetic readings would have the theme of feeling grateful and giving thanks. The themes were quite varied. Once when it had rained heavily the Saturday night before the Sunday Evensong, I began with a reading whose first line was "God washed the world last night!" Then continued readings were presented related to cleansing, forgiving, creating a void in order that good things could come in. I still remember Evensong as one of my real pleasures at Virginia State.

In an English literature class in which we were studying Shakespeare, I sat next to Horace Sims, a very friendly student who would walk down the hill to the Campus Grill with me between classes to have a beverage and discuss reading assignments. We had no student union building on the campus and the Grill was the place to go for refreshment, to take a break. Sims was an older married student and one day he told me he wanted to introduce me to a friend of his. I told him to invite this friend to join us at the Campus Grill one day and I would be glad to meet him. Shortly after that conversation Sims brought his friend, George Cotton, who had lunch with us. George called me later, which would be his habit for the rest of my time on the campus. This would be the beginning of a rather long courtship.

George had a big car and would invite me, as often as I could get away, to go on drives with him. On these rides, George began to teach me how to drive. We would regularly go out into the country where his uncle had a farm. I would drive around there and occasionally try to learn to ride his uncle's horse. I still laugh out loud when thinking about learning to ride that horse and hearing George say with some impatience, "Dorothy, can't you open your legs wider than that?" I was afraid of being too comfortable on his uncle's horse, and I didn't see the humor in what he said until later—or the ridiculousness. Actually, it was embarrassing.

George Cotton and me, going out to a graduation dance.

Our courtship became important to me, as it was another way to find some relief from the intensity of my campus life and provided some personal interaction, for which I hungered. George would come to campus on Sundays to Evensong and sometimes would sit in the circle at SCA gatherings. I always thought he felt a little out of place in the circle, but he came because I was there. George worked in the motor pool at Fort Lee, Virginia, and would often talk about the big rigs he drove for the military. He never drove long distances, just around the region, so he was back every evening at his home, where he lived with his mother. George had a long stint in the military; he even spent time in Italy. He told me how he started courting an Italian girl and how White soldiers taunted him about that. George said he made a decision to carry a pistol in the glove compartment of the vehicle he drove while in Italy in case he needed to protect himself from the White soldiers.

George in the military.

GOING TO New York City for the first time with SCA was mind-boggling. It's an experience I shall never forget. Back in Goldsboro, to visit New York was viewed as something the rich and famous did; it was like going to another country, another world. I was chosen to join a group of students from other colleges to participate in a student YWCA conference there. Happily, the Daniels were supportive.

Knowing this was my first big trip, Dr. Daniel decided to prepare me for this exciting experience by giving me a lesson in how to keep up with my things on the journey. He said, "Be conscious of how many things you are carrying. As you move about remember what you have. Count them. Three things? If you don't have three things, for example, you know you don't have all of your things. Just remember the number." This was 1954. Now, after having traveled to many countries around the world, I still do that today. *Let's see, I had three things,* I have said to myself while disembarking in China, India, London, Vietnam, Mexico, England, the Soviet Union, and so many other places. The lesson has served me well.

This New York trip was memorable and full of firsts. While we were in this exciting city, I had my first visit to Radio City Music Hall. I shall never forget what I felt as I saw an orchestra rise up from *somewhere* beneath the floor and come into full visibility as they played beautiful music. Seeing that orchestra pit rise lifted me up from my seat! I was so excited and filled with disbelief, since I couldn't imagine how anything like that could possibly happen.

Back at a YWCA conference session in our hotel, dinner was prepared for our group of about twenty students and our advisors. They served fried chicken. I don't know what else, because the experience of eating the chicken took my energy and attention for the rest of the evening. As I was trying to cut my chicken, it shot all the way down the table. My embarrassment was excruciating. One of the counselors attempted to help me through the embarrassment, saying things like "We all have mishaps." It didn't help. You see, we never ate chicken with a knife and fork at my house back in Goldsboro. Chicken was a finger food. As a matter of fact, I don't remember using both a knife *and* a fork at any meal.

I shared this painful experience with Dr. and Mrs. Daniel when I got back to Virginia State. At our next chicken meal back in the residence, Dr. Daniel taught me how to eat chicken with a knife and fork. Now I can clean even the tip of a chicken wing with a knife and fork. Apologies to my vegetarian friends.

A prophetic incident took place that spoke to the acceptance of this shameful pattern of insult, discrimination, and humiliation. Speakers were often invited to give a lecture or presentation at our college gatherings. This was a time when students were required to go to chapel. On one occasion, our speaker was the notable Dr. Vernon Johns, who had been the pastor of the now well-known Dexter Avenue Baptist Church in Montgomery, Alabama. At that time, rumors circulated that the congregation at Dexter was tired of and a little embarrassed at the antics of their pastor, Dr. Johns. He would soon be asked to leave the church, I was told. The congregation could not have imagined what they would be in for—that is, with the preacher who would replace Dr. Johns. If the congregation was tired of Dr. Johns's challenges and political views, what did they, at first, think and feel when they later would hear challenges by their new minister?

Dr. Johns is known to have peddled fresh vegetables and watermelons from his farm between Sunday services. And, according to one of his comrades in the ministry, a wedding party was upset when he reputedly said during the ceremony: "And now before I pronounce you man and wife, I want you all to know that there is a load of fresh watermelons outside and at a really good price." The bride was reduced to tears, the story goes. He often challenged Black people to become economically responsible and independent and to buy from their own people. Dr. Johns did not distinguish between statements appropriate in particular environments or settings and those which were not.

However, Dr. Johns was a most impressive speaker, and respected as a brilliant preacher, theologian, and social commentator. At Virginia State College, sitting right down front in the audience, I heard him challenge the audience in a way that no speaker had ever dared do before. As he stood at the podium, I noticed he was wearing no socks; such trappings of protocol or formal dress had no meaning for Dr. Vernon Johns. (I think now of Mahatma Gandhi in his khadi cloth.) Dr. Johns has been called a "man before his time." When I think about that statement now I have to say that he was in the right time as well as the right place—from Dexter Avenue Baptist Church to an academic setting where the crowd needed to hear his message.

In a most bold and totally unashamed way, he said to the audience, mostly faculty and staff at the college, "You sit rather arrogantly up here on this hill, and you walk through the town acting as though you are oblivious to the fact that you can't even urinate under your own auspices." His rather shocking observation to this audience, some of the leading Black residents of Petersburg, Virginia, and this college community, was clearly an embarrassment to many. He referred to them as the Black bourgeoisie.

His words helped me, however, to focus the anger I had felt since my childhood about our American-style apartheid. Now I was old enough to begin doing something about my feelings and concerns. Certainly I was totally opened to what he said and accepted the challenge. Not being able to urinate under my own auspices, or go into most public places where others could go, had always filled me with seething anger and embarrassment. And I never heard a single *professional* at my college complain about this sorry state of affairs; not even the president's wife as we sat in her big Buick eating our lunch on our shopping trips to Thalhimers department store, where we couldn't eat in the Tea Room.

Much later I would get to interact with Dr. Johns as we geared up to intensify our protest activity. When he was forced out of the pastorate of Dexter Avenue Baptist Church, his wife took a job at Virginia State College in the music department. Dr. Johns would divide his time between Petersburg and his farm in Darlington Heights. He was very willing to be a part of our struggle in Petersburg and was often in meetings or informal conversations about what we were doing or what we might consider doing next. He was very interesting to talk with, always providing a unique analysis of the topic of discussion. I was often anxious to have follow-up explanatory conversations and he was always most willing to engage with me.

The dynamics changed one day, though, when he said to me, "I don't need you for this kind of engagement," meaning political discussions. I understood him to be saying he was interested in some kind of social interaction. As much as I admired his bravery and candor and enjoyed his company, I decided from then on to wait for group meetings or at least have one other person present when I was with him. I couldn't imagine what he meant by "a different kind of engagement," but I really was intrigued by him and I didn't hold the comment against him.

A friend of mine laughingly responded, "You were already 'engaged,' right?" Even while still a student, I had been touched seductively by a much older man. He had been a dinner guest at the college president's residence. The man, a speaker whom I didn't know and whose name I can't remember, came into the kitchen while I was working on the dinner and took an opportunity to quickly put his hand inside my blouse. Then, just as quickly, he pushed a five-dollar bill down my blouse. He never said a word; neither did I. I kept clearing up the dishes as if he wasn't there. He left the house after dinner. I kept the five dollars.

I was in the graduating class of 1954, wearing a cap and gown, right down in front of the other proud marching graduates. But, unlike so many of them, when I looked around, I saw no family member of mine there to see me receive my degree in English and library science. There were, however, very good friends: Alphena Bowen and George Cotton. George Junius Cotton became my boyfriend and a regular suitor for most of my student life at Virginia State since my classmate Horace Sims brought him to the Campus Grill to meet me. George showed up at my graduation with the largest and most beautiful basket of flowers I had ever seen. It was the first time anyone had ever given me flowers. George actually never proposed, but one day he told me he had bought a ring for me and was going to speak to Dr. Daniel about marrying me. I just went along with it. On the day he came to ask for my hand I stood in the hallway upstairs where I could listen to the conversation.

Me in my cap and gown.

Our wedding day.

Dr. Daniel's response to George was very perceptive. He asked George if he was "really sure he wanted to marry me." George said, "I sure do." He told me later that he would have asked the president of the United States for me. As I think about this now, I'm surprised that George felt a need to do the "proper thing" and ask permission to marry me. I don't know how far George went in school; strangely, I never asked him, and he never told me. But it was clear that schooling was not an important part of his life experience.

I decided to marry George because he was a safe exit out of the confused situation in which I found myself. It was like I didn't know how to be out on my own. So I said yes and let him put the ring on my finger.

• • •

Now I had to think about wedding plans. George and I set the date in 1955 for the week of Thanksgiving. Being a holiday week, we could both easily be away from our jobs, me from the job Dr. Daniel had secured for me in the catalog department in the library at the college and George from Fort Lee.

Having seen movies with glamorous stars getting married in long white flowing gowns, coming down beautiful stairways, I envisioned a wedding where I would float down the stairs the same way in something beautiful. I was so excited that there were stairs in the president's residence, and I planned to live that fantasy. My gown was a short one, lacy and quite lovely. Effie, my sister, and Mildred, George's sister, attended me as I dressed.

As I stood at the top of the stairs, waiting for the strains of "Here Comes the Bride" to be played, I found myself thinking, *What am I doing?!* In other words, my doubts about getting married to George, or anyone else at that time, came into full consciousness. Years later I realized why I had that feeling: I was marrying to break the ties to my painful student past, to get away from the Daniels. The Daniels had wanted me to marry a student from my class who was on his way to law school. I have forgotten his name, but I remember that he showed an interest in me, though he never courted me as George Cotton did. George was always spoken of as a "nice" guy, but that didn't mean we were meant to be a wedded couple. I think our relationship had become just a habit, starting about a year after I arrived at Virginia State College. A few relatives had driven up from Goldsboro and the men in the wedding were waiting in the parlor in their rented tuxedos, and the bridesmaids were all in place. So I proceeded slowly down the stairs to the strains of the traditional wedding song, which was played on the grand piano in the living room by a music student I knew.

After the wedding, to complete the fantasy, I put on my new salmon-colored suit with a large hat to match, and George and I drove off to Washington, D.C., in the new Buick George had bought. We had a reservation at a small hotel for the weekend. On that Thanksgiving weekend, after taking off with my groom into the sunset, I coincidentally saw William Hairston on a sidewalk as we were about to enter the hotel. We had performed together in every annual high school play. He was leading man and I was leading lady. Though I hadn't seen him since high school, I felt a real bond with him. Seeing him at that moment, I began to cry. George said absolutely nothing. He couldn't respond. He didn't know what those tears meant and he didn't ask. He must have been hurt, but he said nothing.

Before we left, we shared a simple fare, which Mrs. Daniel had helped me get together. A guy named Robinson (I'm not sure I ever knew his first name) was the chef in my last year living with the Daniels. Robinson would occasionally come over to prepare meals for them. I saw Robinson again months after my wedding in the president's home and he asked me if I had received the twenty-five dollars he had left with the Daniels for me as a wedding gift. I had not, so I asked Mrs. Daniel about it.

"We used it to buy the refreshments for your wedding," she said. I was shocked and angry. This would be the last insult, since now, at least, I felt "grown" and independent as George and I returned from Washington to our own apartment. It was the second floor of a two-story house owned by a woman I remember only as Mrs. Brown. I would no longer accept disrespect or allow myself to be put down; the sense of myself as an independent adult flooded my being.

Working in the catalog department of the library would be my job for the next four or five years. But keeping house with George and going to my job every day eventually was not enough for the life I had envisioned. I didn't know immediately what I would do about my restlessness, but I knew there had to be something else. George was pleased with our life, but I think he realized I was restless, especially as I became more and more deeply involved in community activities, including working with the Reverend Wyatt Tee Walker, the pastor of Gillfield Baptist Church.

George didn't get involved in community activities or church. He didn't seem interested in anything. I suggested once that he take some course at Fort Lee, the army base where he worked. I don't even recall what the course was. He began to do so, but his mother said to him, "Oh, so you don't have enough education for her?" It occurred to me, though, that I should go to graduate school and pursue a master's degree in something. Where would I go, and what would I study? This was the question. As a teenager, I had listened to a radio soap opera situated, as the announcer would say, "on Boston's Beacon Hill." There was something about the way the announcer said that that intrigued me. That's it. I would go to Boston University (BU) to study for my master's degree. I don't think I ever saw Beacon Hill, but I did go to Boston University on the Charles River one summer and enrolled in the education department. Since we didn't have a speech therapist in the school system in Petersburg, I decided that special education with a focus in speech therapy would be a good thing for me to study. This would allow me to travel from school to school and work with students who had speech problems. I could come back to Petersburg and become the speech therapist for all the schools in the city. The interest probably evolved from my having the leading role in the annual school plays, thanks to Miss Gray, my English teacher.

My first experience at BU was a summer session and it was life changing; I came home for a few weeks and went back for a winter session. This time I shared an apartment with two other graduate students. George would come up to Boston once in a while and together we would visit my good friend Alphena Bowen, now Alphena Bowen Clark. My last session was the summer session of 1960. I pondered briefly whether I would stay and march with the graduating class that August or rush back to take up my role as an organizer in our local protest movement in Petersburg. I decided to stay and march with the other graduates. This, I realized, was important for me, since it marked a milestone in my life and marching in cap and gown symbolized something for which I had worked hard and had long envisioned. Little did I know that this inherent desire to have work that allowed me to move about would come to full fruition by meeting a special speaker invited to my church, the Gillfield Baptist Church. The speaker was Dr. Martin Luther King Jr.

July 25
E Ridge Rd
Lackawanna N.Y.

Hello Dorothy
how is You an George
Getting along fine i
hope, i am Doing putty
good, i Got my same
Job so i am Doing ok
Dorothy i had Planed
to Come home in
august but i Dont
Know wher i will a
now, for money is
so Care i Dont Know
wher i Can make it
are not, it Dont
look much like i
Can make it, but
it will nice if You
all Can Get to Come
up here my vacation

*Letter from Mr. Foreman
to daughter Dorothy.*

2

begon the 4th of
august and i Dont see
how i Can make it Down
home, all so i makes
putty good up here but
it takes a lot up
here to live up here,
i had Planed to Drive
Down and now my
Car neds work on before
i Can get very far,
so i just Dont see how
i Can Come Down, so i
will look for You all
this time,
so i say thats all
for you
from Daddy

Chapter 5

MEETING DR. KING

"I'm on My Way to Freedom Land!"

A rather elderly member of Gillfield Baptist Church in Petersburg walked up to Reverend Wyatt Tee Walker, peered questioningly into his face, and asked, "Are you our new minister?" Reverend Walker said, "Yes." The woman said, "Well, son, you ain't lived long enough, to have sinned long enough, to have repented long enough to be telling me what to do."

Reverend Walker told me this story one day as we stood together on the grounds of the church. He was youthful and dressed in his characteristic Bermuda shorts and was holding a set of golf clubs, a perhaps unusual image of preachers at the time. A young *and* handsome preacher was something that churchgoing woman would have to get used to. Hearing "Wyatt Tee" preach would soon help her with that.

Gillfield Baptist Church is a medium-size brick building located in a quite unattractive industrial area of Petersburg. The former Brown & Williamson tobacco factory is directly across the street.

Gillfield was one of the more popular Black churches, certainly when Reverend Walker and I were there. As our new minister he was dynamic, energetic, and knew how to engage the congregation by establishing various church clubs and organizations. Most members belonged to some group in the church.

I belonged to my "Birth Month Club"; all members belonged to one. The Birth Month Club would be a home base, a place where everyone could get to know one another and feel connected. It was structured for building and making friends, for fostering relationships that strengthened a sense of community. However, the Young Women's Parish Club (YWPC) was the organization in which I was most active. The YWPC was a free-flowing group of members willing to take on a variety of spontaneous, creative activities, such as hosting special guests to the church, for example. Or the minister might call on us to be involved in protest activities against segregation.

We would also create and design activities that we thought would be of interest to others in the congregation. The twelve or thirteen of us who made up the YWPC would often get together just to hang out, and five or six members of the group became special friends of mine. We would look forward to getting together after church to share lunch, often at my home. I loved to entertain, and I claimed to be the best cook among us. Reverend Walker would sometimes join us. At these gatherings there was good conversation, lots of laughter, and definitely good food. I've heard Black historians describe Black preachers who were as talented a pulpit personality and as creative as Reverend Walker as "our Shakespeares." Reverend Walker would certainly qualify as that. In November 1953, *Ebony* magazine cited him as "one of America's greatest preachers."

Wyatt facilitated an evolving sense of community, as most churches did at the time, with his wonderful sermons and readiness to discuss them. Our church stimulated an enthusiasm and energy that added much to our lives. Reverend Walker's sermons challenged us to be conscious of the things that impacted our lives—the social problems and patterns that were unjust—and to understand that we, ourselves, had to take the gospel into the places that needed changing. He brought a new kind of energy and focus. A testament to Wyatt's own enthusiasm, commitment, and energy is the fact that he was not only a powerful pulpit personality, but was also the leader of the local chapter of the National Association for the Advancement of Colored People (NAACP), the leader of the Petersburg Improvement Association, and state director of the Congress of Racial Equality (CORE). To many of us he easily went from being Reverend Walker to "Wyatt" after we were enmeshed in the civil rights work on a much larger stage—in our then hometown of Petersburg and on to Atlanta.

In 1954 I made sure I was an official member of all the organizations led by Reverend Walker and I spent time every week involved in planning activities for each one of the social change civil rights organizations. We were not a large town and there was not a great deal of formality in organizing. Since the activities of all of these civil rights organizations flowed together and the membership lists of each were composed of mostly the same people, this made it relatively easy to protest. Sometimes a phone call would bring me to the church to do training alone, though occasionally other members of the church or one of the other organizations would be asked to take charge of an activity or program. We had a lot going on simultaneously relative to our evolving social change demands. This would not have worked had we been too "academic" or formal. We had to work with whoever was available, whoever would show up when there was a need.

This informal way of functioning facilitated our accomplishing a lot in a short amount of time; too much formality or bureaucracy, I learned, could get in the way of making any progress. We were a small contingent of Gillfield church members mostly and we were highly motivated.

Like so many across the country as well as abroad, we paid close attention to the unfolding drama in Alabama, the Montgomery Bus Boycott, which sparked political protest action nationwide. On December 1, 1955, Rosa Parks was arrested on a bus in Montgomery because she would not move to the back of the bus to give a White man her seat. The policy was that Whites would seat from the front and Black people would seat from the back; Mrs. Parks took a seat in the last row of the section reserved for Whites. When a White man got on and needed a seat, the driver asked Mrs. Parks to move to the back. Mrs. Parks refused to move to give the White man the seat she had taken. The driver called the police and she was arrested. Mrs. Parks's arrest drew attention across all the southern states. Black people were incensed, as were their White allies.

Rosa Parks and me.

Before Mrs. Parks was arrested, a one-day boycott of the buses had been planned by the Women's Political Council (WPC). But her arrest so angered many people in Montgomery that a citywide bus boycott was planned. With Rosa's approval, the local NAACP leader, Mr. E. D. Nixon, and the WPC called for a one-day boycott of the buses. They did so by preparing fifty thousand leaflets and organizing groups to distribute them. Preachers spoke from their pulpits about the continuing abuse of Black people on the Montgomery buses and urged their congregations to support the boycott, and they did.

With the success of the bus boycott, Black leaders came together and formed an organization, the Montgomery Improvement Association (MIA), whose purpose was to continue the fight against the abuse of Black citizens, especially in the local transportation system. They now needed someone to lead this newly formed organization, and so they named a preacher newly arrived to Montgomery to do so. This preacher was twenty-six years old and named Martin Luther King Jr. He had arrived in Montgomery to pastor the Dexter Avenue Baptist Church.

Martin Luther King was just about to receive his doctorate from Boston University and hesitated only briefly before accepting the position as leader of the MIA. Given his fascination with the teaching and work of Mahatma Gandhi, focused on the concept of nonviolence; his oratorical skills; and his ability to use language in a way that would impress the highly learned as well as ordinary people who had no experience in higher education, Dr. King was a sure fit for the battle that lay ahead.

It seemed that Black people en masse were greatly energized by the sight of hundreds of Black folk, and a few very committed and supportive White allies, walking everywhere rather than riding the buses. We saw pictures of buses rolling down the streets of Montgomery with sometimes one or two lone White passengers. Many

White people stayed off the buses, not because they were supporting the boycott but out of fear of violence. The philosophy and strategies of nonviolence had not yet infused themselves into the larger community. But the use of nonviolence to protest the gross injustice visited upon the Black citizens of Montgomery would become an inspiring model in many places.

George Cotton.

Montgomery was not the only place Black people were insulted and abused in a local transportation system; the same pattern of abuse was rampant all over the South. My husband, George Cotton, returned to Petersburg by bus from a trip to deliver a tractor trailer from Fort Lee to another military base. When George disembarked from the local bus that brought him back to Petersburg he realized his luggage had not been taken off. I stood by the bus with him as he yelled to the driver, "My luggage was not taken off!" The driver scowled at George in a very hostile manner and sped off toward Richmond, Virginia, about twenty-five miles away. George and I jumped in his car and drove to Richmond to retrieve his luggage. George made no formal protest; neither did I, I'm embarrassed to say. We had not yet fully *come to ourselves* and this was a time when the protest of a Black man would bring no resolution anyway.

Segregation was widespread in Petersburg, as it was all across the South. WHITE ONLY signs and segregation policies were prominent at most public places. If real written signs were not posted, "invisible signs" were enforced just as rigidly.

A major goal of us civil rights activists in Petersburg, Virginia, was to end the denial of Black people's use of the public library. We were granted a few daily hours of "special access" through a side entrance to a lower level into what appeared to be storage space. This especially agitated Reverend Walker. So as head of the local chapter of the NAACP he wrote to the national headquarters asking them to take the case of Black people's exclusion from full use of the public library in Petersburg. The response from headquarters was that they were swamped and could not add another case at the time. Reverend Walker would not accept that nothing could be done at the time, nor would he put off protesting the situation. He began challenging the policy by attempting to negotiate with city officials.

Reverend Walker wrote to the city manager to protest this library practice. He presented petitions before the city council. On June 17, 1959, Reverend Walker read a part of one of the petitions at a council meeting:

> *Mr. Mayor, Members of the Council, friends assembled: We appreciate this space you have provided on tonight's agenda for presentation of our grievances pursuant to the facilities of the Petersburg Public Library. . . .*
>
> *The present prevailing conditions particularly as it affects Negroes of this city and area . . . is the familiar "separate and un-*

equal." A poorly lighted side entrance with the ridiculous sign "Branch Library" is made for all intents and purposes the "colored entrance." Negro citizens, adult and children, are steered to this entrance by the present library staff. In this basement "Branch Library," which is supposedly separate but equal, there are at latest count fourteen places to sit in, three modestly large rooms and one hallway that are considered "space." The illumination is incandescent in character and limited contrasted against the fluorescent lighting of other areas. If you are non-white, the library is closed to you until after 1:00 P.M. when the Branch or "Negro hours" begin.

We petition as the Petersburg Branch of the National Association for the Advancement of Colored People (Membership 1070) and on behalf of the general Negro citizenry, for complete desegregation of the facilities of our Public Library. It is our desire that unless the side entrance is of some convenient use for deliveries, etc., the same be closed and common entrance for all be the rule and practice.

Our appeals were first ignored and then denied. One letter back to us said the library property was "deeded to the city of Petersburg for the edification and use of *White young men and women.*" Reverend Walker was not about to accept this response, so we intensified our nonviolent strategy of attempting to resolve the issue via negotiation.

There was regular correspondence. We learned that the family that deeded the property to the city had no stipulation that it was for Whites only. It was a "regulation" created and implemented by city officials. We continued the pressure with calls and an exchange of letters and documents. I guess we wore them down, because after months of protesting and negotiating, we got a letter indicating that Black people could use the library as other Petersburg citizens did.

We no longer had to take direct action against the library. Planned picketing was canceled and we could turn our attention to another segregated facility, the local Woolworth's store. Black people could shop in the store but were not allowed to sit at its lunch counter. The Woolworth's became a national and popular symbol of the blatant injustice and insult, and the ridiculousness, of segregation in many cities.

On February 1, 1960, four North Carolina A&T College students staged a sit-in at the Woolworth's lunch counter in Greensboro. Their action created a wave of protests that spread all across the South. Sit-ins then became the modus operandi in many places where Black people were not allowed. It certainly motivated us to head to our own Woolworth's in downtown Petersburg. There were many places where Blacks were not allowed entry, though sometimes there were a few that allowed Blacks in the back door or other designated special entrances, as in theaters and the library. I remember an ice cream parlor where I could buy ice cream for my little niece from a back window but we couldn't go inside. But the Woolworth's had a full lunch counter with seats, so it was an easier target. We had a place to sit for the protest.

We strongly protested the fact that Black people could shop at every counter in the Woolworth's store, but could not eat at the lunch counter. To make a statement we conducted a picket line. Picketing, or boycotting places where Black people were treated unfairly, was a powerful form of protest. Woolworth's refusal to allow Blacks to sit at the lunch counter and the exclusion of Black people from full use of the public library were key targets of the protest movement in Petersburg. There was full agreement that we must dramatize the situation to ensure that no one could say they didn't know about such practices.

To tackle the whole segregation system there had to be a target, a focus, and we had to start somewhere. There was no strategy we could come up with that would allow us to tackle every manifestation of segregation simultaneously—the right to vote; the right to try on clothes in stores; the right to get jobs where we spent our money; the right to be served in the order in which we came up to the cash register with our purchases; the right to a fair trial by a jury of our peers; the right to get new and up-to-date books for our children in schools rather than the old, worn-out hand-me-downs from the White schools; the right to get jobs for which we were prepared as well as the opportunity to become prepared—and on and on in this, our country, which purported to be a shining example of democracy for the whole world. With a visible, designated target, what we wrought there would reach into many other aspects of this system designed to dehumanize a segment of the population. A boycott on the downtown stores in Birmingham, Alabama, for example, got the attention of the entire city. Merchants were hearing us at last after many appeals and negotiation attempts had fallen on deaf ears. Such actions raised the consciousness of those who saw, heard, and understood what we were about. And businesses could see the result of such actions in their cash registers. Often when Black people stopped shopping at specific stores many White people also stopped frequenting the boycotted store. As was the case for the Montgomery Bus Boycott, this was often due to a fear of violent disruptions, not some principled desire to support the boycott.

As in many other areas, White people were oblivious to the Woolworth's situation as well as so many other obvious examples of our American-style apartheid. The racist pattern was just the norm. It was what had always been. A later video, *The Nashville Sit-In Story,* which was about a movement led by my friends and coworkers, shows a White woman being interviewed during the sit-in movement in that Tennessee city. With a look of real surprise she says right into the camera, "It never occurred to me that they couldn't sit at the lunch counter." Reactions like this to our protest activity further verified the need for direct action like the sit-ins. People had to be shocked into bringing into consciousness the insult and the injustice of such deeply entrenched patterns—perhaps especially where we could be in one *part* of an establishment but not in another. It took a shock factor to bring to consciousness a ridiculous norm.

Reverend Walker and I had both noted the Greensboro movement and agreed that we were ready to focus on our own Woolworth's store policy. I volunteered to get a group together to make picket signs. We discussed how we would recruit and prepare a small group of participants to picket the store. So announcements were made in all church meetings including our Sunday school. It would become my job to prepare the picketers. We met in a Sunday school class-room in the church, where we made the picket signs and started our first training session. This would be my first "nonviolence" training workshop.

I really didn't know much about nonviolence. Actually, I knew nothing substantive, except that if you got hit, you didn't hit back. People have actually said to me, "I couldn't stand there and take a lick and stick my cheek up inviting another blow," taking literally the well-known biblical admonition to "turn the other cheek." Well, that's not what we did, either! This simplistic interpretation of non-violence leads to a major misunderstanding of it. As I delved into the concept and study of nonviolence, starting in Petersburg, I became intrigued with the central core of its teaching: how nonviolence can become—and at its best does become—an operating principle for every aspect of one's life. Being actively involved in learning about this philosophy opened a whole new world of discovery to me. I found then and still find the study of nonviolence exciting and trans-formative. I still occasionally reread Louis Fischer's book *Gandhi*, and through the years now, I write and speak about my ongoing journey as a dedicated student of nonviolence. My understanding of nonviolence continues to become "a force more powerful," just as the Mahatma awakened people with his observation that "the British didn't take India away from us, we gave it to them." He went on to explain that they must stop cooperating with unjust laws. This was the goal, too, of our Citizenship Education Program: people coming to understand their power, even of noncooperation.

As I was walking with my picket sign in front of the Woolworth's store with seven or eight other people, mostly much younger than I, an elderly Black man leaned toward me and said, "Lady, ain't you got a table at home?" Affronted and motivated by his anger at me for picketing the store, I laid my sign up against the side of the building and engaged him in conversation. "Mister, if your wife was down here shopping and wanted to sit and rest for a few minutes, have a cup of coffee, or use the ladies' room, don't you think she has a right, the same as a White woman, to do so? Should she have to go all the way back home? Your wife can shop at every counter in this store, but she can't go to the food counter to sit down. You ought to be out here helping us fight to change this!" I wish I could say whether this man ever caught the spark, changed his mind, and related to what we were doing, or at least understood it, even though he himself was apparently afraid of our "stirring up things." My questions, I believe, at least left an impression on him, such that he may have felt compelled to think about the matter. After all, I had tried to make what we were doing personal for him.

Equally important was what my immediate response to him did for *me*. This being my first actual physical protest activity, I discovered that as I was challenging this elderly gentleman, I was also strengthening my own resolve and belief in what I was doing. This would not be the only time that our protests would evoke a negative response. The "Black bourgeoisie," as Dr. Vernon Johns called the people "up on the hill" at Virginia State College, could be heard making comments like "I wish those nappy-headed kids would get out of the street with that mess." Mind you, they weren't really describing our hairstyles, since Afros had not yet become popular. To say someone had nappy hair was pejorative.

I was excited about what was happening in my town. It felt important; I felt useful and very much needed. My church life had become so much more than the Sunday-morning service. Actually, all the protest activity I had become heavily involved in made church involvement more meaningful; the message of the sermons, though always enjoyable, now had increased relevance to what we were actually living through. One could enjoy the artistry in the delivery of a sermon, the mental or spiritual stimulation and the sense of enhanced community by virtue of being active in a church community; but one could also find real purpose and meaning for his or her life by becoming involved in the "movement" activity. Church, religion, community, spirituality — all conjoined to enhance the meaning of what we were doing.

I know Reverend Walker noted my commitment to all that was going on. He knew he could trust me to stay the course with him in all that he was about. This is undoubtedly the reason I was chosen to train volunteers for our picket line. In fact, I think I volunteered, as opposed to having been chosen. The minute Reverend Walker expressed an idea, need, or plan, I was right there with him to help get it going. So, now that we knew we wanted to put a picket line in front of the Woolworth's store, I readily responded that I would train participants and help plan it.

Back at the church, we had recruited people to come to a meeting where we were going to discuss and demonstrate what nonviolence was about and what nonviolent protest could do relative to the goal we had set — to break down the segregation system. Mostly young people came and this would be my first attempt at conducting a nonviolence training workshop.

Thankfully, I would soon come to know that nonviolence was so much more than "not hitting back" physically. My own sense of nonviolence that I gleaned from the teaching of Gandhi was that one certainly does "hit back," though not physically. The hitting back is done in the context of the fullness of the spirit of the doctrine, the philosophy and strategies of nonviolence. It is a different way of "fighting" injustice. It is contained in the goal of wanting to win over opponents to one's cause. I had interesting challenges and success in helping participants understand and accept some of the basic principles of nonviolence. The most resistance came from the understanding that one must accept suffering without retaliation. This was easier if they related this basic principle to the cause—our goal in a protest. Avoiding violence of spirit was another principle that served us well. For example, during one protest, James Bevel, our fellow team member and one of the foremost practitioners and teachers of nonviolence, showed no anger toward a policeman clearly wanting to hit us as we were walking down the street monitoring a demonstration. He gently asked the policeman, "Excuse me, sir, have you got a cigarette?" This demonstrated a simple but brave counter to the stance of the policeman.

Our protest activity was making news. A *Look* magazine photographer showed up at one of my training sessions. Years later, I discovered a photograph of me from that session pulling a girl's hair and blowing smoke over her, though I find smoking rather repulsive now (I used to smoke then, just a little; it was a "glamorous" thing to do at the time). We had to slightly harass training-session participants in order to see if they could take abuse without retaliation. If so, she or he was an appropriate candidate for our protest.

As I immersed myself in a serious study of nonviolence and later saw the *Look* photograph, I hoped that none of my SCLC friends and coworkers at a later stage of my development would ever see this very simplistic interpretation of nonviolence. I know now that none of them knew anything about nonviolence, either; most of them did not know as much as I knew intuitively or spiritually. But we had to start with what we knew, what we had. The movement was happening! Martin Luther King Jr. was teaching and preaching about this exciting concept and philosophy in Montgomery and elsewhere. The whole country started to listen. Howard University president Mordecai Johnson gave a lecture on Gandhi and nonviolence that not only helped shape the Montgomery Bus Boycott but ultimately influenced freedom struggles in many countries around the world. It was a concept influencing a movement in which everyone, old and young, could participate.

REVEREND WALKER told me that he was going to invite Martin Luther King Jr. to come to Petersburg to speak. Having become deeply interested in nonviolence and having followed the Montgomery Bus Boycott and his leadership there, I was excited by the news.

"Mass meetings" were becoming the norm in every locality where a civil rights struggle was going on. People who were not actively involved came in large numbers to these night meetings to get the scoop on what was happening in the town. Our Petersburg movement was building up steam, so Reverend Walker decided to invite the increasingly popular Martin Luther King Jr. to Petersburg to be our mass meeting speaker.

Seldom is there just a speech or sermon when it comes to special programs at a Black church. There is always something added to make a program fuller and more interesting, even entertaining. There is often music, poetry, and dance, and flowers are always added to the stage. I recited a poem before Dr. King spoke.

Banquet-style meals usually follow such special programs, even if held in someone's home. Even in places where we had a good restaurant, there was some pride in preparing and serving a feast of a meal in a residence. For special guest speakers, especially for preachers, such meals were most often planned and served in the parsonage, the preacher's residence.

After the mass meeting at the church, the Young Women's Parish Club served the dinner for our guest of honor. This was my first time meeting Dr. King, who had received an enthusiastic response to his speech at the church. As I observed him at the dinner, I thought him to be an unassuming, gentle man who was easy to converse with. He was quite engaging in conversation, very open and ready to share his thoughts with those of us serving the meal and who had been a part of the program. We certainly wanted him to know how angry we were about the way Black folk were treated. He was a conscious presence interested in everyone, and he made a point to ask who the woman was who had recited the poem on the program. I walked up to his place at the table and told him I had come across the poem in a magazine somewhere and that a notation indicated the author was a teenager, but the name was unknown. I shared some lines from the poem again, telling him that it spoke to me when I was feeling anger and resentment about the exclusion of Blacks from the public library as well as other public places:

> We look out upon the world, eyes deep with pain
> But there is no despair in them or bitterness
> We see millions wronged and hear their cries
> And power crazed men sit throned like gods
> While justice turns away her face and weeps
> But theirs are tinsel crowns already tarnished
> For coursing underneath the turmoil and the hate
> There lies a heart that beats and bleeds for it
> That hopes and still believes

Theirs is a faith that will transcend all wrong
For measured by eternal deathless things
The death knell for these times already rings
That ears like ours may hear, and listening hope
And hoping pray and wait

"I say this poem a lot, and usually change the last line to 'pray and *work*,' " I told him.

I would later learn that Dr. King loved poetry; he loved beautiful language and the songs of our people. He relished the exchange of philosophical and theological ideas that pointedly expressed the longings and experiences of mankind.

Before Dr. King left Petersburg the next day he urged Reverend Walker to move to Atlanta and work with him to help develop the burgeoning new organization he and his colleagues were working to expand, the Southern Christian Leadership Conference. Reverend Walker agreed to go to Atlanta and work with him if he could bring the two people who worked closely with him in our local protest movement. That would be me and a fellow named Jim Wood.

I was very interested in this opportunity, excited, actually, to move to a new place and immerse myself in the freedom struggle and in an organization whose principal goal was to "redeem the soul of America." Having followed the protest activity in Montgomery to change the segregation pattern on the buses and hearing the voice and words of Martin Luther King Jr. as he supported, encouraged, and inspired the people there, it seemed like a great opportunity. Of course, Dr. King was gaining the attention of not only the people of Montgomery but of people all over the country and even abroad. Many people, especially from across the southern and border states, were seeking the help and guidance of this preacher who had been catapulted into national prominence by guiding the people of Montgomery in their struggle for freedom and justice. Here with us in Petersburg, this wonderful speaker and preacher told us he needed a strong organization and a good team to be able to respond to the many requests now coming to him for help and support. In so many cities and towns at this point, people were working to change the abusive patterns and the oppression under which we lived.

Jim Wood.

I don't remember having any hesitation at all, and told my husband, George Cotton, that I would like to join them for about six months. In September 1960, a few weeks after marching in the procession at Boston University to receive my master of education degree, my husband drove me to Atlanta. George stayed a few days and then drove back to Petersburg alone. We never really got to know each other. He didn't seem to relate to the things that took my attention—nor the people. I stayed in Atlanta for twenty-three years. The civil rights movement became my life.

Chapter 6

GREW LIKE TOPSY

I know a change is going to come.

—OTIS REDDING

I wouldn't take nothing for my journey now.

—AN OLD AFRICAN AMERICAN SPIRITUAL

GETTING SETTLED IN Atlanta was not easy. Looking for a place to live brought unusual challenges. After my husband left to go back home to Virginia, I made a fast decision to move out of the motel where the two of us had stayed for a few days. I inquired about places where I could rent a room until I learned the area. At one place, a very nice house where I had been told the owner took in roomers, the owner scrutinized me for an extended time, and then told me, "I'm sorry, I do take in roomers, but I'd be too nervous to have a single, good-looking woman in here. I don't know enough about you." Then, as I was walking down Auburn Avenue a boy snatched my pocketbook. *What have I done?* I asked myself. This was my first week alone in Atlanta.

I soon found housing at Dora McDonald's house. She was Dr. King's "girl Friday," a term still used in the 1960s to designate a female secretary or assistant. Dora invited me to rent a spare room in her cozy house. Dr. King once said, "Dora could be the secretary to the president of the United States." I don't think I ever told her that. I hope he did.

My stay at Dora's house, which lasted less than a year, was uneventful. It truly was just renting a room, a clear business arrangement until I could find my own place. We did not interact as friends, just workers in the same organization. We each had our own car and drove to work separately. This was mostly because Dora's work required her to be in the office constantly, to manage Dr. King's schedule, including the many calls from people wanting to see and talk with him. It took all of her time to keep him organized—or at least trying to keep him that way. And I would soon be required to travel the region.

The first day I walked into the SCLC office it became quite obvious that this was a *movement* office, which for us meant that there was, early on, not a great focus on office organization. However, this would improve as SCLC evolved. I met Ella Baker, Lillie Hunter, and Ernestine Brown in this developing office. Miss Baker, as I called her, was working as the executive director. Lillie and Ernestine were secretaries. Along with Dora this was the entire SCLC staff at the time. Ernestine and Lillie reported to Miss Baker. The SCLC main office organization was very loosely structured.

I worked long hours at the SCLC office as Reverend Walker's administrative assistant. This would change when my job description changed. My work ultimately would require a lot of travel. Simultaneously, I was exploring possibilities for my own apartment; I started to get to know the city pretty much on my own.

Eventually, I would be in my own apartment, then a rental house, and much later my own first home, for which I paid one dollar. The house was on East Ontario Avenue, off what was then called Gordon Street, a main thoroughfare. I received the house through a program designed to "give" long-empty houses to people who would commit to fix them up; a list of required repairs was handed out at a city council meeting. Homeowners were selected by a lottery conducted by the council. I was excited to become a first-time homeowner. Since my work came to require extensive travel it was a great feeling to return home to a place I owned. (Gordon Street is now called Ralph David Abernathy Boulevard. Many of the streets in Atlanta are named for civil rights leaders, fitting since it was home base for the SCLC-led segment of the movement.)

I grew to love living in Atlanta. I used to tell my friends how I loved to travel, and eventually I would get the opportunity to visit many places, including other countries. This would come much later, but I always felt a sense of peace and relaxation as I arrived back home in Atlanta. Atlanta came to really feel like home, and I know now it was because I was growing into our work and feeling energized by it. I realize now that unconsciously I was on the cusp of something big and important. This was also because of the connection I was making to others on our growing team. So a feeling of *family* was emerging. This too was appreciated and it enriched my life.

With three new people—Reverend Wyatt Tee Walker, Jim Wood, and me—descending into the SCLC office on Auburn Avenue, I soon felt settled in—to the work, the environment, and the soon-to-be-growing staff. I felt I was in the right place and doing the right work, work I was destined to do.

THE SCLC office was a rather small space. On one side of the office sat Wyatt, the new "chief of staff"—the title he would take for himself. The rest of us—Jim Wood, Miss Baker, Ernestine Brown, Lillie

Wyatt Tee Walker, Ann Walker, and me.

Hunter, and I—had desks in a large outer section. Dr. King was in the process of moving to Atlanta from Montgomery, Alabama. When he was finally settled in Atlanta, we moved into a larger space in the same building. This allowed Dr. King and Reverend Walker to have a larger space, which would provide them some privacy.

Miss Baker, then in her early fifties, had been a phenomenal organizer for the NAACP before joining SCLC. She had set up NAACP branches all over the South and headed the NAACP branch in New York City. She came to SCLC with great experience and an impressive organizing track record. But Miss Baker would soon show unhappiness with the new arrivals—especially with the men. But I felt as though she and I became friends while she was in this Auburn Avenue office.

The prevailing paradigm at the time in the organization and in the larger society was that men were the leaders and women were the followers and supporters. As Miss Baker said to me, she was not of a mind to be "second to a bunch of chauvinistic men," men who saw women's roles as subservient to theirs. Women were not expected to bring their own creativity, wisdom, and ideas to the table. This pattern of behavior and this way of thinking were not acknowledged consciously by most of us despite how common it was in the organization at the time. Early on we regarded this cultural pattern as "the way things were." We felt a little uncomfortable with these sexist attitudes but wouldn't speak about it until much later in the development of our movement. Miss Baker reacted negatively to this pattern of male chauvinism right away and did not hesitate to speak to me about it. As one of the earliest of feminists, though she didn't use the term, Ella Baker was most unhappy. The atmosphere of male dominance in which she suddenly found herself was clearly not where she wanted to be. Her resentment was palpable.

Miss Baker would often express her feelings with a couple of us when we could take a little time to share lunch or a beer, which she really enjoyed. And she wanted her beer served just as she ordered it. "Don't pour all the beer in the glass," she once told a waiter. She wanted a little poured at a time so the rest of it would stay cold in the bottle. Once, a young man who knew her slightly chided her for having an alcoholic beverage, speaking of what being under the influence would do to one's body and spirit. Ella said, "Have you ever drunk beer?" The young man said, "No." Ella said to him, "Well how do you know?" Enjoying a beer with Ella Baker was a rare and pleasant moment of relaxation in the midst of our social change struggle; I was grateful for her presence, for I could see and feel her wisdom, her consciousness, and learn from her experience.

Miss Baker would soon move on to other areas of work. With Reverend Walker as chief of staff, Miss Baker saw no role in the office for herself. She never challenged Dr. King directly, from what I saw, but the men felt her resistance to their dominance and chauvinism, or sense of full authority. I'm not sure they understood that one could describe their style as dominating and chauvinistic. The modern women's movement did not emerge fully until the 1970s. Before Betty Friedan's bestseller *The Feminine Mystique* (1963) and Gloria Steinem's work, among others, women treaded rather lightly on such issues, though at the time they were often blatantly treated unequally. I looked forward to a fuller exploration of gender inequities within Black culture and broader American culture. Some women felt that fighting segregation had to be our priority early on, with no time to take on the chauvinism of men—Black men especially. Our major goal was getting rid of American-style apartheid. Some articulate Black women felt we could not deal with racism and chauvinism at the same time.

Me at my desk at SCLC.

Miss Baker would soon leave SCLC's main office. Actually, she was asked to work with the students who were being convened at Shaw University in Raleigh, North Carolina. This was a historic event because it led to the founding of the Student Nonviolent Coordinating Committee (SNCC). This meeting put on full display Miss Baker's ability to organize. The deep respect this committed freedom fighter had for ordinary people who were treated unjustly in the American apartheid system was very clear in the way she would help students and others realize their own power. She would ask what *they* saw, what *they* wanted, pushing them to find their own voices. This approach meshed naturally with our teaching styles in the Citizenship Education Program, which I would later direct. This is why Ella Baker and I got along well. She and I could discuss anything together; nothing was too delicate.

Spending time with Miss Baker deeply enhanced my respect and appreciation of her. I can remember so vividly her telling me how she would arrive very early in the morning in a little rural town and sit anywhere she could find. One of these times, she told me, she was on a railroad track waiting for the town to wake up. Then she would find the leaders in the community with whom she had come to work. She would help them come to know that they were not alone and that many people in the southern and border states had the same challenges. As I've mentioned earlier, these challenges included the exclusion of African Americans from the benefits of full citizenship. Miss Baker had left SCLC by the time I was director of education, but we still interacted. We connected.

AS ADMINISTRATIVE assistant to Wyatt Walker, I found that the job was not a small one. Wyatt produced enough work for two or three administrative assistants, with massive numbers of documents to be typed and processed. I'm a fast typist, but the work generated by Reverend Walker was still enormous. We were contacting heads of other organizations as well as petitioning public officials to support our desegregation goals. I often felt overwhelmed with the amount of paperwork Reverend Walker generated and put on my desk, but I was not clear about what else I could move on to in the organization.

One day in the office, after I was with the organization for a little less than a year, Dr. King pulled a chair up in front of my desk and proceeded to ask me a lot of questions. He wanted to know how I got involved in our local movement in Petersburg, about my schooling, my church membership, my family, and my hobbies. He mentioned again the poem he heard me recite back when he visited us in Petersburg and shared how he enjoyed poetry. A major change was in the offing.

A few days after that conversation with Dr. King, I was asked to pay a visit to the Highlander Folk School in Monteagle, Tennessee. This was in early 1961, when Highlander was being threatened with closure because it was "conducting illegal activities." We knew the "illegal activities" amounted to allowing White and Black people to come together. Even selling whiskey was included in the phony charges. These trumped-up accusations were eventually used as a pretext to shut down this popular folk school, founded and run by Myles Horton. Highlander was in the midst of a difficult court battle because of these charges and it was clear that they were fighting a losing battle—the writing was on the wall. The state would win.

Highlander Folk School had first made a name for itself when it opened its doors to the United Mine Workers who went on strike in 1933 in Wilder, Tennessee. At Highlander, the strikers came to understand their rights to fight against the inhumane conditions in which they were forced to work. In doing so, their determination to solve their own problems and their connections to one another were both strengthened.

In 1932, Highlander's founding year, the focus was on helping workers fight for just and fair wages and safe working conditions— to bring into focus problems and concerns of laborers. The facility was a rather rustic but comfortable building that housed workshop participants as well as providing workshop and study space. Everyone would convene in the large gathering room for meetings and meal service. There was a kitchen and two bathrooms.

When I arrived at Highlander I met Septima Clark, a public school teacher in Charleston, South Carolina, who had been fired because she would not say whether she was a member of the NAACP. We had a very rewarding and pleasant time together. Septima offered me tea and we had a long chat as we waited for the fifteen or twenty people who would soon be arriving for a scheduled workshop. She was extremely welcoming and gracious.

One of the things Septima shared with me was a painful event on Johns Island, one of the Sea Islands along the South Carolina coast. A young Black boy had been shot and killed by a White man because he had accidentally run over and killed the man's dog. I wanted to know who else knew of this atrocity, so I spoke with Frank Adams and Scott Bates, who indeed were aware of the story. Adams was coauthor with Myles Horton of *Unearthing Seeds of Fire*, about Highlander and Horton, and Scott Bates was a noted professor, historian, writer, and activist who lived in Sewanee, Tennessee. They had both interacted with Septima and Myles for many years. Both of these men were longtime board members of the Highlander Folk School.

After this horrible shooting, Esau Jenkins, an enterprising businessman on Johns Island, realized that the people there had not risen up in righteous indignation about the killing of the Black boy because they had no political power. Esau decided he would help rectify this situation. He realized that in order to have political power the people of the island must be registered to vote. To be registered voters the people were required to sign their names in cursive letters. They also needed to understand the goals of elected politicians.

Esau Jenkins had a motel, a grocery store, and a restaurant/club called the Progressive Club. It was regularly used as a meeting place for various civic groups. He used an old school bus to transport people from the island to their jobs in mainland Charleston. He would hang the application form for voter registration in the front of the bus to familiarize his passengers with the requirements to become a registered voter. He would distribute copies of the literacy test for them to take home and study. Esau would also discuss the questions with his passengers on the bus even though the questions on the literacy test were designed to intimidate these African Americans of Johns Island. Esau wanted them to be prepared until we could get to the next step—getting rid of the ridiculous, intimidating, and irrelevant questions.

The ability to write in cursive was a requirement for voting in some locations. So, here I am, teaching men and women to do just that.
(Photograph © Bob Fitch)

Esau Jenkins had met Septima Clark at a conference at Highlander and discovered that she had worked as a teacher and had been fired. He recruited her to work with him and the people on Johns Island in his effort to enhance their ability to become literate enough to read the voter registration application form. A famous photograph shows

Septima holding the hand of an elderly man as he practices writing his name in cursive letters. On Johns Island basic literacy was a major component of teaching *political* literacy. The major goal remained helping people to register to vote and realize the connection of voting to political power, and how having such power—or not—impacted every aspect of their lives. The killing of an African American boy or the infliction of other atrocities without any legal repercussions should never happen again.

With Esau and Septima's help, the South Carolina Sea Islanders became excited about learning. They started to hold citizenship education sessions around kitchen tables and in churches and beauty parlors on Johns Island. People on the other islands could feel the change among the people of Johns Island and wanted to have similar sessions where they lived. This especially would be true for Edisto and Wadmalaw islands.

Soon Esau and Septima realized the need for a central place where people could be brought together from different locations to learn to solve their problems. The Highlander Folk School philosophy was especially ideal for doing this. This unique school was a place where people could be brought together and realize they had the same problems.

Esau and Septima got to know Myles Horton, a White seminary-trained educator. His colleague Dr. Harry Ward at Union Theological Seminary in New York urged Myles Horton to go to Denmark to study the success Scandinavians were having in running folk schools. Highlander Folk School would base its philosophical underpinning on what Myles had learned. Steeped in the Socratic method of teaching, he was greatly energized by what he learned in Denmark. So he brought the concept back to Tennessee, where it would serve labor organizers and ultimately civil rights activists who made their way to Highlander to be introduced to this bold experiment in grassroots problem solving by the people themselves. This would be a real trans-formation—a change from waiting for and expecting an "expert" to come into a community to fix things.

As history has shown, Myles was the ideal person, with the right attitude, philosophy, and conviction to make Highlander a folk school that could meet a real need of grassroots people hungry to learn—to realize they did not have to live as victims. People could come together for any good purpose to study and learn.

Myles readily opened Highlander for Esau and Septima's grass-roots citizenship training program, designed to help the people of the South Carolina Sea Islands learn what they needed to know, especially so they could register to vote and realize the power they themselves had to solve their own problems. The Highlander phi-losophy was unique in its ability to help people learn to do just that. It was *people empowering* and still is. Myles became more and more committed to the folk school approach to teaching and learning.

Dr. Lillian Johnson, though she had been a college president, was intrigued with the notion of a folk school and was the owner of the school's lovely property, with a ten-acre lake and cottages in the woods along with the big house that became the main building. I say "though she had been a college president" because Myles's theory was that for-mally trained educators could not do the kind of teaching that was required for the empowerment of grassroots populations like the peo-ple of the South Carolina islands. But Dr. Johnson clearly understood and accepted the concept. In 1932 she gave the property to Highlander with Myles as the guiding light that would bring into being this unique and creative learning institution. In a new location, Highlander con-tinues today in 2012, a training center doing work from the same basic philosophy—helping people realize their own power to solve their problems.

• • •

THE DAY Dr. King was sitting across from me at my desk and questioning me very intensely, it turns out he was checking me out as a potential team member to help develop and expand the Citizenship Education Program, the grassroots training effort started by Esau Jenkins on Johns Island. This was a pivotal moment. My Highlander work would set me on the road to a program that would spread across the southern and border states. I was happy to have my work be focused on this important grassroots training.

I visited Johns Island and enjoyed immersing myself in the culture of the islands. The people of Johns Island were predominantly African American, and, I was told, some of them were functionally illiterate like the people on the other South Carolina Sea Islands, such as James, Wadmalaw, Edisto, Yonges, and Kiawah islands. Formal education was not available to them, but one could attain a strong sense of culture through the language, music, strong vestiges of African cultures, and other practices that these islanders, perhaps more than any other Blacks in the country, maintained for countless years after being forcefully brought to the Americas. I used to enjoy visiting the churches in the area and hearing the Gullah speech and songs sung like nowhere else. Especially in Moving Star Hall on Johns Island, the older people would often gather and there would be powerful singing with shouts and clapping. Guy Carawan, a fantastic White folk musician who learned and then shared across the South the songs of the Sea Islands, describes the clapping as "hypnotic rhythm made with feet on the floor and clapping." We would go to little wooden churches in rural areas and feel the entire structure shake from all those feet, shouts, and claps.

A very special pattern of clapping always accompanied the singing, a rhythmically methodical clapping that produced distinct and different sounds according to the way the hands were brought together in the clap. Hands fully flat together produced one sound; if the hands were crossed with a pocket for air, it would be a bass or heavier sound. When only the fingertips come together, a lighter sound, perhaps a tenor, was produced. Learning and hearing about this rhythmical clapping held over from older times in Africa was exciting. Guy Carawan told us that the best singers were often invited to travel to other cities to perform. They'd return home with some money in their pockets but not enough to avoid going back to their jobs taking care of White families and doing field work on farms, the jobs most available to them. No one offered to manage them in a way that would help them move out of poverty, though this African-style music might have become a career path for them.

ONCE ACCEPTING this grassroots training initiative, the SCLC team recruited people to attend workshops from all the southern and border states. We greatly enhanced the curriculum, and continued to work from the philosophical base that Myles Horton gave to the early initiatives. We also greatly enhanced the learning opportunity and general content of the training. This allowed us to continually adapt to the basic needs, wishes, problems, and concerns that the workshop participants brought to this learning environment. The goal of every five-day session was the same: to help people discover their own power.

Protest actions against segregation were going on all over the South. Occasionally we would initiate contact with activists, but often they would call SCLC feeling the need for a particular kind of leadership. They saw SCLC as being very effective and successful at bringing more media attention to them.

Guy Carawan with his guitar, accompanying a session at a Citizenship Education Program workshop. Seated, far left, is Septima Clark. We still have a good laugh these days when I joke with him, saying, "Guy, you know I thought you were just a skinny little White boy who just loved to hang around Black folk. But when you picked up your guitar and opened your mouth to sing, I remembered how you brought us all those songs from the Sea Islands of Georgia to our protest movement in Petersburg, Virginia. I knew then I would love you! I loved to sing with you and noticed what your gift of music did for us then and now." Getting to know Guy definitely helped me with my prejudice against White southern speech patterns.

A strong focus would be on basic things like how to run a meeting, how to successfully negotiate, the importance and nature of politics, how governing decisions are made, how laws are made, and how to assess whether a law was just and understand the basic documents on which the country was founded. These were regular themes in CEP workshops. Student development of self-awareness, self-empowerment, and techniques in breaking down the walls of segregation and exclusion were always in the mix. These adult civic learners brought their specific problems to the classroom. So we designed a lesson plan that went beyond the basics, based on the real needs and goals presented. The basics were always covered, but we also helped participants draw up plans of action specific to their identified local issues.

Twenty people attended the workshop on my first visit to Highlander. Once settled in their rooms, the participants soon came together for dinner. After the meal people were invited to introduce themselves and share their experiences and feelings. One of the most memorable remarks was made by a young Black man who said, "I just sat down with my plate and a White woman came and sat right next to me and struck up a conversation. This is the first time a White woman sat next to me and talked to me just like I was anybody else."

The year 1961 was a time of rigid separation of the races, a time when in many places and situations Black and White people never interacted with each other with mutual respect, and, certainly, would never sit together to share a meal. There were exceptions, but not in public establishments. At Highlander, however, since its founding in 1932, the climate was a welcoming one, to all people. Excluding anyone based on race was alien to Myles Horton and the concepts he was espousing.

Highlander was invaded more than once by law officers breaking in on meetings for no real reason, only ones they would concoct to bring charges against this wonderful folk school. The harassment was constant. When they were charged with selling beer, Septima said they did *serve* beer but that it was part of a closing celebration. This was regarded as selling by the state. (I never saw Septima sip even a glass of wine.) In any case, it was and is clear that the state had the goal of shutting down this wonderful institution because it would not mesh with the racial segregation policies that existed at the time.

Not everyone appreciated the racial openness of Highlander, and this was the reason Myles sometimes got attacked. He told me that attackers once broke his ribs.

The state of Tennessee clearly had it in for Highlander. The powers that be were not about to stand by and allow such a place to continue—after all, segregation was still the law. They brought the organization to court and there was a long battle; the sham of a trial ended with the state confiscating the school's property. Until the organization was shut down, the state was not through with its harassment of Highlander. After the false charges of selling liquor, the state sought to revoke Highlander's charter. The handwriting was on the wall; the *system* had won. The state auctioned off the facility thanks to a panel of racist jurors and the blatant, pervasive racism of the time.

The harassment was constant and carried out in a number of ways, including labeling the school as communist. The cases of harassment I am aware of not only in Tennessee but all across the southern and border states could fill many pages here. There was a system in place in many regions that supported very creative ways to harass, attack, and brutalize people who interracially came together for any purpose. Even a first lady was not immune from the smearing. People of my generation still remember the large billboard on a major highway with Mrs. Eleanor Roosevelt's photograph and that of Dr. Martin Luther King, with a caption indicating they were at that "communist school" in Tennessee. At the memorial service for Myles, who died on January 19, 1990, one supporter said, "They wouldn't know communism from rheumatism." There was great laughter.

Because of Andrew Young's work as a leader of youth programs for the National Council of Churches, Myles Horton had asked him to join the Highlander staff. Myles saw him as the ideal person to become education director at Highlander. By the time Andy had made all preparations to move from New York to Tennessee, Highlander at Monteagle was no more, the property now sold. Septima said "even cans of peas were confiscated from the kitchen." Details of this blatant racist misappropriation of "justice" are well documented in Frank Adams and Myles Horton's *Unearthing Seeds of Fire*.

Andy is an excellent negotiator and set in motion a process that would allow the innovative education program started on Johns Island to continue. Though he had planned to answer Myles's call and to come south to work for Highlander, he now started to look for other ways, other venues, other supporters, and especially the funds to not only keep the education program going, but to greatly enhance it. Ultimately, through his contacts and connection to the United Church of Christ (UCC), Andrew Young was able to get the Field Foundation, which had been supporting the training initiative at Highlander, to transfer the funds to the UCC to pay his salary, provide stipends for and pay the expenses of participants, and eventually pay the salaries of all of us working with the Citizenship Education Program.

This innovative program would now be situated within the SCLC. Technically we, the program staff, were employees of the United Church of Christ, but only in the sense that the National Church Organization was a conduit or channel for the grant funds for running the training program. In reality we were all SCLC staff, as citizenship education was what this organization, SCLC, was about: that no segment of the population, no man, woman, or child, would ever have to suffer humiliation and treatment designed to designate one as less than any other citizen, that systems in place that institutionalized racism and oppression could be changed—America could be changed. At SCLC we set out to do just that, greatly expanding into a ten-state, region-wide program to achieve this goal.

The thousands who came through the CEP workshops were important members of the "ground crew," as Dr. King referred to social change workers in the southern and border states. The ground crew would be recruited, developed, and deployed when needed to do organizing work in all those states. From Esau Jenkins's bus routes, to gatherings at the Highlander Folk School, and thence to the SCLC training center—the Dorchester Center in McIntosh, Georgia—a bold and creative initiative evolved that became a major energizing force to mobilize massive numbers of people who would tear down the walls of segregation. America would be forced to be true to what it had set as a major founding value: *we the people* would never again be brutalized and deprived of basic rights and all of us could function as respected contributing citizens. This "birth defect," as Condoleezza Rice dubbed it, that America was born with would be healed.

We didn't really know where our intense work would lead, yet we were energized, committed, focused, and determined, and held on to our goal of building a new and different America. See how far we have come, even though the journey toward the ideal continues.

Chapter 7

WHY NOT YOU?

I'm gonna do what the Spirit says do
I'm gonna do what the Spirit says do
What the spirit says do, I'm gonna do, Oh Lord
I'm gonna do what the Spirit says do!

IN 1961 SCLC put a team together that would ensure that the Citizenship Education Program would continue and become stronger, because the very concept was deeply embedded in the heart of the civil rights movement. Our full-time team consisted of Andrew Young, myself, Annell Ponder, Septima Clark, and Bernice Robinson, Septima's cousin, who had been brought over to Johns Island as the first citizenship school teacher. B. J. Johnson, Ben Mack, Carl Farris, and Victoria Gray Adams were also soon to join the CEP team. Indeed, this great transformative movement evolved from a spirit and consciousness of people already working against a brutal and unjust system. A special strengthening occurred when we recruited broadly, connecting people who were dealing with the same injustice.

We planned a residential training session designed to help people discover their capacity to solve their individual and community problems. Andy, being a minister of the Congregational church, knew of an old school building that had been property of the church in McIntosh, Georgia. This historic site was the Dorchester Academy, built as a school for freed Black Americans. When it was no longer used as a school, the church turned it over to the community for use as a community center. Andy negotiated to have it made available to us to use as our training facility for the Citizenship Education Program, which we, as SCLC staffers, would now be responsible for running and expanding—both the curriculum as well as geographically across all of the southern and border states.

This former academy building was and still is a grand old structure, representative of single-facility school buildings of times past, when students slept on the upper floor and teachers on the lower floor. There were classrooms and a large gathering room on the first floor. There was a large kitchen, where the food was prepared and served buffet- or family-style in the gathering room.

At least fifty or sixty people attended each workshop, occasionally more; once I had to secure rooms at a nearby motel for an overflow. Though we don't have an accurate number I believe that more than eight thousand people sanctified this space with what we did there. People came from all the southern and border states. Those who came were there:

- To learn to no longer feel like a victim because of race, poverty, or any unjust system.

- To discover their strength and to live from it, not from perceived weaknesses brought on by comparison to anyone else.
- To accept that we the people have power only waiting to be awakened.
- To realize government is by the people, but only if we are conscious of this right and actualize it.
- To learn how to build coalitions.
- To learn how to build a "movement" for positive change.
- To strengthen confidence in "the rightness of our cause."

We would ponder these questions:

- What does it mean to function as a citizen in these times?
- Do citizens in fact have real power? What is this power? Can they know this power?
- How do we work together in this decade of unavoidable diversity?
- What does diversity look like now?
- How is it different from earlier times?
- What is the role of government; indeed, what *is* government?
- What is the role of the citizen? Do citizens have real governing responsibilities?

Based on the relevant issues of the people attending, we invited those with special information or skills that a particular group needed. People who knew how to "work the system," as one participant called it. For example, upon hearing the distress of one family who had trouble getting officials to test their well water, we invited someone who dealt with just that issue. After a discussion where people said they would rather put their money under their mattresses because they "didn't trust banks," we invited someone from the bank just down the road from us in Hinesville to give a presentation on the importance of banking. People were able to learn the various benefits of and documents used in banking. There was humor once when one participant said, "I don't trust those White folks; I'm gonna still put my little bit of money under the mattress—oops!" She exclaimed, "Now y'all know where it is!"

Getting the word out about the Citizenship Education Program, which would now be convened on a monthly basis at the Dorchester Center, brought exciting and interesting challenges as we plotted the course of our work. In a real sense, it was the local community struggles for justice that provided the platform upon which Dr. King stood—synthesizing, interpreting, and projecting a vision with a voice and message to which people en masse could relate. Our CEP often provided the local "ground crew" in cities where we were called to work, our SCLC staff being the main crew. Without the activism of local people and their decisions to tackle structures of oppression, our roles, including that of Dr. King, would have played out very differently.

Let me tell you a little story about the ground crew. When I was sitting next to Dr. King on a plane once, he looked out the window as workers outside were scurrying about putting bags and boxes on the plane and generally checking on things. He said, "Look out the window, y'all; that's the ground crew. If the ground crew didn't take their work seriously, we could conceivably be in real trouble, never getting where we want to go. Their job could be as simple as tightening a screw that needed to be tightened. That ground crew is just as important as the pilot. That screw could be as important as any other mechanism that keeps this plane in the air."

Not surprisingly, at the next stop, we would soon be treated to a speech whose theme was "The Importance of the Ground Crew." He described all the ordinary people involved in working for social change as the ground crew. As the audience applauded him, he'd say he may have become the pilot, but his work could not be effective if it were not for all of us, the ground crew. He told all of us staff and colleagues, and especially the people he would come to address in church meetings all across the South, how important their work was in organizing and working for social change in their communities: "You may keep inviting me to come and share with you, and hopefully encourage and support your efforts, but just as a pilot flying a plane must have a functioning ground crew, you are the ground crew in our great and important struggle and we couldn't have a movement if you do not do what you are called to do." CEP graduates were key members of the ground crew of the civil rights movement. Their work in various communities along with Dr. King's voice and leadership provided the glue that bonded us together all across the southern and border states. A massive and powerful movement for change was the result.

To determine whom we should invite to come to our five-day training sessions, we decided that we needed to go to designated cities where local leaders were carrying on their struggles against segregation and oppression and the denial of participation in the political process. We would respond to some of the many calls and invitations that had come in to the SCLC office and specifically to Dr. King. Every community wanted him to come and help in their local struggle. Often, for the CEP participants, Andy, Septima, and I (people sometimes assumed on first seeing us that we were mother, son, and daughter) would get in a car and be on the road meeting people, ending up in several of the cities from which SCLC had gotten a letter requesting help. This was one major recruiting tactic. Once a group had come to a five-day workshop, they would then recruit for the next month.

The local leader or contact person would gather a small group to listen to us share why they might benefit from an experience in the CEP five-day workshops. Often the local leader was a preacher, a small businessman or -woman, or an officer of some club or Black organization. There was no e-mail then, of course, so people would simply respond to a phone invitation. Sometimes we'd be given a slot in a church service to explain our work. After sharing the goals of the five-day program we would then extend an invitation to those gathered to join us in the next month's CEP training. Sometimes we would attend a quartet sing. Quartet singing was a very popular form of entertainment across the South. These performances were also a good venue to seek support for and involvement in voter registration efforts. I remember once even recruiting in a pool hall. Andy shot a few balls as he and I talked about a local voter registration drive.

There was always a positive response, always some people who wanted to come, to get involved, to find a place where they would meet other like-minded people. I think a special attraction of the Dorchester Center was that people heard they would be getting together with people from other places who were involved in the same kind of struggle. Occasionally, there would be questioning looks, and perhaps looks of doubt. After all, some of the battles looming before us had been going on for a long time and here we were saying we had a program that would strengthen their efforts—whether their efforts revolved around the denial of the right to vote, being shut out of public places and jobs where they spent their money, or the rampant mistreatment in the criminal "justice" system. I know that some people signed up because it provided an outlet toward something better.

Recruiting was very easy in most places. The meetings set up for us included highly motivated people who were eager to hear what we had to say. Once a group had participated in a five-day workshop, for the next scheduled workshop we had only to call a former participant to find out if there were others in their communities who wanted to know about this opportunity. Former participants would urge others to avail themselves of the privilege to have this experience. The majority of the sessions were held at the Dorchester Center, but occasionally we would convene at the Penn Community Center, depending on where the participants were coming from.

IN A citizenship education session, people learned to redefine themselves. They arrived feeling like victims but went home having shed every vestige or sense of the victimhood that was clearly programmed into Black people through our American-style apartheid.

Dr. King said more than once, "It's a terrible thing when a country so structures itself that a segment of its population is treated as though it is less than other citizens; but it is even more cruel when these habits, patterns, and laws are so embedded in the society that this mistreated part of the citizenry so internalizes these patterns—this mistreatment—that it believes and accepts these distorted definitions of itself." In so doing, in internalizing this oppression, massive numbers of Black people were living out of a deficit of consciousness of who they were. In addition to erasing this "programming," the goal of the CEP was to help people learn to live with a new consciousness, and to become contributing, obligated members of society.

WHILE THERE were deep, sorrowful, and serious moments, there were also moments of great joy and laughter in the workshops and in various other settings. For example, sometimes we had participants who were preachers. It was common for African American preachers to declare that they had "a calling" to go preach. Dr. King knew such preachers and could have fun joking about their call. One preacher said he was plowing on a farm one day and looked up and saw "GP" written in the clouds. The preacher told us, "I know God was telling me to 'go preach.'" When Martin heard one of this man's sermons, in the midst of raucous laughter he said, "I think God was telling him to go on and plow!" I still laugh when I remember Martin asking me, as we were driving on a "people-to-people tour" with Johnny Mathis on the car radio, "Dorothy, how long is the 'twelfth of Never'?" I don't recall my response, but he helped me out by saying, "Well, it's a long, long time." We had a great time, with a lot of fun and a great sense of fulfillment as we taught, learned, and organized. We were onto something big. We felt like family.

For a full eight years the Dorchester Center would be the site of a marvelous experiment in teaching, learning, undoing the effects of brainwashing, and organizing for action. This educational experience was unique because it was closely tied to a powerful social change movement of people. Indeed, it could be touted as the base upon which much of the civil rights movement was built, along with the focus and work of other powerful social change organizations. The NAACP, CORE, SNCC—all of us working toward the same objectives would help America itself move closer to its promise of great moral values, making real the promise of our experiment with democracy.

On a recent visit back to the area of McIntosh, Georgia (it's now called Midway), I walked the grounds remembering us at break time during a workshop, playing volleyball together. I strolled around on the upper floor, then I stood for a very long time in the large gathering room on the first floor, where I recalled the thunderous sound of singing. We took the same energy we used to play and sing into the towns and cities of our country, creating and enhancing powerful social change movements in the hometowns of our participants. Those attending a workshop joined others, meshing goals and the spirit of resolve that would one day, unbeknownst to us at the time, change the whole country for the better. This is what flowed from the actions, the work, and the resolve of the people who started local protest movements and who spent five days in a training session in which they were transformed.

IN THE 1950s and 1960s, Black people still had *"no rights which the white man was bound to respect."* This was set as precedent in March 1857 when the United States Supreme Court, led by Chief Justice Roger B. Taney, declared that all Blacks—slaves as well as free—were not and could never become citizens of the United States in the *Dred Scott v. Sandford* case. Justice Taney, who was a staunch supporter of slavery, wrote the court's majority opinion.

In our civil rights struggle in the 1950s and 1960s we were working against vestiges of this decision of so long ago. It is amazing to me how ancient, unjust, and violent policies can impinge upon life in the twentieth and twenty-first centuries. Many people still react with shock and disbelief when a study of our movement reminds them of how patterns currently operative can have roots from so long ago.

In a recruiting session with a group gathered in the home of some friends of mine, Albert and Eunice Minnis in Norfolk, Virginia, I got some very helpful advice. Years earlier, I had done student teaching with Eunice. Her husband, Albert, said to me after my recruitment presentation for CEP participants in their living room, "You just told us here in this room about an interesting program and you're inviting local leaders to come and participate in it, and you closed by telling us you would pay the expenses of those of us who would like to travel to Georgia—your Dorchester training site—to participate. If you reverse that, and let that fact be known in the beginning—that you will fund the trip—people can hear you better. You see, most people are thinking as you are explaining the program whether they have the money to travel and stay away for five days or not, already concluding yes or no before you finish based on their economic situation. If they know that up front, they'll hear you better." Why didn't I think of that! I already had a master's degree from Boston University, and I'm not sure Albert Minnis finished high school. But I know he was a good businessman. He had a lucrative business selling used auto parts to sometimes major car repair shops. When anyone would ask him what work he did, he'd say, "I deal in junk. I'm a junkman." It's incredibly exciting to realize continually that learning is forever—that is, if one is open to it.

Moments like this deepened my understanding and realization of the many people from whom we can learn. I continue to appreciate the fundamental philosophy of the CEP and Myles Horton's modus operandi, which fueled the spirit of the teaching and learning that was so integral a part of the Highlander experiment since its founding. Formally trained teachers would not make appropriate CEP teachers, I heard Myles say more than once. They were too programmed to follow an "institutionally scripted" approach to teaching and learning. Many formally trained teachers would not even be comfortable interacting in the home of a "junkman."

Being truly open to learning, interacting with people *where they are,* honoring the fact that everyone knows some things, is a trait that made for excellent citizenship school teachers. I understood even more deeply Myles Horton's approach to fundamental, grassroots education, and a part of that concept was even clearer as I realized that Albert Minnis was the kind of person who would make an excellent citizenship education teacher in his community. We could all learn from Al, both the teachers and other students. What I learned in Al and Eunice's living room made me a better CEP instructor and a better recruiter. He was just the kind of person we were looking for, though I got to know many such "philosophers" in the eight years of this training model.

I was very much at home, really flowing with this approach to people and learning, plugging into their capacities as opposed to some perceived deficit by others or by themselves, thanks to the programming of the culture of the time. Perhaps it was because of my own upbringing and because I never got steeped in the teaching methods of some public school systems anyway. I have been hungry for and open to learning and having new experiences for as long as I can remember. And being the director of education for SCLC, I enjoyed the opportunity to share this nonformal learning approach.

One time I was attending a conference in Atlanta and during a break a colleague of mine told me he was going to Senegal to the first African World Festival of Black Arts. I said, "Going to Africa! Wow! What a wonderful thing to be able to do! I wish I was going." My friend said, "Why don't you?" I walked away from that conversation pondering that question: *Why don't I?* Something was stirring inside of me. I had never considered that traveling to Africa or any other country was simply a matter of a particular mind-set. *Why don't you?* This too was a moment of transformation, a moment of realizing that I could change the way I thought of possibilities. I went to the festival in Senegal and have been going to other countries ever since. I'll never forget sitting on the stoop of the hotel, and a tall, handsome man was next to me. It was Cab Calloway!

*At one of SCLC's annual conventions, we decided to pay tribute to Septima Clark.
She was our senior teacher in the CEP. We presented her with
a bouquet of roses and a crystal bowl. She deeply appreciated being honored,
but later on, she couldn't resist whispering to me, "Dorothy, why does
anybody think I need another bowl?" And I laughed.*

That little question "Why don't you?" is one that I came to use
many times as I worked with the adults who came to our five-day
citizenship education workshops. As I noticed someone caught up
in the pattern of seeming to only complain, especially about the way
some official had treated them, I'd ask, "Why don't you have that
job?" Why aren't you on the school board, on the city council, in
the legislature, in the mayor's office—and on and on. I'd work with
participants in our workshops in a way that sometimes shocked them
into thinking outside the box.

I remember when a housing committee was needed in Ruleville,
Mississippi, Fannie Lou Hamer's hometown. Mrs. Hamer would

just walk out into the street and shout, calling neighbors' names like, "Bessie, how many can you sleep?" or "Margie, how many can you sleep?" On and on, she shouted until she had secured enough housing for all the (mostly White) students who were on their way to Mississippi from elegant northern colleges and universities to be part of the "Freedom Summer." The focus of the Freedom Summer was an effort to strengthen the political consciousness of the people of Mississippi, especially African Americans. As previously indicated, there were many obstacles put in place to keep African Americans from participating in the political process. Freedom Summer was launched and led by activist Robert Moses. His work contributed greatly to changing the cruel system operating in Mississippi.

Another SCLC annual convention moment: (right to left) Wyatt Tee Walker at the podium, me, Ralph Abernathy, Juanita Abernathy, and James Bevel. Hosea Williams enjoyed telling people that "Dorothy was the first one on our team to stop straightening her hair."

Chapter 8

"THE COBWEBS COMMENCED A-MOVIN' FROM MY BRAIN"

"Ain't You Got a Right to the Tree of Life"

The day started like any other day at the Dorchester Center. Buses were pulling up on the grounds, cars were finding their way there, bringing people from all across the South to see what this week's training session would do for them. They were farmers, preachers, students, homemakers, beauticians, seamstresses, sharecroppers— and they were all African American. All African American because we were living in a time of rigid separation of the races. It was illegal or at least dangerous for Black and White people to come together in equal relationships. This was 1962, and their arrival was a response to the call that if they would come together for a Citizenship Education Program workshop, they would go back home stronger and more enlightened about how to tackle their problems. As people got off the buses or out of their cars, they were greeted by me, Annell Ponder,

125

B. J. Johnson, Andy Young, Septima Clark, and sometimes others of our team. Once settled, the new arrivals were served a great southern meal of fried chicken, okra, lima beans, greens, corn bread, and apple pie, prepared by Mrs. Beulah Devette, who lived right there in the neighborhood, just across the street. Afterward we would all gather in the great room of the Dorchester Center.

IN THIS great room we would begin with a community sing, a gathering song or two. Songs from our actual life experiences would come to play an important role in all that we did in the civil rights movement. It was now time to start to get to know one another—who each one was, and not only where each had come from geographically but *what* each had come *from*.

People were often very dramatic in the way they would introduce themselves, sometimes through heartfelt prayers for "the oppressors," and for the suffering they were enduring: being treated as noncitizens, nonpersons. After Mrs. Fannie Lou Hamer's first workshop with us, she would return bringing others from the delta of Mississippi. An introduction was often done with the inclusion of a song. Mrs. Hamer, a robust woman with a full, rich, booming voice, would start a song and we'd all join in. I remember the first time she told us that her husband, "Pap," as she called him, took her to the next county because she had been threatened with violence if she didn't stop the foolishness of trying to get other tenants on Mr. Marlow's plantation to learn to register to vote. Pap did take her away, but one day she called Pap and told him to come get her, that she was not going to run from home and hide because she was "sick and tired of being sick and tired," tired of being abused and treated like dirt. Pap went for her and brought her back home, where she became more active than ever.

There would always be a song to help express the feelings evoked by what people shared. The song could be by the person sharing or by someone else who felt strongly about what was being shared. There were often "sorrow songs" that helped to tell a story like Mrs. Hamer's and that of so many others.

When anyone would strike up a song, everybody would join in. What I call Mrs. Hamer's signature song, "This Little Light of Mine," would always get everybody energized. But then, *all* the singing seemed to do that. Everyone knew the most popular songs and they were sung spontaneously. This was a common occurrence in Black churches—spontaneous singing. One often-sung sorrow song was "I've Been in the Storm So Long":

> *I been in the storm so long*
> *I been in the storm so long, children*
> *I been in the storm so long*
> *Gimme little time to pray*
>
> *Oh, let me tell you, brother*
> *Just how I come along*
> *Gimme little time to pray*
> *With a hung down head*
> *And an aching heart*
> *Lord, gimme little time to pray*

Then other names would be called with supplications to understand:

> *Let me tell you, Sister/Preacher . . .*
> *Just how I come along*
> *. . . Please gimme little time to pray*

As people began to feel more and more comfortable in this new environment, a bonding occurred, and in this atmosphere people began to articulate specific reasons they had accepted the invitation to come to the Citizenship Education Program training. We heard, for example, "When we go down to the courthouse, we're treated like dirt, like they don't see us as people." (Well, they didn't.) "They'll test everybody's well water but mine," one woman shared. "The pavement stops once it gets through White areas," another told the group. "We work all year on the man's crops," one preacher said, "and at the end of the year, he says we owe *him* money."

We heard about "whore's hollow" from Mrs. Annie Devine from Canton, Mississippi. It was called "whore's hollow" because bodies of young Black women had been found there after they'd been sexually abused and killed. "The books in the Black schools are so old and worn-out, they ain't about nothing that's going on now. And the buildings are so raggedy, not much teaching and very little learning happens there," another woman reported. "The Black kids have to work in the fields; else we get put off the place. They don't care whether Black children get an education or not." And from another: "When any of us do want to try to register to vote, the place always closed." Or, "Our children have to go off to Chicago or somewhere to find work." And, "If we can learn anything in this citizenship training that will change our sorry lot in life, I'm glad to be here." These were the kinds of feelings being voiced by those who came to these opening sessions.

I know there were a few who came because it was a free trip and some who came out of curiosity, but most of the people were there out of hope that they could find encouragement and help for the struggle for justice they were in back home. It was clear they were committed to changing things. Mrs. Viola Smith said, "I already decided God didn't intend for me to live like this; the way we have to live."

"There's an old song that speaks to what I feel," someone re-flected, wishing he could sing it then. "It asked the question," he said, "about how can we sing the Lord's song in a strange land? But we're struggling, and I have faith enough to run on and see what the end will be." He was referring to a musical version of the 137th Psalm:

> *By the rivers of Babylon,*
> *Where we sat down*
> *And where we wept*
> *When we remember Zion*
> *Where the wicked carried us away*
> *Captivity required of us a song*
> *How can we sing King Alpha's song in a strange land?*
> *So, let the words of my mouth*
> *And the meditation of my heart*
> *Be acceptable in thy sight, oh Lord.*

With these expressions of pain and hope and even celebration of coming together, we, the staff, started to share our intentions, the goals, for this five-day experience, how we were all going to learn together and how we would work from the real-life experiences they brought with them—that we all brought together. We told them, "We will explore approaches to understanding some of the root causes of some of the problems, and realize things that you can and must do to change things."

We wanted to make the basic documents on which our country— yes, *our country*—is founded come alive. We intended to establish and deepen the concept and awareness of ourselves as *citizens*. No more being a victim. We wanted them to see themselves no longer simply as "consumers" of government, but rather to see the government as "us." "I think you will leave here after a week feeling like 'obligated members of society.'" I would always say, "There is something *you* must do. We envision that you will discover your capacity and, indeed, your obligation to help solve the problems we face as communities, as a people, as a society, coming clearer and clearer about the fact that if things are going to change, you will have to change them."

Our hope was that we all might begin the creation of a vision of new institutions that, by virtue of a new consciousness, and a redefinition of ourselves, we would help develop. And where they were already in institutions, people could take this new awareness to that place where making a difference would be inevitable. Though there were no quick fixes, we must *be* a part of the changes we wanted; we must be the change. We told them that you must "cast down your buckets where you are," as Booker T. Washington advised, and in this context see what's right in front of you, as most of you are already doing—putting your energy on what you see that's not working for one segment of the population. Once you see yourself as *citizens* you will function in newer, more effective, and more powerful ways. And if they didn't want to listen to speeches and sermons related to the movement, the songs would get them.

A Pivotal Curriculum Session

Having studied at a two-month-long seminar at the National Training Laboratory in Bethel, Maine, and in the "human potential movement" sessions at the Esalen Institute with Will Schutz, a social psychologist who headed Esalen's residential program, and others, I had become convinced that there were unique and dramatic ways to make a point in teaching, methods that were sure to help people reach new realizations. Any good teacher knows that just "telling" something is not as effective as when students struggle to understand a concept through serious dialogue. This may be even more true with people at an age when they have already established their style of learning and are already set in their ways. So, being highly motivated to help them *open themselves* to new ways of learning, to help them discover the joy of new realizations and become ready to teach others, I wanted the session on "Being a Citizen" to really grab them.

I therefore envisioned and designed a session aimed at delving deeply into the concept of citizenship. As usual, we opened the morning with me and B. J. Johnson leading the group in a song. Sometimes someone in the group would offer a morning prayer to start the day, but there was always powerful group singing as well.

As I stood before the group of forty-five or fifty people, occasionally more, I began by saying, "Tell me, what does the term *habeas corpus* mean?" I walked around the room for a few minutes, looking directly at anyone who seemed to be really curious and searching for an answer. Very shortly, if no one came up with an answer, I would answer the question: "*Habeas corpus* is a term used to demand that anyone holding an individual, as in an arrest, 'produce the body,' that is, they must 'bring the person before the court.'"

Then came the key, serious question: "What's a *citizen*?" My session on the meaning of citizenship began, revealing an example of a teaching method that could be instructive for anyone setting up a local CEP class. And this is exactly what each was requested to do once back in their community. For the better part of the morning the group would grapple with this question, this concept of citizenship. "Someone who doesn't break the law," someone answered. "If you treat your neighbor right," or "Following the Ten Commandments," someone else would say. "Well, you ought to vote," I can still hear a preacher from South Carolina say. "Yes," I confirmed. "You ought to vote." "If you don't break the law" and "It's my God-given right"—those two answers were always in the mix of the definitions of a "citizen."

Somewhere in the midst of this discussion, slowly but surely we'd get to a point where someone would mention something about a major law in the land. "Yes, the supreme law of the land," I would be so glad to be able to confirm. "And what is that law?"

It didn't take very long for someone to say, "Oh, yeah, the Constitution." This statement would take the group into a full discussion of this "supreme law." Everybody was familiar with the terms *Constitution* and *constitutional rights,* because many of even the poorest people had a television—at least a black-and-white one. And in the early 1960s everyone heard people "taking the Fifth" in televised court hearings. We'd have a big discussion about what this "taking the Fifth" meant. Watching and hearing people speak of the right not to self-incriminate helped us affirm the fact of this supreme law. We would have a general discussion about the term *Constitution,* which would now be written in big letters on the chalkboard or flip chart. Copies of sections of the Constitution were distributed to every person.

This document was used to enhance reading skills as well as to help people come to know its meaning for our lives. This was an important part of the lesson, as these emerging citizenship education "teachers" would be expected to work with people back in their hometowns. Some of them were often functionally illiterate. So, reading sections of the Constitution served more than one purpose.

The group started to realize what we'd been missing—a real consciousness of the "law" and claiming and affirming that it belonged to Black folk, too! Coming to realize how claiming and internalizing the message of the Constitution could be applied to the struggle for social change was fundamental to the goal of empowerment. And empowerment is what we were about.

It would soon become time to move to the structure of this

supreme law of the land. What comprised it? Someone had mentioned amendments, especially the Fifth. "Yes, it has amendments," I would affirm. *Amendment* would be written on the chalkboard. Visualizing the term, writing it, and using it in a sentence was a helpful technique that I knew from classes in high school; we knew that *seeing* a term as well as using it in sentences enhanced retention of its meaning. From a full discussion of amendments we would highlight those amendments that were directly applicable to the struggle of every participant in the workshop. Amendments are "add-ons," or changes, one man said. When an omission or a need was recognized, a proposal to address the missing item or concern would be developed. It was now time for a discussion of the Fourteenth Amendment, which was related to what we were about: citizenship.

You could actually see the comfort level rise, the satisfaction at the realization that this "supreme law of the land" we had identified establishes one's citizenship. We would read aloud together that *"all persons born or naturalized in the United States . . . are citizens of the United States and of the state wherein they reside."* Another important provision of this amendment was this: *"Nor shall any state deprive any person of life, liberty or property without due process of law, or deny to any person within its jurisdiction the equal protection of the laws."* Though the Fourteenth Amendment actually failed to protect the rights of Black citizens, it did lay important groundwork for the changes fought for and won in the twentieth century. We had to insist it be applied to us as well. This was a fundamental reason for the struggle that changed our country.

When participants started to internalize the Constitution's declaration that no state can take away your privileges of citizenship, one saw a change in the very faces of many in the room. This was true even though Supreme Court Chief Justice Roger B. Taney wrote in 1857 in the Dred Scott case that the framers of the Constitution believed that Blacks had "no rights which the white man was bound to respect." Taney further stated that even the phrase "all men are created equal" was not meant to include Black people. This statement actually provided a challenge to participants in our workshop. It motivated people to roll up their sleeves and work harder with a determination to make this quite wonderful document include them, too. As Dr. King so powerfully challenged the country, "America, be true to what you said on paper!"

The people in the room began to realize from these statements in the founding documents that each one of us has the same rights as every other person in the country. This right is inherent: *being a citizen* is legally based as well as a *God-given right,* as someone had offered when we started the discussion. One could actually see confidence emerging; people were being strengthened, and there was a kind of lightness about the room, a kind of joy found in the challenge to make these words include us.

We now needed confidence in the growing realm of physically challenging demonstrations—of marches and protest activity in which so many in the room were actually involved back in their hometowns. So the study of the First Amendment was the next order of the day. *"The right peaceably to assemble and to petition the government for redress of grievances"* was one of the most meaningful and necessary discussions we had, as these very grassroots people confirmed. Now when the call went out for people to gather for a protest or demonstration, there were people all over the South who knew, with confidence, that our cause was just and that we had the legal right and even the obligation to "petition the government for redress of our grievances." Translated and practically speaking, for Black people at that time the First Amendment was saying to us, *We have the right to march from Selma to Montgomery to say "we ain't gonna take it no more!"* What had seemed to be rather mysterious or perhaps even meaningless declarations in the First Amendment, like a lot of apparent mumbo jumbo, took on real meaning in people's lives and our struggle.

So, people who had lived for generations with a sense of impotence, with a consciousness of anger and victimization, now knew in no uncertain terms that if things were going to change, *they themselves* had to change them. They now had the consciousness of a firm philosophical as well as legal basis for challenging oppressive systems and even accepted the *obligation* to work to change such systems. The truth that no one had the right to dominate and oppress them was an important truth to internalize. To realize their responsibility to assume the role of a citizen, accepting all that it meant, was necessary. Participants were internalizing the realization that everybody can't be an elected official, but everybody can vote, everybody can hold elected officials accountable and help remove them from public office when they are not accountable. Everybody can study the issues—inform themselves—and even see themselves holding public office.

To massive numbers of Black people, government had seemed like something rather mysterious, and certainly as somebody else's business. In our CEP sessions government was now being demystified. People who had lived for generations under an oppressive system were starting to redefine themselves as well as their concept of government.

As I've mentioned before, I already had a master's degree in special education from Boston University, but I learned more about how to function as a citizen, how to live and work from this consciousness, as I worked with the people who came to the Citizenship Education Program.

Four Young Men in Black Leather

One day a group of four young Black men walked late into the session I was conducting on the Constitution of the United States as it relates to citizenship. My image or stereotype at that time of young men in black leather clothes, chains, and boots who rode motorcycles came swiftly to the fore. I was nervous, lest they were violent. These young men grabbed copies of the Constitution from the resource table and began throwing them on the floor and yelling, *"We don't need this damned racist document! We need our own government, our own laws. You're wasting these people's time!"*

I'm not exactly sure how we stopped their interruption of my session, but there's a photograph of me somewhere, and Delores Harmon, who was working as administrative assistant to the program, said, "Dorothy, you looked scared!" I was. But I soon gathered my courage and started to dialogue with these young men. "Are you all coming for the Citizenship Education Program we're conducting here this week?" No response to my question; just more rude and violent rhetoric. "You're welcome to stay if you will take a seat and you're welcome to participate in the discussion we're having about the relevance of the Constitution to our lives, to our struggle." Somebody in the group started singing one of Guy Carawan's songs, "Ain't You Got a Right?"

They seemed to calm down a bit. These young men took seats and looked questioningly at us and listened. At one point, when the dialogue turned to some specific action concerning a bridge people intended to tackle once they got back home, one of these fellows said, "You just ought to burn the f—— bridge down!" I must have no longer felt intimidated by them because I thought my comeback to that suggestion was very clever. "Okay," I said, "we'll hear you, and you are welcome to participate, but you must find a more intelligent and respectful use of language if you're going to participate. And now take note of this: Miss Lucy over there was speaking about that bridge as the route they take going to work every day. If you burn the bridge down, do you have some engineers ready to rebuild the bridge or some plan in place to involve and support Miss Lucy and her husband? Besides, you may feel powerful destroying the bridge, but what is your goal? How does that action feed into a plan for the area?" He had no ready answer, but I had a plan for the afternoon in which they could play an important role if they stayed. They did.

WE'D PLANNED a "trust walk" for after lunch. Everyone was to pair off with another person. I don't remember the name of the most vocal of the group of young men, but I asked him, the one suggesting burning the bridge, to specifically walk with Miss Lucy. "Now the goal and purpose," I emphasized, "is to listen to your partner share with you why she or he came here to this CEP session, and what their vision is for continuing their struggle for change when they get back home. In other words, what does your partner want to have happen as a result of the struggle he or she is involved in?" They were advised to then change roles. The listener would become the speaker. When we reconvened, each would explain only what *the other* had shared of their goals and vision.

We did this exercise more than once as a way to enhance appreciation of one another. It was an exercise in really listening and dialoging and doing it respectfully. It was a way to realize that there is more than one approach to dealing with and solving problems. We had a long and intense discussion about possible results of various actions we would take and whether our actions moved us toward our goals. The leather jacket guys never articulated goals; they were just deeply angry. And at first this was the only energy they were bringing forth.

It was very difficult for anyone afterward to continue speaking as though his or her opinion or approach were the only one. Even the act of walking with another person, if following the directive, created a space such that each had to really *see* and *experience* the other, as well as see the other as worthy of being listened to and with energy as valid as theirs. Once we reconvened, anyone not able to say what their partner had expressed got the message and started to show at least a little embarrassment if they had not followed the plan. These guys in the black leather jackets projected a different attitude now. They realized a need to garner some modicum of respect, even from Miss Lucy, which they'd never get if they made her feel she didn't know anything, that her feelings didn't matter, that her life and way of working didn't matter. I concluded that they started to understand that if they really wanted to change the status quo, they needed to see and relate to the whole community and hear the views and concerns of others. Otherwise they themselves would be isolated. They would create no *movement*.

"Tell me, what is habeas corpus?" I suddenly threw out at the group. They looked surprised, probably having forgotten that this was the question with which I had opened the session on "Being a Citizen." No one could provide an answer. I was very glad they couldn't, because a part of my plan was to demonstrate to them at least one effective way of teaching. After all, a major purpose of the CEP was to help participants in this training experience become teachers themselves once back home. The expectation was that many would create their own citizenship education classes, whether around their kitchen table, in their beauty shop, the basement of their church, the back of the little corner store—wherever they could find the space to accommodate the regular convening of a group of people who wanted to feel more empowered and no longer a victim to the oppressive and dehumanizing environment in which so many of our people lived. We expected them to become *citizenship school teachers*.

"Okay," I said. "Now I ask you to answer this question: What's a citizen?" There would ensue a rewarding discussion of the meaning and ways of functioning as a citizen. The sense of confidence in the room was palpable. People realized they didn't need anybody's permission to fight for the right to vote, or to go in establishments licensed to serve the public. They realized that they indeed had the right to march from Selma to Montgomery if necessary and to express in different ways that "we will no longer tolerate the abuse of this oppressive system." Mrs. Topsy Eubanks said, "The cobwebs commenced a-movin' from my brain!"

"What I've attempted to demonstrate is a teaching method that will help you to help people redefine themselves," I said. "I trust that what you have expressed in here today—what you have experienced here—you realize that, with your help, the transformation occurring for you, people back in your home community can also experience. I emphasize now a teaching method that may serve you very well. You see, I quickly told you the answer to the first question I asked—about habeas corpus; I didn't expect or want you to remember the answer in order to show you what happens if you throw out your answer to a question compared to what can happen when and if you want people to come to a new realization. To really internalize a new awareness, you should set up a 'dialogue situation' in which they are forced to struggle with a concept until they truly get it. Real learning comes from inside a person. The best teacher ultimately is one's inner self. The lesson is realized. It is remembered. It is internalized. It is truly the learner's.

"The teacher's job is to create a climate—a learning environment."

I would sometimes call Dr. King and ask him to come over to the Dorchester Center and meet and greet the forty or fifty people, sometimes more, who had been studying with us all week. I especially wanted him to be there on the last day, when the group would set up our large gathering room for a closing banquet. The group could be very creative, scouring the area for decorative greens and local flowers and planning a program that would reveal to Dr. King what they had experienced and learned during their five days with us. Participants were encouraged to plan skits, and share with the group how they had grown in confidence and skills to enhance the social change work in which many were already engaged back in their hometowns.

CITIZENSHIP EDUCATION CLOSING PROGRAM

OPENING PRAYER: Grace before food is served: "For the rich experience we have had this week we give thanks" and "We give thanks for this generous table and pray that those who have no food will come to experience the bounty and generosity of the earth."

The Menu

DRINKS:
  Mind Cleansing H_2O
  Transformational Cranberry Juice

APPETIZERS:
  Civic Duty Cheese and Crackers
  Diversity Fruit Platter

SALAD:
  "We the People" Tossed Salad

ENTREE:

Citizenship Baked Chicken with Nonviolent Milk Gravy

Freedom Singing Green Peas

First Amendment Mixed Vegetables

Constitution Sautéed Mushrooms

Clear View Buttered Carrots

Reconciled Corn Bread

DESSERT:

Voting Rights Apple (or Sweet Potato) Pie

Desegregated Chocolate and Vanilla Ice Cream

Nonviolent Coffee and Tea

Human Rights Chocolate Mints

Closing Speaker: Dr. Martin Luther King Jr.

CEP certificate.

Dr. King often joined us for the closing and it was great fun for him and for us. Of course, he knew we expected him to give the group a big send-off with a rousing speech of encouragement. I will never forget one powerful statement he used to cheer them on in their community work on this last evening. He told them, "Nobody can ride your back if your back's not bent!" They were standing tall now, with greater confidence and awareness of their own power. There was no sense of being a victim. You could see a difference in the faces of everyone who had spent the week training with us. I was always especially pleased when Martin could come over.

WE WANTED the last day of our training sessions to be fun and festive. Andy loved to dance and so did I, so sometimes during the week when the studying was over we'd move the chairs and tables and put on some recorded dance music and have almost a dance competition. Having this close-up time with Dr. King, when he was able to attend, on the last evening together in an informal setting and feeling his pleasure in being with all of us, even seeing him throwing a few balls over the volleyball net, contributed to the joy of coming together in a CEP workshop week. Most important was the transformation that was so obvious in everyone who had spent the week in the workshop. Those of us who were the teachers grew as well, both in confidence and in teaching and learning techniques.

I still smile when I remember what fun Martin was; he could be really funny, even joking about some of the ridiculous ways that racism showed itself. For example, once when we were driving on a "people-to-people tour" recruiting and speaking, with four or five of us in the car, he said, laughing heartily, "I know how we can solve the race problem: we should get a law passed requiring everybody to marry someone of a different race!" I could see he was in his element when he had time to just hang out with us—his team and CEP soon-to-be "graduates." We always scheduled the "playtimes" in the afternoon. Dr. King was very gregarious and clearly enjoyed the relaxed atmosphere at our workshops.

Dr. King at the Ping-Pong table. He was a jolly fellow
who loved to relax and play.

Back in their hometowns, our "graduates" would get others to join in the effort to break down laws and patterns of segregation. These would be the places where protest movements would grow. Sometimes we would follow them home to help and support them in their local organizing and protests and help them set up their local CEP class.

These towns, large and small, would become the hotbeds of movement activity: Albany, Savannah, and Atlanta, Georgia; St. Augustine, Florida; Birmingham and Mobile, Alabama; many towns in the Mississippi Delta; towns in North and South Carolina; and towns in Tennessee and Virginia. Actually, none of the southern and border states was untouched by our CEP recruitment and training efforts.

ONCE WE had participants from an area, these "graduates" would become the recruiters for the next month's training session. They delighted in returning to their hometowns and telling friends, neighbors, and fellow church members about the fun and rewarding time they'd had at our training center. These gatherings always included enjoying Mrs. Devette's great meals, the joy of meeting people doing the same protest and organizing work we were doing, the singing, the laughter, and sometimes the tears.

ONE MORNING I had a group of visitors in a session on the meaning of citizenship. The group was from the Putney Graduate School of Teacher Education, located in Vermont. Having heard of the birth of this adult grassroots training program and knowing of Myles Horton, who loved this way of helping adults discover their own power, they came to spend a full day to see for themselves what we did. The professor with the group of graduate students said to me at the end of the session, "That was a brilliant piece of teaching." I've shared an account of this session in speeches in many places around the country, especially as I've often been invited to give talks to teachers and educators. Though public school teachers have complained to me about how they have to stick to a structured, preset curriculum, or teach for an upcoming required test, they also speak of being determined to make their teaching more relevant, more interesting, and more creative for themselves and their students alike. Citizenship Education Program training focused on the real needs and experiences of people's lives in the midst of a powerful social change movement. Indeed our graduates were key in creating the movement that changed America. They went home feeling and singing an old song often heard in Black churches in the South—"I'm Gonna Do What the Spirit Says Do!"—but with an on-the-spot made-up verse: *"I'm gonna vote if the spirit says vote!"* On and on expressing joy in their newfound determination.

This is a story within a story, which was never documented with cameras. But that was for the best when you consider that had it been widely known what we were doing, we would have been harassed and even shut down, just as Highlander Folk School was. Citizenship Education Program training was the base upon which so much of the civil rights movement was built. Thousands of people came through our sessions, and their hometowns were never the same again.

Chapter 9

THE REASON I SING
THIS SONG

The reason I sing this song, Lord
I don't wanna be lost, you know
The reason I sing this song, Lord
I don't wanna be lost
You know, the reason I sing this song, Lord
I don't wanna be lost,
No, I don't want to be lost in the storm.

Henry Brownlee jumped the fence at the plant where he worked when he heard a group of us singing during a small marching demonstration in Savannah, Georgia. Brownlee, as we called him, said that when he heard us singing "I woke up this morning with my mind stayed on freedom . . . hallelu, hallelu, hallelujah!" "I couldn't seem to hold myself back. I just got caught up in what y'all were doing. Somehow, it got to me. When I jumped that fence, it wasn't long before I knew I wasn't ever going back in that plant."

I hadn't known this until I asked him one day how he got interested in civil rights movement activities. Henry Brownlee became one of our most devoted staff members working around the southern region. He went wherever he was needed to assist in local community organizing efforts.

The music, the communal singing that drew Brownlee to the movement, was a very powerful organizing tool, affecting many people as it did Brownlee. The singing that became a symbol of the civil rights movement often involved songs sung by our ancestors, but with new lyrics we created to address our current situations, concerns, and actions. The old songs took on new meaning and became a source of power for the men, women, and children who added their voices to the chorus. Legions of people were moved by communal singing, in new ways that often surprised them. Like Brownlee, they became moved to assert themselves politically and socially. This was true even when they had heard and sung so many of these songs before in the churches, at least in the original versions, and associated them only with religious worship.

THE MOST famous song of the civil rights movement is of course "We Shall Overcome," but there are many such songs. They have affirmed and reconfirmed our commitment to work until our country overcomes the blight on our promise as the greatest experiment of democracy and the greatest country in the world. Though a signature of the American civil rights movement, "We Shall Overcome" is now embraced and sung all over the world.

A Langston Hughes poem, "Freedom's Plow," and the song that flows from it put forth the vision of a world in which people of every land live free. *"May all peoples know its shade."* The journey, the vision put forth in Langston Hughes's poem is the same vision articulated by

Dr. Martin Luther King, by Nelson Mandela (for a nonracial South Africa he projected), and by Mahatma Gandhi in South Africa and India. This poem also prophetically gave us this popular paraphrase of one of Hughes's lines: *"Keep your eyes on the prize! Hold on!"*

We sang songs grounded in Black church culture in our movement, but there were secular songs that were important to our efforts as well. The incredible importance of the music in the movement was no surprise to me since the people most deeply involved were steeped in the Black church tradition. Singing, especially communal singing, was integral to the Black church experience. It was an activity engaged in most naturally. If we look back into the history of the Black church in America we can see the important role that the church and religious or spiritual expression played in the most brutal of times, from being held in bondage to the many attempts at freeing ourselves. The singing provided great and varied support; it expressed many moods, serving many purposes.

"Come, let us rebuild the wall of Jerusalem and suffer this indignity no longer," we read in the Bible (Nehemiah 2:17–18). The King James Version reads, *"Come, and let us build up the wall of Jerusalem, that we be no more a reproach."* We had been living in indignity, and when this modern-day movement took root, we African Americans and our allies sang out of our sorrow, out of the indignity of living as oppressed victims. "I Been in the Storm So Long, Gimme a Little Time to Pray" was sung out of sorrow, with others of the same predicament and with those who saw and felt our plight. This experience caused a bonding, a camaraderie that gave strength to the burgeoning resolve to do something about our challenge, to *"Hold on . . . to see what the end would be."*

In Exodus we read how Miriam the Priestess sang with the people to celebrate the journey out of Egypt. We too sang from the sheer joy of participation as well as to celebrate a "coming out of bondage." Examples of lines from some of these songs are *"Freedom is a-coming, oh yes!"* and *"If you miss me from the back of the bus, and you can't find me nowhere, come on up to the front of the bus, I'll be riding up there!"*

We sang away our fear and sorrow with "I'll Be Alright." We sang of our hope and joy: *"Freedom is a-comin', oh yes!"* We sang to motivate and challenge ourselves: *"Which side are you on?"* (We borrowed that from the labor movement and used it to urge those who hung around yet seemed hesitant about jumping in and fully participating.) Music energized us when we were tired: *"Pick 'em up and lay 'em down, all the way from Selma town,"* which I learned as Len Chandler walked with his guitar near me on the Selma to Montgomery march. The call-and-response song "Certainly Lord" became a very effective song of challenge. In regular Sunday church services one could hear lyrics such as *"Have you got good religion?"* In movement mass meetings these lyrics became *"Did you register to vote?"* The audiences would respond *"Certainly Lord!"* On and on it would continue: *"Have you been to the polls? Will you go to jail? Do you love everybody? 'Certainly Lord!'"* Always the answer was *"Certainly Lord!"*

New lyrics were created on the spot by anyone who thought of lyrics posing questions pertinent to the possible or pending actions, or that reinforced a concept being taught. For example, the song "Do You Love Everybody?" was especially pertinent after a CEP workshop session or mass meeting dealing with nonviolence. We were teaching that "the essence of nonviolence is love." The response returned was sung with great energy and commitment and resolve. It was sung rhythmically and with beautiful creative harmony. We couldn't always tell whether everyone who echoed back the refrain *"Certainly Lord!"* would do what was requested if called on—or if they had in fact already done so. But the song was energizing, and motivating. We would always sing at the start of a workshop session and often close a session with a song as well, with lyrics flowing from what we had been studying. Much of the time class sessions and discussions in different settings would spark a song. The mood would often dramatically change from pondering what one could do to bring about the change we had discussed to one of declaration (approaches in terms of specifics would come in later sessions). But the song "I'm Gonna Do What the Spirit Says Do" affirmed that people were opening to possibilities that they could and would become active in working for positive change in some way.

At the height of the civil rights movement, with young and not so young people engaged in protest activities in many places, a group of young people from Albany, Georgia, came to the Dorchester Center to participate in one of our Citizenship Education Program workshops. This group had been expelled from Albany State College for participating in protest activity. One of these students was Bernice Johnson Reagon, who would later earn a doctorate degree at Howard University and found the renowned a cappella singing group Sweet Honey in the Rock. From this group of expelled students I got the impression that everybody in Albany was a great singer, because every one of them seemed to have a powerful solo voice and together they created a style of singing that was unique and beautiful and captivating. These students from Albany introduced me to a song that spoke so directly to why we sing: *The reason I sing this song, Lord, I don't want to be lost.* Singing together created an important feeling of connectedness, of camaraderie.

Here again, lyrics were created that spoke so directly to what we were about: *"The reason I pray so hard; the reason I go to jail; the reason I register and vote."* One could name any necessary activity and end with *"I don't want to be lost."*

You couldn't hear or sing these songs and not be touched and stirred by them, finding new places inside yourself that propelled you into a new consciousness, places from which you would feel and act in new ways.

The original Freedom Singers: (left to right) Cordell Reagon, Bernice Reagon, Rutha Harris, and Charles Neblett. They invited me onto the stage to sing with them.

Many of the songs were staples of the Freedom Singers, who were Cordell Reagon, Bernice Reagon, Charles Neblett, and Rutha Harris. Since I love to sing and was often called on to lead song sessions with various gatherings in church mass meetings and demonstrations, I relate strongly to an observation by civil rights activist and musician Julius Lester: "In the music, the beauty and the pain wrap around each other; it seems to want to take us somewhere."

Once younger people, pop musicians, and DJs created and introduced new songs with the same messages as those sung in church and in the mass meetings, music became even more important to the movements of the 1960s and 1970s, expressing the suffering, the hopes, the goals, and the achievements, step by step, of this great civil rights struggle.

Radio DJs were extremely helpful to the cause. They could not necessarily safely speak of or openly support the movement activity. But they did attend our mass meetings, so they knew what was going on and supported our efforts, not least when they'd play Sam Cooke's "A Change Is Gonna Come" or Nina Simone's "Mississippi Goddam": *"They keep on saying go slow; do things gradually"* and *"I don't want to live next to you; just give me my equality."*

Marvin Gaye's "What's Going On?" beautifully combined gospel, rhythm and blues, soul, and jazz. This was a song that changed the face of popular music. One of the lines from this song—*"Only love can conquer hate"*—is directly related to the essence of nonviolence. Sam Cooke wrote "A Change Is Gonna Come" after he heard Bob Dylan's "Blowin' in the Wind" in 1964. Curtis Mayfield stirred a lot of people as he sang the challenge song "People Get Ready."

Younger people brought popular modern tunes to the repertoire and wrote new ones, sometimes almost playfully mocking oppressive laws, such as James Bevel's "Your Dog Loves My Dog":

> *My dog loves your dog,*
> *Your dog loves my dog*
> *So why can't we sit under the apple tree?*

The songs interpreted what was going on around us—what we were doing, what we were struggling for—and at the same time reaffirmed our goals of abolishing a violent system and becoming free of oppression.

James Brown singing "I'm Black and I'm Proud" reaffirmed our determination to "take the ugly" out of Black and spoke to the system that perpetuated the notion that Black people were not worthy human beings because they were *Black.* The music signaled a shift in consciousness and changed motivational paradigms, helping African Americans redefine and express our natural selves' way of thinking, feeling, and being, and even how we groomed. We gave one another permission to stop straightening our hair—to reveal our true features and be "Black and proud."

Afro hairdos became very popular and were worn by the famous, such as Abbey Lincoln and Angela Davis, and everyday people alike. Could we have had the powerful impact on the culture without our freedom songs? I very much doubt it. After singing we were different. We felt different; we lost any residual fear; we were motivated and determined. There came a knowing that we would go on and continue "to see what the end would be."

MUSIC OPENED us. It allowed us to feel alive. We learned that when you feel alive, you can act. This is what happened to Henry Brownlee when he jumped that fence to join us. The singing he heard touched something in him, propelling him into a new way of seeing himself and a new kind of work he could do in the world. A speech relates to one's intellect; a song goes straight to the heart and soul.

Bernard Lafayette likes to tell a story about being in jail in Mississippi. The jailer ordered the protesters who had been arrested to "shut up that singing" or they would have their mattresses taken away. This only resulted in the singing getting louder and even more defiant. For example, the "prisoners" would create musical responses on the spot. In the state penitentiary in Parchman, Mississippi, sounds reverberated throughout with "prisoners" singing, *"You can take our mattress, oh yes! You can take our mattress, oh yes! You can take our mattress, you can take our mattress, you can take our mattress, oh yes; but we will have our freedom, oh yes, we will have our freedom, oh yes, we will have our freedom, we will have our freedom, we will have our freedom, oh yes!"* The jailers knew that protesters prepared for their arrest by always having a toothbrush and toothpaste with them. So when the jailer said, "If you don't stop that singing, we will take your toothbrush," Bernard, with mouth half closed, likes to demonstrate for those of us who were not there, *"You can take our toothbrush, oh yes; you can take our toothbrush, oh yes; but we will have our freedom! Oh yes!"* At this point we can laugh at such recountings or stories as well as at other events in our struggle. And we note that the humor of these times is another example of how we kept our spirits up. Now this may be a poetic creation by Bernard, but even if so it reveals an important dynamic of the movement— creativity and fun.

There were other concerns among those incarcerated with Bernard. For example, some of the demonstrators worried that additional protesters had not gotten arrested and joined them. Where were they? Why are other demonstrators not following us here? An on-the-spot stanza was created when they realized that busloads of arrested demonstrators were indeed arriving at the prison at that very moment to join them. With great joy, the prisoners sang *"Buses are a-rolling, oh, yes; buses are a-rolling, oh yes; buses are a-rolling, oh yes; buses are a-rolling, buses are a-rolling, buses are a-rolling, buses are a-rolling, oh yes! And we will have our freedom, oh yes! And we will have our freedom, oh yes! And we will have our freedom, oh yes!"*

Another song that stands out for me is one that a Baptist preacher sang regularly in mass meetings in Birmingham, Alabama. This was Reverend Jesse Douglas, whose signature song was "I Told Jesus It Would Be Alright If He Changed My Name," meaning that one would indeed be changed if one accepted the challenge of fighting for justice:

> *I told Jesus it would be alright if He changed my name.*
> *I told Jesus it would be alright if He changed my name.*

Yes, I told Jesus it would be alright if He changed my name.

And Jesus told me, "The police dogs will bite you, if I change your name."

Jesus told me, "The police dogs will bite you, if I change your name."

Still I told Jesus, it will be alright, and He changed my name.

And I'm no longer the same,

Since He changed my name.

In the Southern Baptist tradition, when one declared he or she had gotten religion, they also testified that they were "no longer the same." The same was true when you committed to the struggle for justice.

This song goes on to suggest other penalties people will suffer if they continue to fight for freedom and justice: *"They will throw you in jail, if I change your name; people will talk about you if I change your name / Still I told Jesus it would be alright and He changed my name / And I'm no longer the same, since He changed my name."*

On occasion I have heard people complaining about the singing. "We need something more radical—more powerful," one could sometimes hear. As I travel the country, I sometimes still get questions suggesting the irrelevance of the singing. These come from people who have not allowed themselves to become immersed in the history, the story of the great struggle that rearranged the social order in the country. Perhaps one would have had to have been personally involved to understand this profoundly helpful, even saving, tool.

IN A PBS documentary about our movement anthem, "We Shall Overcome," one woman expressed her doubt and even rejection of the song until one day, after listening to the song with an open heart and mind, she said, "It touched me." Many people, upon *really listening* and *really hearing* the song, singing it and incorporating the spirit of the song in their own being, felt its power. This power was not available through violence of any kind and for some, not felt through the many speeches in some of our mass meetings. Even if one didn't want to listen to speeches and sermons related to the movement, "the songs would get them," a woman in a CEP class said to me.

Pete Seeger, the famous creative folk singer and freedom fighter, noted that our anthem "We Shall Overcome" is "sung in countries

Pete Seeger and me.

around the world." I too have personally experienced this—the universality of this song now. Our songs incorporated the very *spirit* and goals of the movement. Songs were healing; they were prayerful; they were challenging.

When I consider the words of our anthem today, I know that there were indeed profoundly important reasons why all of us "freedom fighters" sang this and many other songs. In a real sense, we sang our way to freedom. We sang because we were free in spirit. Free because we were *in community.* And nobody, nothing, would "turn us around." There was an exciting momentum and resolve generated by the songs.

Music and musicians advanced the movement. James Brown is owed a debt of gratitude for what he did in the aftermath of the assassination of Dr. King. There was talk of a scheduled concert of his in Boston being canceled because of worries about violence breaking out there, as it had in many cities. After the news of Dr. King's death, James Brown convinced the sponsors in Boston to let the show go on by broadcasting it live, free of charge. No one would have to buy a ticket. James Brown singing "I'm Black and I'm Proud" and his incredibly fancy footwork just may be the reason most people stayed home rather than taking to the streets of Boston on April 4, 1968, the day Dr. King was killed.

I HEARD Seal, the award-winning singer of soul music, say in an interview with Tavis Smiley, "Great leaders can speak to the mainstream; great music gets into your bloodstream." This is exactly what the freedom songs did for us in the civil rights and other human rights movements. There was a song written for Nelson Mandela while he was incarcerated at Robben Island in Cape Town, South Africa. The refrain sung with great power was *"We're gonna sing Mandela free!"* And so we did. People were singing the song with this refrain in many places around the world.

Andy Young's statement, "The reason communism did not catch on in the South was that those organizers did not sing," may be exaggerated, but I know that something deep and profound happens when people sing together, and sometimes when they just listen to singing with an open heart.

Chapter 10

THE ESSENCE OF
NONVIOLENCE IS LOVE

I love everybody
I love everybody
I love everybody in my heart

"I COULDN'T JUST stand there and let somebody hit me and stick my other cheek out and let them hit me again." I have heard this as a critique of nonviolence so many times in various settings and I would respond, "Well, I couldn't, either." This sentiment represents a misinterpretation of the "turn the other cheek" advice. I have attempted to respond as frontally and as strongly as I can to correct this erroneous assumption ascribed over the years to this biblical advice.

The phrase "turn the other cheek," attributed to Jesus, is a teaching taken from the Sermon on the Mount. Since we can probably all agree that Jesus taught through parables, I have great confidence in my assumption that what Jesus meant is that one should turn the better side of one's nature to a situation. People can transform a dis-

161

ruptive and potentially violent situation into something good; one can extricate anger and violence, turning a possibly violent exchange into a force for peace and healing.

My response to the critique would get looks of surprise and questioning. Most people were usually deeply locked into their very narrow interpretation and misunderstanding of active nonviolence. For the most part, however, the people who participated in our Citizenship Education Program workshops were receptive to the theory and the strategies of nonviolence as a "force more powerful." But those who were not were in for an interesting awakening. The teaching in which many had been immersed from childhood in their houses of worship meshed directly with the tenets of nonviolence. Participants realized that they had heard it before in Sunday school lessons and in sermons: the admonition to "love your neighbors as you love yourself." In the churches they had been imbued with the philosophy that love is the greatest value and that this love is given without regard to what the other person does or whether the other person shows love in return. We came to see that love is healing and we agreed that racism is a sickness, and we should work as healers.

The CEP students connected to this new understanding of love, the concept of "love being the essence of nonviolence." They started to see nonviolence as a potent force for change and that inherent in this philosophy was the *responsibility* to confront injustice. People in our movement would come to learn that love in the sense we were now hearing it described was the same kind of love espoused by the teachings of Jesus, "to set at liberty those who were oppressed" and to do good to those who persecute and abuse you.

MOST PASTORS of the day in the churches frequented by members of communities in which there was a lot of movement activity could regularly be heard comforting members by assuring them they would get their reward "by and by"—in a place called heaven. Those who had accepted this projection, this teaching, were in for a great and important awakening! A transformation that would change their lives, would change the way they understood what was required of them in order to relieve their suffering here on earth. This future healing, this relief of suffering on earth, would no longer have to be put on hold until after they died and "got to heaven." When many preachers transformed their thinking, when they accepted that "God didn't intend for some people to be treated as *less than*," the tone of their sermons began to change. Of course there were many who did not change their view. There were, for example, the "men of the cloth" who would use the Bible to justify racial discrimination. Some White preachers used a passage in Genesis, especially "God made the beasts of the field each to his own kind," to justify their racist views.

When grassroots preachers came to Citizenship Education Program sessions and understood nonviolence, when they saw that it meshed with the biblical teachings they quoted on a regular basis, there was an important multiplier effect: their congregations could now deepen their understanding of how they could make their religion *political* and their politics *spiritual.* They understood why they needed to do so. This is exactly the position taken by Mahatma Gandhi. Though we could still hear a few increasingly isolated preachers preach a gospel of "pie in the sky," of getting our reward "by and by," a transformation was taking place that would enhance our recruitment efforts for workers in the struggle for justice.

Someone would occasionally challenge the nonviolent way in our CEP sessions and in our direct follow-up work back in communities with our graduates. As Gandhi acknowledged, there certainly were other ways of confronting evil and injustice. In the book *Gandhi's Seven Steps to Global Change,* by Guy de Mallac, the author lays out Gandhi's philosophy and some important reasons why active nonviolence became the option of choice:

1. One could turn away from an evil situation, actually ignore it. Gandhi said this is cowardly and that he would be in favor of fighting rather than running away from or not confronting an injustice.
2. One could be neutral. We already have too many people who are silent. This option "ignores both justice and injustice."
3. To capitulate, to give in, to succumb to what is, is another very problematic option. Gandhi came to see this option as the worst choice.
4. To fight, obviously, is another option—returning violence with violence. Since no healing of situations would flow from this choice because violence begets violence, and since transformation and healing is the goal, this choice is not in keeping with the philosophy of nonviolence.
5. The last possibility, "which is for the brave," is to respond nonviolently. Proponents and activists who believe in nonviolence see this response as requiring the greatest courage. Responding nonviolently requires a special understanding of human characteristics and possibilities. Working from this understanding, this option, one has a special kind of caring for the "other."

Gandhi spoke of his evolving philosophy as "an experiment" with truth. His politics were indistinguishable from his religion. His religion made him political. Satyagraha returns good for evil until the evildoer tires of evil. When he was attacked by a violent crowd in England, he did not ask for the perpetrators to be prosecuted.

"Gandhi never sought to humiliate or to defeat the Whites in South Africa or the British in India. He wished to convert them," wrote Louis Fischer in *Gandhi: His Life and Message for the World.* This principle of nonviolence was most important to us as we conducted workshops designed to help participants understand why expressing anger and hostility toward opponents would not serve their purpose nor that of the larger movement. Our stated purpose in SCLC was to win the White establishment to our cause.

Gandhi often stated, "At the root of innumerable wrongs in our civilization is the discrepancy between word, creed, and deed. It is the weakness of churches, states, parties, and persons. It gives men and institutions split personalities." Gandhi had achieved balance because in his world, creed and deed were one; he was integrated. That is the meaning of integrity. "The truth shall make you free"—and also *well,* he taught.

I came to interpret this statement as learning the truth about ourselves, the truth about those objecting to our goals, and daring to "speak truth to power." The best movement workers blended together the ideas of Gandhi, King, and Thoreau to create a clear philosophical structure that would be easy for us to study, to learn, and to teach. Dr. King laid out these basic principles in his book *Stride Toward Freedom:*

- First, that nonviolent resistance is not a method for cowards. It does resist.
- Second, nonviolence does not seek to defeat or humiliate the opponent, but to win his friendship and understanding.
- Third, a nonviolent attack is directed against forces of evil rather than against persons who happen to be doing the evil.
- Fourth, nonviolent resistance exhibits a willingness to accept suffering without retaliation, to accept blows from the opponent without striking back.

- Fifth, nonviolent resistance avoids not only external physical violence but internal violence of spirit.

Dr. King was very pleased that in workshop sessions where nonviolence was the focus I adapted these principles and we had many opportunities to experiment with these basic tenets. One time when he attended the last day of the five-day workshop he was upset because he thought that I did not use his writings and that I referred more to Gandhi and Thoreau. "You never use my books," he complained. I made sure it didn't look that way again.

BECOMING A *satyagrahi,* as Gandhi referred to practitioners of nonviolence, was an ongoing process. *Satyagraha* is a *tatpurusha* compound of the Sanskrit words *satya*—meaning "truth"—and *agraha*—meaning "insistence" or "holding firmly to." Once someone has this awakening, one is different; a transformation begins that is both humbling and empowering. It helps people in the Black Southern Baptist church tradition to understand the passion with which Reverend Jesse Douglas in Birmingham would sing in mass meetings "I Told Jesus It Would Be Alright If He Changed My Name." He was singing about the transformation that occurred after internalizing this philosophy of nonviolence. I'm also reminded of how another song from the Black church tradition of many years ago spoke to our experience. I think I heard my grandmother sing these lyrics: *"I looked at my hands and my hands looked new; I looked at my feet and they were new too."* Also, *"Since my soul got a seat up in the kingdom, it's all right."* By pondering the metaphorical meaning of so much of the language of our historical religious tradition, we could believe and accept the tenets of nonviolence. To perceive ourselves as victims could no longer prevail. Changing the way we thought about ourselves and now others—even those who oppressed us—caused Black people to no longer live with the stooped stance of oppression. We were energized and motivated to work for change.

MUCH OF what I had begun to reject as a teenager, concepts like "residing in the Kingdom" and accepting suffering here because I would get my reward in a place called heaven, I began to transpose, to give these expressions new and different meanings. Jesus "changing my name," "looking new," having "a seat up in the Kingdom," and so many other articulations came to be interpreted in a way that made sense to me. Specifically, most of these phrases came to mean for me that a transformation could happen right now, right here. The now "Christian" teachings of Jesus that "the Kingdom is within you" and that "the things I do you can also do" came to be the real message for us in the movement. These really were the same messages we sought to get across.

The message of nonviolence was internalized for thousands through teaching, studying, preaching, singing, and actively taking a stand. For us nonviolence and the religious or biblical teachings blended into the same message. For these and many other reasons, Black people in the Bible Belt in which this great civil rights struggle was unfolding could relate to Martin Luther King Jr. and those of us working together with him. They could relate to our talk about the meaning of nonviolence for our struggle. As Martin emphasized many times, his "Pilgrimage to Nonviolence" was greatly facilitated by his study and love of Jesus' Sermon on the Mount.

Nonviolence, as massive numbers of us came to feel it and understand it, flowed from ancient teachings. Now we were hearing and accepting that these teachings meant we even had a *responsibility* to confront injustice. To accept injustice would be denying another helpful teaching: "We are made in the image and likeness of God." Attributes of God as good are found in the *core teaching* of all the great religions of the world.

Nonviolence provided grounding, a base from which we could struggle for justice, strengthening and empowering ourselves. Because the essence of this philosophy of nonviolence (love) was familiar, we could accept talk of love in this new context. As we internalized the theory and philosophy of nonviolence, we felt stronger; our confidence was enhanced. Dr. King spoke of "projecting the ethic of love to the center of our lives." This broader interpretation was projected night after night in mass meetings, and it really clicked. After all, this revolutionary movement unfolding in and all around us was now the central focus and activity of our lives.

I came to a realization as I internalized this concept of love: I actually could look at a policeman in Birmingham or St. Augustine, Florida, and feel compassion instead of hostility or fear, even as I was being beaten (or at least after our attackers stopped or we were able to leave). I eventually came to see the policemen as being damaged by the racist programming, structures, and institutions in and around which we all lived our lives. Just as important, I realized I was opening myself to seeing how this understanding of love was so deeply changing *me* that I related to people differently in every place where I interacted, including business, personal, and family relationships, with friends, and even with strangers in public places.

I REMEMBER sitting in my living room in Atlanta reading a book by Eric Butterworth, who suggested that the mother of a child killed by a drunken driver would one day need to forgive the driver in order for her to be whole again, and that "one day Jews would have to forgive the Holocaust," and that "Black folk would one day have to forgive slavery." At that point I put the book down and burst into tears, since those statements shook me to the core. They caused me to take a hard look at how I was living my life and doing the work in which I was engaged. I realized that I had come nowhere near the position of forgiving White folk for the Black experience suffered in America. I wondered if perhaps I even enjoyed having that experience to hold over White people. The stupidity of this did not mesh with my evolving image of myself.

Reading Butterworth's admonition to forgive, I knew that I no longer wanted to play the role of "the angry Black woman" for White people. Yes, *for* them. It was like an epiphany, an awakening. I realized that the way I was living my life and carrying on my work in the world was actually keeping me from evolving into my best self. It was also keeping White people with whom I interacted from working on themselves and the institutions they managed. In some strange way, I was facilitating this. Absorbing my anger, feeling guilty, was for them. I realized a sense of coddling, a sense of *"We know, Dorothy. You're okay with us."* I felt I was treated protectively and that somehow this was strangely insulting and demeaning.

I've never forgotten how this awakening caused me to look inward, to work on myself. At the time, I was on the board of directors of the Atlanta YWCA and three or four members of that board and I had become really good friends. At one point I was the only African American woman in that little circle of friends, and Eric Butterworth's statement caused me to look at what I represented to these White friends and how I played my role with them. Being the rather angry Black woman, I played that role to the hilt. In my emotional outbursts about racism I came to see that some of my White friends were actually being entertained by my playing that role. What I exuded was real; I felt locked into the role of always being the one to express the hurt and anger of Black people. If they were not enjoying the way I related, they certainly must have held this one view of who I was and what I brought to the table. Was this all of me? I asked myself. Is this all I am good for? Is this the totality of my identity? Am I being helpful in our stated mission "to redeem the soul of America"? To help remove the scourge of racism? Could I be more helpful in healing the sickness of racism by bringing to the fore all of my skills and talents?

Additionally, I felt that in some strange way they were all absolved of any responsibility to actually *do* anything about racist practices. After all, if they felt a little beat up on by allowing me to always express the woundedness of Black people in our meetings and even when we were simply together as friends, actually *doing* anything about it would not be a priority.

These former friends might not be able to relate to my sense of my experience with them, but it is very clear to me. This is just one of the experiences that helped me begin to realize and accept that transformation is possible for anyone. I understood better how I could work in a way that would help move us all toward healthy community.

In that moment I knew I would find another way, a more substantive way, a nonviolent way to be together with my friends and coworkers. This would include fully knowing who I was, and having confidence in my own worth. It included understanding in a new way the scriptural teaching that I am *made in the image and likeness of God*—and God as the spirit of love and compassion and forgiveness. With this knowledge, this new consciousness, I now knew that I would "speak truth to power." I understood now that I would work in a way that caused White people with whom I interacted to see the role they were playing in maintaining oppressive institutions and structures. I realized my complicity and knew I would immediately begin a new way of being together with these friends. If I continued to work with them, I would work in a way that helped us *all* confront injustice. I would no longer let their blindness to the plight of oppressed people go unchecked because they "took care of me," honored *me*. Nor would I allow them to blame the victims of our racist culture.

As I became clear about the change that had occurred in me, I felt sure that others too could experience change in their perceptions, their expectations of others, and the way they had been programmed. I understood that what had happened to me is one of the tenets of nonviolence: the *power of truth* both about oneself and one's actions and the importance of facing honestly the situations in which we find ourselves and speaking truth to power.

I understood more completely how it is possible for the worst of evildoers to change. Understanding this, bringing it to full consciousness, helps to keep the faith in nonviolence, that potent essence, *love*, as a method of bringing about change. One realizes that it is even more powerful and effective if it becomes a way of life, not just a strategy for practitioners. One takes a chance with love, with trust in the humaneness of all, trusting in the knowledge that there is within all of us a spark of divinity. The nonviolent practitioner seeks to ignite this spark. This is true whether one calls it nonviolence or not. Actually, the change begins to simply happen.

I had an opportunity in Johannesburg, South Africa, to meet Dr. Pumla Gobodo-Madikizela, a clinical psychologist who shared her story with the congressional delegation I was privileged to be a part of. Her story is a powerful example of a transformative experience and discovery of how forgiveness is possible even in light of the most brutal atrocities. No, it is not easy, but in her book, *A Human Being Died That Night: Forgiving Apartheid's Chief Killer* (2003), Pumla reveals her "profound understanding of the language and memory of violence and of the complex issues surrounding apology and forgiveness after mass atrocity."

She began a journey with Eugene de Kock, the former commanding officer of state-sanctioned apartheid death squads in Pretoria's maximum security prison, where he is now serving a 212-year sentence for crimes against humanity. I was spellbound as I took the journey with her, reading her account of an extended series of visits to the prison where she spent hours in conversation with De Kock. She moved from fear and anxiety as the great iron doors clanged shut behind her to tenuously beginning a series of long conversations. She noticed the opening on both their parts and eventually saw a flicker of regret emerge in De Kock. Though he was known now as a "monster," Pumla and he eventually began to connect via their humaneness after many visits; their dialogue led to a beginning of openness and connecting as two human beings. De Kock was also known as "Prime Evil" for his state-sanctioned crimes against massive numbers of Black Africans. His crimes were revealed in great detail before the powerful Truth and Reconciliation Commission (TRC), which was a part of South Africa's national experiment in reconciling and healing.

Pumla Gobodo-Madikizela served with Archbishop Desmond Tutu on the Human Rights Violations Committee of the TRC. Her training and deep understanding of the language of violence and forgiveness, along with her determination and persistence in getting inside the mind of a man capable of such murderous atrocities, provided a deeper understanding of the teachings of Mahatma Gandhi and Martin Luther King Jr. for me. This is especially true as I ponder what it means to forgive; what happens when nonviolent practitioners are willing to hang in there, to go through the really difficult moments of dialogue and experience. Having the courage to have conversations with even such a violent opponent as De Kock and noting that even one such as he, with his confession of massive murderous atrocities, comes out a changed person, is encouraging to those of us who are committed to continue to work for a peaceful world.

I share Dr. Gobodo-Madikizela's experience as it is a powerful example of courage and commitment through nonviolent communication—coming to see the "other" as human, as being worthy of reentry into the human family. It is an example of how a person can evolve from a place of fear and anxiety, as Dr. Gobodo-Madikizela did, and after many hours of conversation find herself inadvertently reaching out to touch her opponents's hand. Slowly a transformation had occurred in both her and De Kock. With her persistence, her dedication to "get inside the man," she eventually tapped into his humaneness. He even asked with apparent pain and concern, "Did I kill any of your relatives?" Pumla said, "No."

We too had to make these kinds of discoveries throughout our civil rights struggle in America, and to learn that by holding on to the principles of nonviolence, even our most violent opponents had the potential to tap into their own humaneness and higher moral values.

Mahatma Gandhi's freedom movement work in India, England, and South Africa flowed from his realization that any system that perpetuated oppression of any person or people must be confronted and challenged. So his experiment with *satyagraha*, or truth force, became the tool of nonviolence, a philosophy he developed and used with a strong belief in the humaneness and even sacredness of the life of one's opponent.

Dr. King said he was fascinated with how Gandhi took his love ethic and applied it to places needing radical social change. He talked about how he was especially influenced by Gandhi's great Salt March to the Sea. By adopting this *satyagraha*, we were allowed in our struggle for justice in America to connect with or tap into the deeply buried attributes of caring, compassion, and humaneness of our opponents. Though this new awareness is often not immediate, something stirs in the opponent; something forces them to begin to examine their own values. I know that in a nonviolent encounter the practitioner begins to be seen by the opponent as a part of the same human family. Many opponents have acknowledged that they saw the righteousness of our cause as we protested our mistreatment, but needed to garner the courage to act on this awakening *in themselves.* This hesitation was especially true when racist and oppressive views prevailed throughout their own communities.

As opponents, even sometimes violent ones, began to embark on a new understanding of what it meant to be humane in relationship to Black people, our CEP participants were strengthened as they began to accept the damage that racism had done to White Americans. They were damaged in having been programmed into a false sense of superiority; Black Americans had been damaged by the deeply entrenched system touting Black people as inferior. Both had to be healed, and Black people, through our movement, along with our White allies, were taking the lead. CEP participants came to understand all aspects of this erroneous programming. This knowledge strengthened their commitment and provided them greater confidence in working to change the American-style apartheid back in their hometowns and ultimately the nation.

"Is this America?" Fannie Lou Hamer of Ruleville, Mississippi, asked when she challenged the Democratic National Convention in 1964. With her powerful voice and organizing skills, Mrs. Hamer was one of our star Citizenship Education Program graduates. Her simple question was powerful. It still is.

A WONDERFUL result of understanding and accepting nonviolence was that we could see that those who espoused separation of the races and responded with violence to our nonviolent protests were expressing their need for self-fulfillment and to find meaning for their lives. Since they had been programmed into such thinking during their young and formative years, we realized that their beliefs had to be held up for them to see so they could reassess the path they had chosen. In doing so, even violent opponents could see that following the law or a custom was no excuse for acting brutally toward Black people. A law in which we had no input we understood was no law at all.

As adherents of nonviolence, when we encountered a brutal policeman in Birmingham or a violent White person in St. Augustine who was threatening or doing violence to us protesters, both of which I experienced, we were able to see our opponents as *themselves* having a great need for healing. We had hope and faith that they too could change and be transformed. Our movement activity sometimes helped violent opponents realize the error of their ways and live more fulfilling and honest lives.

We would realize that we are all members of the same body, part of the same reality. If we truly accept this Gandhian philosophy, we'll see that our opponents, when we could be in dialogue with them, may even have a part of the truth as Gandhi taught. With this awareness we are able to truly respect our opponents and listen to their views, understanding where they're coming from. Even though we could not approve of their behavior or accept the false principles on which they based their actions, we could create a space, a climate, in which dialogue could take place. We saw that we really could hate the violent deeds but still love the person, an agape sense of love. (*Agape*, the Greek word for "love," was embraced by Christians to describe a self-sacrificing love of God.) When such space for dialogue was created and we moved toward nonviolent direct action, we became so imbued with the philosophy and vision of reconciliation that throughout a campaign we maintained our caring, loving image of our opponents and considered them to be still a part of the same human family. This belief, deeply embedded, is the reason we could even submit to their violent response to us, never returning violence with violence. Our vision and our commitment to our goal were the philosophical and spiritual bases upon which we now firmly stood.

IN AN early workshop session held at the Highlander Folk School, a White man nervously came in with his teenage son. He was most welcome, though he did not know that initially. As people introduced themselves and it became his turn, he told the group that he had been an organizer for the Ku Klux Klan and that he had come to see the error of his ways. He said he now wanted to help us in our efforts to break down the walls of segregation. Someone inquired as to how he came to change his mind. I don't remember his response but I remember the seriousness and honesty with which he shared his journey. I remember trusting the candidness with which he responded to our questions. He certainly felt our welcoming spirit, which must have reinforced his commitment to work for change.

On the other hand, there was Preacher Red, a White man whom I came to know when he rang our phone at the SCLC offices. He said, after someone handed me the phone, "My name is Preacher Red and

I want to speak with someone high up in your organization." I can laugh now and be moved near to tears simultaneously as I recall my response. At that time I was the education director for the organization, but my response was "Andy! Someone on the phone wants to speak to someone 'high up.'" Andy said, "Ask him if you're high up enough." But that's another part of the story. When I told him that I was the education director, he asked if I would meet him at a restaurant, since he said he needed to talk with someone who worked with Dr. King. He was from Appalachia and probably wasn't clear about the segregation policy even in Atlanta. I agreed to meet him at Paschal's, the popular Black-owned restaurant that of course welcomed everyone. We could not yet eat in "White" restaurants. The civil rights bill would come later, in 1964.

I told him how he might recognize me and what I would be wearing. As we sat down he quickly and very nervously began our conversation by saying, "I want you to know that I hate Dr. King." Even with such a comment, he didn't seem threatening, only nervous. When I asked him why he hated Dr. King, he said, "Because Dr. King is leaving us out. We have just as many problems as you all have. Our problems are not based on color or race, but my people are mistreated and suffer just as much because we are poor." I cry now as I remember this.

This very grassroots preacher from Appalachia caused a very special awakening in me and other members of our CEP team. When I told the rest of the staff about the encounter, they, like me, were moved. We immediately began looking for a White person to join our staff who would begin recruiting in Appalachia for White participants to come to Dorchester Center and participate in our CEP workshops.

Just as Black folk en masse had been programmed to live as though they were not legitimate citizens of the United States of

America, poor Whites have also been subjected to abuse and general denigration because of their poverty and lack of education—the "outcasts of society," as Gandhi referred to any people mistreated and not given their due as legitimate members of society. I heard and felt Preacher Red's sincere desire to be a member of the whole human race. He expressed a part of the truth that we might not have taken into account given the legacy of slavery and the horrors of its aftermath. We had been working from the knowledge that poor Whites and Blacks had been pitted against each other; poor Whites had been infused with the notion that Black people were their enemy and inferior to *them*. Preacher Red represented the White people whose wrath we had experienced many times. As a matter of fact, poor, sometimes illiterate, Whites were often used to do the violent dirty work of the "White establishment." In any case, some radical adjusting in our CEP recruitment was in order. *"A change is gonna come,"* sang Sam Cooke.

WE WERE about to take another giant step forward toward living in what we knew to be the *Truth.* It must have taken a great deal of courage for Preacher Red to come to us. White people who would fraternize with Black people at that time would be brutalized as severely as Blacks often were. Preacher Red's challenge to us was accepted. Hiring a young White man to recruit White people from Appalachia to begin coming to our Citizenship Education Program was soon to follow. I can still remember my feeling and emotional response when the first group of White people did indeed join us at the Dorchester Center to participate in a CEP workshop. I cried as they entered. I cry now.

Personal transformation is most often not spontaneous, and it is not easy, but most of us began to approach our movement work with a new understanding and even a deepened commitment. Most important, we had a new and different view of the opponent. Though one may not be ready to call it love, an experience such as this begins the process of redefining one's own set of values and definitely enhances the ability to see and respond to the violent person with a surprisingly different attitude, totally without fear, and actually look at such a person through eyes of love with *agapic energy,* as civil rights activist Diane Nash proposed we refer to nonviolence.

As I sought to help participants in our CEP workshops become conversant with the terminology of nonviolence I realized that we needed to apply important aspects of nonviolence to actual situations in which they were involved back home, situations they shared with us in the CEP introductory sessions. How could we make the tenets of nonviolence real for them? I pondered, and I realized that the philosophy and the principles of nonviolence could be shown very clearly by involving them in some simple exercises and presentations based on problems they had shared. There were often preachers in the sessions. Most of the preachers who came were not seminary trained but many had done rather in-depth reading of the Bible. They too came to see and understand a clear connection or similarity between many of the teachings in the Sermon on the Mount and the lessons of nonviolence:

"Blessed are the peacemakers, for they shall be called sons of God." Our movement was definitely about establishing peace, but we had to come to an understanding of what *real peace* is. Peace without justice, we knew, is not peace at all. The preachers and all of us came to fully realize, to understand, and to teach that there can be no peace without justice, and people in the training program had no trouble highlighting manifestations of injustice. Indeed that's what the movement was about—ending injustice so real peace could be established.

"Blessed are those who hunger and thirst for righteousness, for they shall be satisfied." The massive numbers of people who got involved in movement activities most certainly had a thirst for righteousness; that's why they were involved. People knew things were not right. And trainees developed stronger and stronger confidence and satisfaction in the knowledge that our goals would be "satisfied."

"Blessed are those who have been persecuted for the sake of righteousness, for theirs is the kingdom of heaven." This statement was encouraging as movement activists were indeed persecuted. And as we know, some were even killed.

Mass meeting speeches and sermons drew heavily on these and other teachings of Jesus and also those of Mahatma Gandhi. Along with a strong cadre of preachers, we had many activist leaders and teachers on our SCLC team. All of us, listening to the powerful voice of Martin Luther King Jr. and seeing the quiet, determined action of thousands of nonviolent "soldiers"—workers for justice— in many cities and towns, now realized that something great and powerful was happening in our country.

BEFORE OUR training program wound down, around eight thousand had come through our doors. With such large numbers of committed participants, we were feeling incredibly empowered as never before. All of us were helping to keep the large nightly gatherings informed and motivated so that more and more joined the ranks of protesters, marchers, and volunteers for going to jail. The mass meetings became the place to be every night—for the teaching, for the singing, for information, for recruitment, and for the building of community this powerful movement afforded.

• • •

WHEN I'M asked about using nonviolence in a protest, I respond to the inquirer, "What do you want to work on?" My question, in response, mostly seems puzzling and surprising. I realize that I need to introduce the pattern of organizing a nonviolent campaign. We used various forms of this pattern in the Citizenship Education Program and sharing it helps provide insight into the use of nonviolence in a specific instance or event. There are specific steps in organizing a nonviolent campaign. They include:

1. *Clearly identify the issue.* This takes some real focus, for if a student says to me, "I want to work to get rid of drugs," I realize the need is to help the student pinpoint or really focus the issue. "Do you mean you want to work to rid your neighborhood of the crack house down the street? Or do you mean you want to tackle the drug cartels that move drugs from country to country?" A helpful discussion often ensues.

2. *Gather all pertinent information.* In workshops we would go into great detail, including role-playing all the places from which information relevant to the issue might be gathered.

3. *The education step.* Identify "who needs to know." At first we used a mimeograph machine to make leaflets to distribute information relative to what people needed to know. It was a big surprise to realize after distributing the leaflets that some communities had many adults who were functionally illiterate. So we had to use a variety of communication tools such as radio announcements and personal announcements at church and social club events. Remember that this great social change movement took place before personal computers and the Internet.

4. *Personal commitment.* Is there an emerging camaraderie? Is time being found to break bread together? Or to sing a little or to meditate? Working in a way that helps people feel connected is

important in organizing. And this is what would be happening—organizing, expanding the working group.

5. *Negotiation.* Intense training in how to negotiate was often provided in our most successful efforts to bring forth change. The language, the approach taken, the clarity of the goal, and an awareness of what can be given up all require intense focus. Selecting the member of the team who was most skillful in this task was very important, as was the awareness that opponents must be treated with respect and must not be left feeling put down or that they'd gained nothing. In other words, no protest occurred without this process.

6. *Direct action.* No, we didn't just have a march. And a march or any other direct action would ideally occur only as a last resort. So confrontation would only come after we carefully assessed whether all other possibilities had been exhausted.

7. *Reconciliation.* This concept was always critical in an effective nonviolent campaign because reconciliation was always the goal.

Each one of these steps could require hours of dedicated time in order to have an individual or group become comfortable in carrying it out for a successful nonviolent campaign. Indeed in the beginning a local movement could sometimes require weeks and months of preparation to come to fruition.

The grassroots people we taught at the Dorchester Center became the ones who would "make the movement" that changed America. As Emil Hess, a wealthy White businessman whom I met in Birmingham, Alabama, said to me shortly before he died, "Birmingham catapulted America into the twenty-first century." Our graduates, who came from all across the southern and border states, were key players in bringing about this dramatic and powerful change in our country.

As they headed home, as cars and buses were being loaded and pulling off, I remember Andy and me crying as we waved and sang, "This May Be the Last Time":

> ... *We work together*
> ... *We learn together*
> ... *We grow together*

For some it was ...

Standing, left to right: Andrew Young, T. Y. Rogers, James Bevel, Fred Bennett, and Bernard Lafayette. Seated, left to right: Hosea Williams, Martin Luther King Jr., and me.

Chapter 11
_____

DR. KING AND THE TEAM
OF WILD HORSES

We are building up a new world.

—From a traditional song, paraphrased
by Dr. Vince Harding

*One day I'm going to see my child enjoy spinning around on that
bar stool in that ice cream store just like that little White boy!*

—Hosea Williams

MARTIN CALLED US a "team of wild horses," we who
made up the leadership team of the Southern Christian Leadership
Conference, and we were indeed a diverse group with different personalities and different talents that evolved into a highly effective
group within the organization. Part of the team that would be convened to sit around the conference table in what was called the executive staff meeting included: Dr. King, of course, Ralph Abernathy,
Andrew (Andy) Young, T. Y. Rogers, C. T. Vivian, Hosea Williams,

Jack O'Dell, and later Fred Bennett and me. Afterward, Jesse Jackson participated when he could get to Atlanta from Chicago. Septima Clark would be invited to join the executive staff meeting when she was in Atlanta. Charleston, South Carolina, was her hometown.

Some other members included state field secretaries who had their own staff and volunteers. These included, among others, Golden Frinks in North Carolina and Herbert Coulton in Virginia, who did a highly effective job traveling the state to organize and recruit participants for the Citizenship Education Program as well as attending the workshops himself.

Some of the team members were gentle, scholarly, and reflective; some were rambunctious; and some were aggressive. All had strong egos, which were frequently on display. Some had advanced degrees and were seminary graduates, some had smoldering and defensive personalities, but for the most part any negative traits were kept in check by the incredible personality, charisma, love, and wisdom we saw in Martin Luther King Jr. Somehow we were all able to find a niche for ourselves on the King team; the glue that held the team together was that all of us had found greater meaning for our own lives and there was a surprising and energizing likability visible among most of us.

Martin was clearly our leader. He was the grand patriarch, and we all had great respect for him. We saw in him an ability to decipher and analyze a concern or a problem in a way no one else on the team would or could. He could cut through all facets of any issue and get right to the core of the matter, and he could explain the pros and the cons in an easily understandable and acceptable way. We were always anxious to hear what he would say after the team debated an issue—and they were sometimes very heated debates. He had a clever and incisive way of speaking. I liked the way he used language and the way he used the rhythm of words to make his point. Sometimes there was silence afterward. Often there was nothing more to say after he spoke. But this was not in the way some preachers in workshops would kill a meeting with arrogance. When the team got quiet after Dr. King spoke, it was because he was convincing — coming from a place inside himself that we couldn't counter, nor did we want to. He had a way of taking the good ideas from the various points of view and cleverly synthesizing them into an extensive whole.

Dr. King was a real people person. He was comfortable with people in general, and people loved being with him. That includes the men and the women on our staff as well as others with whom he interacted outside our organization. We loved to be in dialogue with him. It is difficult to put into words what we all felt. We enjoyed the camaraderie; we benefited from his insight. What he brought to each discussion was always refreshing, different, wise, and fun. He was indeed our guiding light in the struggle for freedom and in building a committed team.

*Dinner at Dr. King's home was common. I am seated to his right, then
Libby and Randolph Blackwell, and Coretta (opposite Dr. King).
To her right are Jean Young and Andy Young, with their child between them.*

Martin appeared unassuming and gregarious, yet he had an intangible magnetic quality. How do we adequately describe qualities like this? I don't know, but there was something that made many people want to be with him. I think it is because he had a way of really "being present" when he spoke to you. I remember observing him when we walked down Atlanta's Auburn Avenue, where our office was located. It was near juke joints, pool halls, and pork sandwich shops. He would often stop and would appear very much at home talking with the guys who hung out on the street there. He had the special capacity to feel comfortable "dining with kings" as well as speaking with guys well into their wine.

People worldwide knew of his oratorical skills. He held audiences spellbound as he articulated his vision and spurred people on to greater commitment to fight for the transformation needed both here and in other countries. No one was untouched by his powerful and poetic expressions. We clearly saw and felt his commitment to the struggle for more noble values, for individuals as well as nations.

Yet Dr. King could be so playful, the life of the party. When he was named Man of the Year by *Time* magazine, the article stated that he was humorless. Nothing could be further from the truth. He loved to be with us, his energetic and creative inner circle. This was true with the larger extended team as well, many of them field staff and organizers assigned all around the South. Our work with SCLC was not just a job, it was a total life commitment. It was work that gave our lives richer meaning whether we were part of the "ground crew" or had a fancy title. He loved being with all of us and we were happy being with him in meetings and when we had a little downtime.

We felt he was our best friend. He needed us as friends as well as coworkers to help him bear the incredibly heavy burden of leading this powerful social change movement in which we were involved. A few of us knew all the various aspects of his personality and of his life and he needed us close to him in just this way. The world may stand in awe of him, but he needed us to help him.

The powerful oratory, dynamic speeches, and visionary observations he could make so readily are what the world knows of Dr. Martin Luther King Jr. His undergraduate, seminary, and graduate education, steeped in philosophy and theology, strengthened his ability to lead a movement that would inspire people in this country and around the world.

He was especially influenced by proponents of nonviolence, by scholars who had a deep understanding of nonviolence and pacifism, although he saw nonviolent direct action differently from pacifism. Scholars, theologians, and those who had a passion for social justice were the most impressive to him. He read the works of great philosophers: that of Plato and Aristotle; Walter Rauschenbusch's *Christianity and the Social Crisis;* and A. J. Muste's pacifist positions. He was exposed to the philosophy of Nietzsche, whom Dr. King saw as glorifying power. He read the works of Reinhold Niebuhr and was particularly interested in his understanding of social ethics. I was always impressed with his confidence in arguing against positions with which he disagreed. He had clear reasons for positions he took.

While he was in seminary he left his campus and went down to Philadelphia to hear Dr. Mordecai Johnson, the president of Howard University, give a speech. What he heard in that speech would set him firmly on the path to becoming one of the greatest orators, speakers, and visionary leaders of the twentieth century. Dr. Johnson's sermon "was electrifying," Martin said. Dr. Johnson had recently returned from India and in the speech he spoke of the work of Mahatma Gandhi and his methods, which energized the people of India and freed them from the yoke of British rule.

At Boston University he was exposed to other proponents of nonviolence. He said the dean of the School of Theology at Boston

University, Dr. Walter Muelder, and Professor Allan Chalmers had a passion for social justice. His education exposed him to a wide array of great theologians and philosophers, some with whom Dr. King had profound disagreements. By studying such a diverse group of thinkers he developed the skill to select which ideas made the most sense to him given his own deepening passion for social justice. Dr. King's fascination with the work of Gandhi would be extremely important preparatory work as he accepted the call to pastor the Dexter Avenue Baptist Church in Montgomery, Alabama, though he had no idea of what awaited him there.

His interests and study prepared him to play a pivotal role when Rosa Parks was arrested for not standing and giving a White man her seat on a bus in December 1955. I find it almost mystical and certainly fascinating when I ponder how it all happened for him—the studying, the going to Montgomery to pastor a church, and being called on to offer leadership in a protest effort even though, as Martin himself said, "I neither started the protest nor suggested it." This protest of the mistreatment of Negroes (as we were called then) on the buses of Montgomery would catapult this young preacher into the role for which the world now honors him.

The story of the Montgomery Bus Boycott is well known, so it is not my purpose here to detail that historic and surprising event. I would only highlight that Martin Luther King Jr. was immersed in a philosophy that afforded him the spiritual and the philosophical underpinnings from which he could bring forth a message that would project goals and interpret events and motivate and encourage Black people to walk rather than ride the buses in indignity. This eventually would include a few White allies. My sense is that from Montgomery to Soweto, from Washington, D.C., to Vietnam, Martin's voice could be heard speaking for many whose suffering was neither seen nor heard by those who benefited by putting others down. And what a powerful voice it was. Not only was Martin's message and challenge to the world heard, it was put forth in a most powerful and even poetic way.

I believe it is true that if Rosa Parks had not refused to move to the back of the bus to give a White man her seat, there might not have been the Martin Luther King Jr. we know today. The people of Montgomery just might not have continued to "hold on," just might not have continued their struggle for 381 days in a massive nonviolent protest action, had it not been for this young preacher who eloquently expressed what the people were feeling. Martin Luther King Jr. interpreted the deeper and broader meaning of our struggle, the struggle of African Americans. People walking in Montgomery, those watching in Memphis and in many other cities around the country, were energized in new and exciting ways. African American people suffering under the yoke of our American-style apartheid would intensify their efforts to defeat this cruel system.

Dr. King could spontaneously quote philosophers and theologians, calling up ideas that had impressed him, sprinkling his speeches with quotes from many of them. Many of the most powerful speeches he made were without a manuscript. Sometimes he would have little scribbled notes on a scrap of paper. Even when he had a manuscript he was often most impressive when he set it aside to speak extemporaneously.

Reverend Ralph Abernathy, who was Dr. King's longtime friend, played a strategically important role in what I call our "King Team." They had the kind of deep friendship that I don't believe could ever have been broken. I've never seen anyone so willing to lay down his life for a friend as Ralph was willing to do for and with Martin. I believe Ralph would have taken that bullet for him if he had had such a choice. I say this as I was regularly with them and observed how Martin and Ralph's friendship was displayed when we debated various actions SCLC should take. Always these discussions and debates took place in the awareness that arrests and jailings and even worse were inevitable. Ralph was ready to walk with him anywhere, anytime.

Dr. King was jailed seventeen times as he led the struggle for freedom and choice. Ralph was with him each time. Martin wanted Ralph's support during those tumultuous times and he needed Ralph as a witness should Martin be subjected to violent actions on the part of the jailers.

Ralph had this same degree of devotion with others in his world. Once at a barricaded street a rather crude police officer said, "I'll let you through, but no one else." Ralph said, "Well, I won't go either, then, because my choir members are right behind me and they need to get through."

Ralph's commitment and devotion could not be missed even though I also recognized his jealousy or perhaps resentment as Martin's star shone brighter and brighter, the world recognizing his powerful leadership for the freedom of oppressed peoples everywhere. It seemed that Ralph could not help feeling somewhat slighted. After all, he was indeed always at Martin's side and ready to play any role that called for his skills.

Reverend Wyatt Tee Walker was a skillful and creative preacher. He was an energetic, take-charge guy who aggressively moved into the role of managing the organization during the years 1961–64. He became, as several of us did, indispensable to Dr. King. Wyatt's leadership was seen as a top-down, militaristic style, which some staffers seemed to have resented. Some staff members viewed him as the executive who dictated and then expected them to take orders. In a social change movement, that is a problematic and difficult model and people resisted it. Taking charge, assuming the authority of his title, Wyatt, as executive director, and chief of staff, as he coined it, was impressive, but as the movement evolved his style would cause both admiration and conflict with team members who also had strong egos.

The entire top or executive staff were leaders in our own right. Most of us had come from positions of authority, whether as Baptist and Methodist preachers or community organizers. Most of us had been key players in local or regional organizations.

I frequently observed the interplay between all these men around the executive conference table with surprise, amusement, and sometimes annoyance at their grasping for power and their need for one-upmanship. At the same time I recognized and admired every one of them. I appreciated the diversity, the talent, and skills each one brought to the table. Even though there was real camaraderie, and Dr. King did not have an authoritative bone in his body, I sensed that most of them competed with one another to impress Dr. King. They each wanted to show Dr. King that they were the most incisive, creative, and helpful person on the team, that they had the best ideas. There seemed to be the need for some of them to prove their greater value to our leader. However, there are clear exceptions to this pattern: Andy Young, for example, and Wyatt Walker, who both had great confidence in who they were as individuals and in the roles they came to play in the organization. They simply went ahead doing what they saw needed to be done even though there were some members who did not relate to or understand their approaches. I know too that some of the posturing was because of the tremendous respect and high esteem in which Dr. King was held by every one of us. Still, some of the posturing certainly came from a need to be "top dog" in the leader's eyes. I kept quiet amid heated debates most times, so much so that Dr. King even asked Andy once, "Why doesn't Dorothy say much in executive staff meetings?" Andy responded, "She has no need to compete with these guys. She's comfortable and confident in her work with the training program."

I had been aware of male chauvinism sometimes among our SCLC staff group. Although I had the title of education director, when the executive staff met and one of the men wanted coffee they would say, "Dorothy, would you get the coffee?" or sometimes the request would be, "Could you take the minutes?" But it was Jack O'Dell, a male team member at the table, who said, "Excuse me, Dr. King, Dorothy needs to stay. She needs to stay at this table and be part of this discussion. She's the education director. Let's call in the secretary to take the minutes and get the coffee or whatever." I will always remember that Jack O'Dell had the insight and the candidness to challenge this practice and view of the role of women. Many women today would never consider themselves second to men, but that was a concept that women had to struggle with in earlier times.

I am amused at myself and embarrassed when I recall my initial response to the telephone call from Preacher Red in 1963. Remember, the modern-day women's movement had not yet occurred. I would never respond by calling Andy or anyone else now the way I did with the call from the Appalachian preacher.

James Bevel was a devoted student of nonviolence. He could quote Gandhi and translate his teachings and experiences right into our "march for freedom." Once, in the midst of several simultaneous organizing campaigns and protest actions, Wyatt sought to "assign" James Bevel to one city when he was already providing leadership working in another. Bevel used very strong language to tell Wyatt he could not tell him not to go back to a community where he had made a commitment to the people. Bevel said he was returning to Mississippi, where he had been working, and that he had just come to Atlanta for a few days only because Dr. King had called all the key organizers in for a planning and strategy meeting.

Wyatt wanted to fire Bevel on the spot and sought Dr. King's approval. That approval was not to be had. Dr. King saw Bevel as a creative and dynamic organizer and preacher, one who would debate Dr. King on theological and philosophical ideas, both popular and unpopular. Dr. King was entertained and stimulated by Bevel's style and the creative way he saw issues. Bevel did not want to be ordered to go into a "battleground"—a place where violence against Black people was rampant and where he might be required to give his life. Such a decision would have to be one's own choice. After all, this was a nonviolent *movement* where people worked from commitment and *spirit* and from an understanding of nonviolent principles. This work was not something one could be ordered to do.

I was with Bevel and Dr. King once when Bevel knew that Dr. King was exhausted and needed to get away to rest. I'll never forget

James Bevel making a point to Wyatt Tee Walker and me.
He had very creative approaches to activism and nonviolent theory.

the way Bevel spoke to him, urging him to take some time away from the struggle to recharge. Bevel said, "You know, Jesus knew when he needed to stop and get away. He would even go up in the mountain and be in isolation to renew himself. That cat knew how to take care of himself!" Dr. King enjoyed Bevel's "familiarity" with Jesus, his ability to speak of biblical characters as though they were just people who hung around with this "cat" who could preach a powerful sermon. Yet there were times when we were taken aback by Bevel's style, his independent thinking and candid use of sometimes irreverent language that might have threatened the reputation of our organization.

For example, Bevel was asked to fulfill a request for an SCLC speaker at a Catholic religious conference. After Bevel's return, Dr. King got a call in which one of the conference planners reported, in great distress, that Bevel had "defamed the name of Mary" in his speech. Back at the office, when Bevel was confronted with this report of his use of disrespectful language referring to "the Mother Mary" and of his "defaming the name of Mary," he responded, "When you got the call, Dr. King, did he say which Mary he was talking about? The Mary whose children in Mississippi are living with bloated bellies because they can't get enough protein? Is it that Mary who has to work twelve and fourteen hours a day and who gets paid a fraction of what she's worth; or that Mary who spends her days taking care of White folks' children, leaving her own children unattended because that's the only job she can get; or that Mary who got raped by the White overseer on the plantation and felt she had to stay there lest she be put out of that shack of a house she lives in with her husband and seven children—or are you talking about that Mary who lived over two thousand years ago? Which Mary was the caller talking about? Which Mary did I defame?" This too makes me cry as I remember Bevel's response to the complaint.

Bevel was angry but so creative in his response. He was engaging and challenging and absolutely brilliant. To my knowledge, no one brought this episode up again. Knowing Dr. King, he may have quietly found a way to have another preacher on the staff offer an apology, or did so himself. I don't know. Later on we did have to take some loving direct action against Bevel. We were all left rather speechless as we experienced Bevel's analyses, his metaphors, his sermons, his way of shocking others into seeing our concerns about people living in poverty and other abuses.

Jack O'Dell, an incredibly important staff member of SCLC, was involved in fund-raising efforts. As the director of the CEP I regularly invited him to come to monthly workshops, because he brought a unique perspective to the program, and not just because of his fund-raising know-how, but also because of his background as an accomplished historian. Jack had the ability to assess individual CEP participants' knowledge in order to design sessions with the group around old and current social and regional political histories. Jack would talk about the history of the struggles for change. He often referenced W. E. B. Du Bois's book *Black Reconstruction in America,* which helped participants understand and relate to what had happened before our current efforts to break down the walls of segregation, discrimination, and injustice. For example, he talked about the fact that P. B. Pinchback, a Black man, served as lieutenant governor in Louisiana in 1871, and how Pinchback won a seat in the U.S. Congress twice, but was denied it. Julian Bond, a leader in our modern freedom struggle, was likewise denied his seat in the Georgia legislature and had to go to court to gain it. Jack reminded the group that we had an earlier civil rights bill in 1883. It was encouraging for the CEP workshop participants to learn of hard-fought victories of the past and that they too could change their status, that they could fight the unjust system by accepting their right to do so. Jack O'Dell's teachings in the workshops were very helpful and stimulating.

As previously mentioned, Andrew Young, a Congregationalist minister, became indispensable not only to Dr. King and the SCLC but to the whole organization—actually, to the whole movement. Andy was not the "boss type." His style was one of winning people over. When Andy arrived in Atlanta, he scheduled individual talks with each of the CEP staff members. Andy and I had a long conversation and by the time it was over I knew I had a friend and a talented coworker. I was meeting someone who loved people, a kind and generous man who gave of himself and supported others. Willie Bolden, one of our field staff organizers (now Reverend Willie Bolden), became emotional when he related an incident to me. Willie and Andy were talking one day and Willie mentioned that he did not have the money to buy tires for his car. Andy handed Willie his credit card and told him to buy whatever he needed. This is the same Willie Bolden who shielded Andy from some of the blows he suffered when he was being viciously attacked during one of our night marches in St. Augustine, Florida. I was watching that beating and knew that most of the marchers walking had to stay in line, except the one who we saw trying to shield Andy by taking the blows if necessary. It was Willie Bolden who rescued Andy. This does not negate the times much later when I could get upset with Andy, but what he brought to the civil rights struggle could not have been bought or paid for. He was like the brother I never had.

Andy also brought a sense of fun to the CEP workshops. On most nights at the end of an intense day of working, studying, and learning, it was Andy who would put a record on the phonograph and regale us with the music of Louis Armstrong, Ella Fitzgerald, and others. We would dance the night away, and Andy was right there with us, outdancing everyone.

After some exciting years (1961–64) with CEP it became clear that Andy was ready to move on and begin working with another part of SCLC. This was a painful realization for me. Every month I planned in detail, coordinated, and scheduled the five-day sessions. Some CEP scheduled sessions were based on basic material relevant to every community, but most important, a weekly curriculum was designed to have a focus on the local struggles participants were engaged in in their hometowns, and which they would describe for the group present.

On one particular day I was complimented on the quality and content of a training session I called "Being a Citizen." This was my favorite session to lead. I found myself wishing Andy were present. When I mentioned this to Andy he replied, "I don't know why I'm here," referring to the time he spent with CEP that week. Initially, I was both hurt and angry when Andy made that comment, but I soon realized that Andy was just what other sections of the organization needed now. He was a very special member of the King Team and Dr. King was already in the process of utilizing Andy's skills in other areas within the organization. He would no longer "belong" to the Citizenship Education Program.

Dr. King acknowledged that he himself was being pulled in too many directions around the country. He said he was not meant to be the manager or executive director of the organization. It was evident Andy Young had the necessary skills and interest to assume some of the leadership and guidance of the organization. Although I had been aware of Andy's moving away from the special program CEP and into a leadership role for the whole organization, I now accepted the full realization of the fact. As I look back, I realize I was a little nervous that Andy would no longer be around during the workshop sessions. Even though I always took the leadership in structuring the five-day training sessions, I knew that Andy would be deeply missed. And I very much liked the session he did, which was titled "Why One Vote Counts."

This was an important lesson for me, a life lesson that has carried me forward through many experiences during and since our movement. The lesson is that nothing stays the same, that things change and life requires people to change. Having had exciting years with Andy as a definite part of the Citizenship Educational Program team, I had to release him from that role—my expecting him to always be there—as he moved on to a different position in SCLC.

As I moved toward acceptance of this fact, a peace came over me. I planned the day-by-day, hour-by-hour CEP schedule anyway, and later realized that my near anger at Andy was unimportant and that all of us on the CEP team had become a close-knit group; we were a family. All of us being together for those five days every month, supporting one another, and most of us conducting special sessions—this could not remain the same since the movement was dynamic and we would all eventually be called to other tasks. Andy would still be in communities helping advance local movements and still be working with people who had come through our training program. Actually, we all did that: we were all everywhere SCLC was engaged. Our CEP graduates initiated and energized local community protest movements.

HOSEA WILLIAMS was a classic example of an SCLC staff member with total commitment to the movement. Hosea had developed and directed the very effective work of the Chatham County Crusade for Voters in Savannah, Georgia. I remember the day Andy and I stood by Dr. King's bed when he was at home sick with the flu. We convinced him that Hosea should join our team full-time, and seeing

Hosea's organizing skills we knew he could manage and develop our field staff.

I get teary-eyed even now as I remember Hosea Williams early on, telling me how he felt when he would walk into a drugstore or an ice cream parlor and see little White children spinning around on the stools at the ice cream counter as they enjoyed an outing for a treat with their parents. Black children were not allowed to sit on these stools. This was one more of those manifestations of how the country sought to dehumanize African American people. Hosea was wounded by the fact that his child was not allowed to sit and spin on a soda fountain stool and that as a father he could not provide so simple a treat for his child. It makes me hurt for him and all the fathers and mothers who were compelled to explain to their children that they were not allowed to do such a simple thing all because of the color of their skin.

There are parallel situations today of inequitable treatment of minority children, of poor schools with inadequate textbooks, or children who never see a dentist or who have no outlet for expression in the arts, such as music and painting. I'm reminded of Isaac Stern, a great musician, who said we could stop a lot of inner-city violence if we taught all youngsters music.

Hosea's dream for his child, though seemingly a very simple one, embodied the full essence of why this movement was so vital in the lives of Black Americans. This denial in the ice cream parlor was just one more way of planting the seed of inferiority in the culture and into the very psyche of African American children and their parents. Our determined goal was to protest against and fight to change the deeply entrenched cultural pattern—this manifestation of American-style apartheid. Hosea Williams was hired on the spot as an SCLC organizer when Dr. King heard me and Andy sing Hosea's praises. Hosea was a very large presence on our team, though sometimes challenging.

Though Hosea would become one of the more rambunctious of our organizers, he was also one of the most effective. Andy Young and I were looking around for people dedicated to working for social change and who were already active in their communities. Hosea was a winner on that score. He fit the bill exactly, as he showed such success and determination in his local organizing with the Chatham County Crusade for Voters. He had important success in heightening awareness of the need for political power for African Americans there.

Hosea Williams was a college-trained chemist. He told me once that when he got his first job in a chemistry lab, he walked into the lab and saw a lot of machinery. He was one African American among many White employees. He said these White guys could take this machinery apart and put it together again. Hosea said, "I didn't even know how to turn it on." He added that in the chemistry laboratory in the Black school, the Black students were provided "a test tube and a frog." Hosea might have been joking or exaggerating, but I don't think so. He was driving home the point that deprivation of resources for Blacks was rampant—the order of the day. And even today this has not changed very much. This disparity in school systems is still typical these days, though there are examples of important interventions like that of Michelle Rhee's in Washington, D.C. A great deal of publicity was given to the way Rhee implemented her goal of removing barriers to effective education in the D.C. school system. There was a lot of pushback, but for some the desire to hold on to jobs in the school system was stronger than the commitment to ensuring that the children were receiving an adequate education.

Hosea's energy and success propelled him into a leadership position and he quickly became in charge of and expanded our field staff. He had to recruit people who would be assigned to work all around the South. Hosea had to see that they had the resources they needed, including vehicles and whatever expense money we could afford. Luckily, we who were running the Citizenship Education Program had our own separate grant thanks to Andy Young, the National Council of Churches, and the Field Foundation. Each executive staff member was responsible for an area of focus for our organizing. For example, T. Y. Rogers and C. T. Vivian were the point people for clergymen and affiliate groups. One time we were all sitting around our large conference room table in a planning meeting when Hosea arrived a little late from Savannah. I was sitting next to Dr. King. Dr. King leaned over to me and whispered with a chuckle, "Watch this meeting turn into a fight now that Hosea has arrived." It did. Hosea argued—fought like a tiger, proclaiming he needed a larger portion of the budget given his responsibility for our now large field staff, which he had put together.

I felt Hosea had a need to confront the rest of us. The other guys on the staff were more polished in language and dress, while Hosea could on occasion have a rather rough manner. My sense was that Hosea believed he had to prove that he was the best, the most needed as well as the most powerful. Once he even challenged Andy, calling him bourgeois because Andy's father was a dentist and Andy presents as a rather polished "pulpit person." But this was easy and perhaps necessary in the Congregational church. A seminary-trained minister projects a sort of polish, unlike the scientific profession generally, where people can often go to work in overalls and jeans. In any case, I know that when we needed someone to meet with heads of large steel mill companies in Birmingham or other corporate types, Andrew Young would be the SCLC team member to take that assignment. Andy was very comfortable as a suit-and-tie guy but could also put on overalls and drive a mule and wagon, as he did when recruiting for the Poor People's Campaign.

Reverend Hosea Williams and me.

Yet I don't know what we would have done without Hosea on the staff. We needed his skills particularly in motivating the "street dudes," as we would call some of his recruits. Hosea could get them to join the movement and motivate them to get involved in the freedom struggle. Hosea was very much at home with those street dudes. He would guzzle beer with them and get on the street corner and do all kinds of rabble-rousing to encourage these guys to come out of the juke joints and get involved in voter registration activities. One called "Big Lester" is a case in point. Grassroots people were recruited regularly and became some of our most competent field staffers for SCLC.

Although we never talked about it, Hosea seemed to resent what he perceived to be our personal closeness with the "big boys." Hosea knew that Andrew Young and I were the ones who got Dr. King to hire him, and he didn't like our perceived power to do that. Even so, we were very close; we were like a little family, with the same kinds of knotty issues that most families have. Ralph, Andy, Wyatt Walker, Bernard Lee, and I were everywhere Dr. King was. Hosea, I think, saw that as an inner circle and himself as not really fitting into that. Yet he was a key staff member with great power and presence. Somehow all of our work flowed together, creating a dynamic whole—working with preachers across the region, organizing with locals to help with voter education drives and actual political campaigns, moving teams into an area to provide support in various desegregation efforts, and teaching nonviolent philosophy and strategies in direct action campaigns. We were indeed a team and our work together changed our country.

Chapter 12

ON INTO THE TWENTIETH CENTURY VIA BIRMINGHAM

The Great March on Washington

Come go with me to that land where I'm bound.

We were intensifying protest activity and making sure that those participating understood the behavior necessary for a successful demonstration or protest action, including adhering to nonviolent guidelines. Because we knew any of us could be arrested, we decided to make sure that no demonstrator had anything that could be misconstrued as a weapon. Walking alongside the line of marchers, I requested everyone to put anything that could be so identified in the box I was carrying. I kept this large collection of mostly small pocket knives, nail files, and even small cuticle scissors in a storage closet on my Atlanta back porch. Seeing that collection in that closet for several years and thinking it useless, one day I threw the entire box in the trash can. How I regret that now. You see, I didn't know then how incredibly important what we were doing was. More specifically, I didn't know that many people around the world would study and even become inspired by what we did. We only knew we had to do it.

Another task I took care of was to make sure we were in touch with people in targeted locales. There was a lot of calling back and forth between our staff people and our CEP graduates and people in the places where the buses traveled or attempted to travel. Sometimes local CEP participants would hop on a bus and join the Freedom Riders. SCLC was getting called on and invited to participate in all the major activities that were going on in connection with our freedom struggle. Our offices were very much stirred, agitated, and involved in them, although CORE had the most to do with initiating the Freedom Rides, along with SNCC. Ours was a support role for the Freedom Rides. All of us in our office related to this protest activity, but not directly. Different organizations initiated various activities, but all were an attack on the pervasive system of segregation. At this time we were getting requests to be involved in many and varied activities in the South. There was an increasing need for coordination with groups that were now becoming an SCLC affiliate.

IN JANUARY 1963, Wyatt Walker presented to the SCLC staff members his plan regarding the situation in Birmingham. It was resolved that SCLC should initiate a large and focused challenge to Birmingham's segregation policies and practices. I was glad when Martin asked me to go over to Birmingham and set up some Citizenship Education Program workshops there. He told me he had decided to accept Reverend Fred Shuttlesworth's invitation to come and help him implement the *Brown v. Board of Education* ruling as it related to Birmingham. We had learned an important lesson in Albany, Georgia, and that was that we took a real chance of thwarting our goals for success when we joined a local effort, even by one of our affiliate groups, if we did not first send in a training team to prepare the community and enhance the chances for staging successful nonviolent protests.

Making the contacts I would need was easy in Birmingham because the CEP team, especially Andy and I, had already spent a good bit of time there recruiting people to attend our CEP workshops. We could also recruit participants by placing a call to Reverend Shuttlesworth or members of his Alabama Christian Movement for Human Rights, and we'd have an impressive contingent from Birmingham at the Dorchester Center or the Penn Community Center when we needed to hold a month's training there. Getting time in regular church meetings was easy. Most pastors were glad to give us time and space to explain our program.

People would come to a church meeting to hear what was going on in the protest activity wherever it was happening. It was exciting for people to learn about what was happening, and I was exhilarated for the speakers and organizers to see so many people filling the seats in the church. The next day there'd be a hundred more people, because someone had invited them to come to a workshop or otherwise become involved in freedom movement activity. Interest and energy escalated. People attending became the troops: they came to the meetings, they got involved in voter registration organizing work, they walked with picket signs, they had an experience in jail in Birmingham. People who came to meetings and decided to register to vote, which many had never done before, increasingly saw reasons for doing so after meetings and recruiting appeals. Sit-ins at libraries and lunch counters and the picketing of stores in the downtown area as well as protest marches resulted in many arrests. Hundreds of activists were arrested in Birmingham. They filled the jails, so then the fairgrounds were used as a holding place. That presented a crisis for the city and for us movement workers. We were worried about the kind of care those arrested would receive—would they be fed, would there be personal care facilities, would there be places to sleep, how long would they be held in the fairgrounds? I don't remember how long they were held there, but I *do* remember running barefoot across a road to those fenced-in fairgrounds to hand out a few sandwiches to protesters. Protest activity escalated. More and more people, young and not so young, got involved.

Reverend Shuttlesworth and me.

A PIVOTAL meeting was held in Room 30 of the A. G. Gaston Motel in Birmingham on April 12, 1963. Should we agree that Martin should lead a planned march or allow some others of us to do so; or should we agree with those who thought he should go north to accept a good friend's offer to arrange a series of fund-raising meetings? We had called many staff members together in preparation for one of the biggest marches we had yet scheduled in Birmingham. We were in desperate need of bail money. On Good Friday, the Sixteenth Street Baptist Church was full with people ready to join those already incarcerated for demonstrating against the notorious racism so prevalent in Birmingham. The group gathered in this critical meeting in Room 30 was made up not only of SCLC leadership but also of local Birmingham leaders and businesspeople who had a stake in helping to make this major decision. Should Martin lead the march or go north to raise bail money for those jailed? There were strong arguments for and against his leading the planned march. The strongest argument was for him to go north and raise the bail money we needed. Dr. King listened intently as usual, not saying much at all. But then a surprising thing happened. Dr. King stood up and went into the adjacent bedroom, leaving the rest of us still debating the question. When he came back to join us he was wearing overalls—not the kind of clothes he usually wore. His change of clothes made a definite and powerful statement, answering the question being so vigorously debated. We became quiet now; clearly the decision had been made. Rather than talk, we all stood up, held and crossed our hands in the usual fashion when we sang our anthem, and someone said a prayer. I don't remember any words Dr. King uttered at this moment, but he must have said something. I know we sang quietly and prayerfully our anthem of the movement, "We Shall Overcome." By this time I had tears in my eyes. I think others also cried; it was an emotional moment. Dr. King did not cry, as I've read in some accounts of this assembly. I gave him a big hug, as others in the room also did. And as he headed out the door we were all behind him. He intended to get to the Sixteenth Street Baptist Church, where hundreds were waiting, and lead the crowd on a scheduled protest march through downtown Birmingham.

However, this march was not to happen. As soon as Dr. King was on the sidewalk, with Reverend Abernathy walking beside him, a police officer grabbed him by the back of his jeans and took him to a waiting paddy wagon. He was under arrest.

AFTER DR. KING'S arrest, James Bevel, a very clever strategist, and I would take the lead in preparing the people in Birmingham for the most intense and publicized protest activity we ever staged. This demonstration increased in intensity and ultimately more than three thousand were arrested. It was at this point that James suggested we allow children in larger numbers to participate in marches.

James Bevel and I now started nonviolence training in the basement of the Sixteenth Street Baptist Church with a focus on children. Every day ten or fifteen youngsters stopped by the basement of the church after school. Soon the number mushroomed into many hundreds of school-age children. Children as young as nine and ten stopped by our training session, first out of curiosity and then because they were discovering feelings and possibilities they had not known before—the possibilities of living in a new and different Birmingham. Like me at their age, before I had words for it I knew something was wrong with the way Black people were forced to live. What an exciting experience this must have been for these young children.

What we did in Birmingham and the response to it escalated into an event that would be seen around the world. On May 7, 1963, we planned to march into Birmingham's business district after massive numbers of children had gathered in Kelly Ingram Park. But they were viciously attacked with fire hoses and police dogs before they could leave the park. Worldwide news coverage of the police attacks galvanized support for the demonstrators. More and more people of every age swelled the crowds now at every event—mass meetings, workshops small and large, marches and rallies.

As I was hanging out in Kelly Ingram Park with a gathering of children after school one afternoon, two reporters with cameras asked some of the children what they wanted and why they were demonstrating. I can still hear one very little girl respond, "I want freedom." The reporter chided me, suggesting that I had told the child what to say. My response to the reporter was to invite him to come to the mass meeting that night and see and hear many children excitedly singing songs of freedom. I then said to this reporter that he was also welcome to come to the after-school discussions where James Bevel and I would be every day, to greet and discuss with the children there what the movement in Birmingham was about and what it meant to their lives. They were learning at very young ages— as young as nine or ten—what was meant by nonviolent protest and why it was important.

My training workshops with both children and adults intensi- fied. It was during this time that Deenie Drew, who helped and took care of us in a special way, hauled carloads of us, me along with the children, downtown to walk with our picket signs to maintain our boycott of the stores. The police did not stop Deenie's car, as one would expect, because of two things: we hid on the floor of her car with our picket signs, and she was fair-skinned enough that they couldn't tell that Deenie was African American. She was as light as any White person in Birmingham. Deenie Drew and her good friend Ruth Barefield-Pendleton were staunch supporters of the power- ful Birmingham movement. They even saw to it that demonstrators were never hungry. We looked forward to the good food they would prepare for us.

The young children and other youth were quick learners. They readily understood why they must claim this Birmingham struggle as theirs. And they did so in a most firm and powerful way and continued to picket stores—stores that would not hire any Black people even though we shopped there.

Some young people attended our meetings despite their parents' wishes to the contrary. I can still see a teenager running from his father because he had not given his consent for his son to participate in the movement. I never got the chance to talk to the young man, but James Bevel and I surmised that the father apparently had ordered his son not to get involved. The son had obviously ignored that order. He was clearly outrunning his father—both physically and metaphorically. That father would not be the only person trying to avoid involvement in the movement and to insist his children not be involved as well. But this movement was like a runaway train that could not be stopped. I think of Curtis Mayfield's lyrics: *"People get ready, there's a train a-comin', it's picking up passengers coast to coast."*

I ONCE stopped at a service station to get gas, only to be ordered by the owner to get off his property because police sirens could be heard a ways down the street. This service station owner was a Black man who was angry and apparently scared. He yelled at me, "Get that car off my property!" I did. I'm not sure why I was driving alone, yet once in a while I had to get back to my office by myself.

Sometimes I had to drive back and forth between Birmingham and Atlanta to take care of some needs at the office and there were times when I needed a place to sleep if it was too late to get back to my apartment. On this particular day, a motel owner would not give me a room due to the intense movement activity in Birmingham. He said he was denying me a room because I had no luggage. I only had a very small rolling bag with me at the time. There was a lot of this kind of fear during the Birmingham campaign. The atmosphere was vibrant and tense. I was upset but I understood the fear.

In Birmingham we were on a roll, boycotting every public place that discriminated against Black people. We even boycotted the liquor stores, because they had separate checkout lines for Whites and Blacks. In what was one of the lighter moments, when someone expressed a desire to intensify the liquor store boycott, one of our staffers yelled in protest: "Not the liquor store!" We responded with great laughter. After all, for some of us, a little "juice of the grapes" occasionally could ease us into a few hours of rest as we wound down from the day's activities.

I remember standing in the midst of one protest in Birmingham with James Bevel when a policeman approached us with a most violent attitude, using "nigger talk" and other expletives as he ordered us off the street. As we attempted to explain to him that we were there to keep our campaign workers organized and to maintain calm and order, the policeman continued to rant and rave with a threatening stance. James used the same strategy he had used before, and asked, "Excuse me, sir, have you got a cigarette?" Such a question to the policeman indicated that we saw him as another member of the human family, and that we were not afraid of him. The policeman was shocked into a different manner toward us. Although he never gave the cigarette to James, a human connection was made. This too was nonviolence at work. James Bevel was a brilliant student of nonviolence.

AS THE protests began to cost the city of Birmingham more and more money, the city's business leaders were concerned enough to consider negotiating with Dr. King and the local civil rights advocates and leaders. The leaders of the business community agreed to allow the gradual disintegration of segregation and to release the arrested protesters of Birmingham from jail. Across the country, in the spring of 1963, there were an estimated 930 protest demonstrations in more than one hundred American cities. The actions of the brave people in one southern city, Birmingham, Alabama, intensified this national civil rights movement.

WHILE WE were in Birmingham—this was several days before Medgar Evers was shot on June 12, 1963—we got word that some of our star workers and participants in a recent CEP workshop had been arrested in Winona, Mississippi, as they drove back home from Georgia. Those arrested included powerful activist and freedom fighter Fannie Lou Hamer, and Annell Ponder, one of our CEP teachers. Several others from the workshop were arrested as well. Dr. King had gotten the news of the arrest, and after hearing about the shooting of Medgar Evers, he called from Atlanta advising some of us to go to Winona and see if we could get them out of jail. Andy got the call and he and James Bevel came to me to borrow my car. I was ready to head to Mississippi along with Andy and James. But Andy said only, "Loan us your car."

Asking to borrow my car fell strangely on my ears. I was a little confused and disturbed that Andy would ask to use my car rather than say, "Let's go." If he had said, "We must get to Winona, let's go," I would have said, "Yes indeed." In this instance I would not even have gone to get a toothbrush, which most of us carried all the time. Because Andy said, "Just give us the keys. Bevel and I are going to take care of it," I became a little angry and insisted that I would certainly be a part of this rescue effort. I said, "Those are women in jail in Winona. If Mrs. Hamer is brave enough to challenge Mississippi, I'm brave enough to help get her out of jail." Andy did not accept my response. Again I told him that I was going, too. He insisted I give them the keys instead. I got into my car—I was ready to head to Mississippi. When they finally saw my determination to go, they piled into my car as well.

I was rather insulted to be treated as a child, to be "patted on the head," figuratively speaking, as if being told to "stay here, little girl." I was director of education for SCLC. I felt very close to Mrs. Hamer, and had stayed in her home in Ruleville. She was one of our star CEP participants, recruiting others from around the Delta area. I wasn't about to be excluded from helping to seek her release.

Andy wrote about this exchange between us in his second book. Several other accounts have been written as people pick it up from his book *An Easy Burden.* He wrote that I drove with excessive speed—80 miles an hour—and only gave him the wheel after I saw an eighteen-wheeler approaching. Common sense would demand a Black woman never drive with excessive speed between Alabama and Mississippi! That would have been suicidal from more than one per-spective. I did let Andy share the driving at some point, but that was probably after we stopped to get gas.

Andy also wrote in his account of the incident that while we stopped to get gas I was swishing down the street in a red dress and "wearing provocative high heels." I did wear high-heeled shoes to go to church sometimes but I wasn't wearing them then. There is a photograph of me taken by Len Holt running across the road in Bir-mingham with *no* shoes on, taking sandwiches to children being held at the fairgrounds after the jails were filled. If I had had "provocative high heels" on in Birmingham, I would not have put them on to go to a Winona, Mississippi, jail! As I think about it now, Andy's initial refusal to include me on this journey with them was male chauvinism at its strongest. He doesn't think so.

Andy's recorded recollection of our arrival in Winona is that once we arrived in town, he and James insisted I stay in the car, and that after they returned from seeking out the sheriff, I was sitting under a tree reading *The Prophet*, by Khalil Gibran. Although I did derive comfort from reading *The Prophet*, I did not sit in a swing reading it as they went inside the jail. For years I kept a copy of that book in my purse. If I read it at all in the car it was not when my coworkers Fannie Lou Hamer and Annell Ponder and others were brought from the cells to be released to us.

I was in the foyer of the jail, not sitting under a tree as Andy Young wrote. I thought it would be helpful to make friendly small talk with the jailers as all three of us waited for our friends and coworkers to be released. This was the first time I felt that I could have done physical damage to our opponents—to these jailers. I was angry at them when I realized that they had abused our friends and yet could stand there making small talk with us. Although I do not recall seeing physical evidence of bruising on Mrs. Hamer and Annell, several accounts have been written about their condition. We do know from prior experiences that jailers often used rubber hoses when beating prisoners—striking them in areas covered by clothing. Mrs. Hamer did say they were beaten. We paid the fines and we and our CEP colleagues were soon on our way out of Winona.

OUR CREATIVE, visionary, and confident team member James Bevel had the idea that we should begin to take large numbers of grassroots people on a long march from Birmingham to Washington, D.C.—to the seat of government. The goal would be to state our case and show the determination we freedom movement workers had for the cause of our action. The idea evolved into the March on Washington: SCLC and all the other civil rights organizations were committed to ensuring the success of this new goal. Though it didn't happen the way James envisioned it would, it exceeded everyone's expectations. I think Gandhi's Salt March to the Sea inspired us to do this.

James Bevel referred to himself as a "country preacher" and didn't take too well to "the suits," as he would sometimes refer to leaders of CORE, NAACP, and the Urban League. At one gathering I remember James walking the halls yelling, "Get your Georgia breakfast! Hot biscuits, bacon, sausage, eggs, and grits are waiting for you all! Come and get it; come and get it." This was at an SCLC planning retreat held at the Dorchester Center. And we did go get it, with big smiles of happy anticipation. I find it exciting and stimulating when I consider James's "country preacher" style compared to that of "the suits." I don't believe anyone else could've gotten everyone up and ready for the day's work as James could. He loved to be called the "country preacher." And he dressed the part—overalls and yarmulke.

The call went around the country asking people to prepare to come to Washington to make an unprecedented statement to the government that *"We want our freedom and we want it now."* No greater statement, no greater way of showing the determination of a people had been made in such a way before. How indeed would we plan a program in Washington, the nation's capital, that would justify the call for such a massive gathering?

I PICKED up Dr. King at the airport in Charleston, South Carolina, to join us in a staff retreat at the Penn Center. I told him I wished he had been with us the night before in a wooden rural church to hear a White girl from Vassar College address a group of elderly African American men and women about her vision. She said: "All I want is a better America. I have a dream that one day my little children can hold hands with your little children and grandchildren and play together. I have a dream that they can study and learn together without it seeming strange or unusual." She kept the refrain going for a while and when she finished an elderly man in the church broke out in song, *"I want Jesus to walk with me; all along this tedious journey. Oh I want Jesus to walk with me."* Martin listened intently. I could see both the preacher and the poet working inside of him. Martin's dream still resonates with many people all over the world. I think he was inspired by that White girl's vision. In any case, as we said about a number of preachers on our staff, Martin "could preach the phone book!" His ability to become motivated to create a sermon was unique. He was indeed a poet.

A staff retreat at the Penn Center. That's me behind Dr. King. Ralph Abernathy is to his left and Andrew Young is in the bottom row at the far left, with his arms crossed.

I was glad I was the one meeting Dr. King at the airport and to have the opportunity to share what had gone on in our community work. I was glad that I had the time and space to tell him what the White girl had said in her remarks the night before, especially saying what her dream was. Martin always wanted me or Andy or a close staff person to pick him up because he had observed that a community person would often ask him so many questions that he felt he had made his speech before he had even reached the venue where he was scheduled to speak.

I TAKE a good deal of pride in the fact that the CEP had touched a few thousand people in a way that they were ready and even anxious to answer the call that went out inviting, indeed urging, people to join us on the Mall in our nation's capital. We needed masses of people at the Mall in a show of strength as we made our case for jobs and freedom. Forty to sixty people per month attended CEP sessions, which were designed to help empower them and to remove the mental programming that put forth the notion that government was all-powerful and alien to "we the people." The people came to claim their role as "owners of government." They went away understanding that the job of government is to represent the people; that government works for the people. We had arrived at a new place, a new consciousness, such that together we could make a powerful statement. It was rewarding for me to be at the Mall on August 28 and to witness the culmination of the work we had accomplished in those many months and years of preparation, to see it finally played out in this great March on Washington. My husband, George, at my urging, drove up from Petersburg, Virginia, to be with me and share in the memorable experience of the March. At this time, however, our visits were more out of duty, since the civil rights movement had become all-consuming for me.

Organizers were nervous about the length and tone of each speaker's remarks. Controlling each speaker's allotted time on the stage was seen as critical. There had been a lot of tension surrounding the jockeying for position on the platform and figuring out the order of speakers. Interestingly, Martin spoke last. He did not fight for prominence or to be in the limelight. What a blessing it was that he came last. He took the day. Anyone speaking after him would hardly have been heard, for what he shared of his dream for a new world, a new way of being together, has become a powerful motivator for those who were present as well as those hearing that speech. No one knew that what Dr. King said after he moved away from the manuscript would be heard around the world and that the "I have a dream" lines would be quoted and memorized by everyone from kindergartners to presidents of countries.

I helped type the now famous "I Have a Dream" speech at the Willard Hotel in Washington, D.C. Dora McDonald, Martin's secretary, did not come up to Washington for the event, and since I was an excellent typist I inherited the responsibility. I ran back and forth from my room on a lower level bringing typed pages for Martin's editing. But, even with all that preparation and writing, the closing part of the speech that has become so associated with the great march was delivered extemporaneously; it had not been a part of the manuscript.

The next day I felt actual gratitude that there were no mishaps, like violence, to spoil the day. I had heard that if there had been violence, government officials were prepared to cut the power to the microphones. I saw that people were in a celebratory, joyful, meditative, and reflective mood. The spirit of the Almighty was with us on this wonderful and blessed day.

In spite of the commitment of grassroots people, civil rights leaders, and organizations in Birmingham, which culminated in the March on Washington in 1963, we paid a huge price after the big march for our actions. Back in Birmingham, the police let dogs and water hoses loose on the demonstrators as we heightened our efforts to help Reverend Shuttlesworth tear down the walls of segregation in Alabama and ultimately nationwide.

The home of A. D. King, Dr. King's brother, was bombed and an unexploded bomb was discovered at the Gaston Motel. But the most violent and horrific action took place in September 1963 when the Sixteenth Street Baptist Church was bombed and four little girls lost their lives as they were primping in their finery for the special children's day service in the lower level of the church.

Where in the world do we go from here? some of us wondered through our pain and tears. But we would go on. The violence would not stop us. It did not stop us. As Emil Hess said, Birmingham catapulted America into the twentieth century.

Chapter 13

"THE SPIRIT WAS MOVIN' ALL OVER THIS LAND"

THE YEARS 1964 and 1965 marked a turning point in the nation and the civil rights movement, and was a time of exciting developments as well as grief. It seems that in 1964 and 1965 major challenges to a system based on grossly unfair laws and patterns intensified. More and more people were motivated to get involved—to bring increasing energy and focus to our determination to make democracy real in America. People would even call our office and offer to bring groups south to join whatever actions we were planning. The Putney Graduate School group is one example of this—they were most interested in the training we provided activists.

It seems that the zeitgeist truly was upon us; there was a momentum that could not be quelled. I believe many people across the country were waiting, even if sometimes unconsciously, for someone to take the first step.

With Dr. King as our highly respected leader, SCLC responded when Dr. Vincent Harding called from St. Augustine, Florida, requesting our help there in challenging segregation. The city of St. Augustine was preparing for a racially segregated celebration of its four hundredth anniversary in 1964, despite the fact that the Black community there had engaged in nonviolent protests against segregation for several years. This intense protest campaign was waged under the leadership of Dr. Robert Hayling, a dentist who was president of the local SCLC affiliate that called for our support. When we heard that the people in St. Augustine knew about our training workshops, we were excited. Consequently, SCLC field staff people were assigned to go there to intensify local efforts to help open public accommodations and recruit people to send to our CEP workshops.

In response to Dr. Hayling's call, I arrived in St. Augustine to assess the situation and to provide a tighter focus for the existing movement before Dr. King arrived. By the time Dr. King came to St. Augustine, twelve or thirteen CEP classes and workshops were up and running, filled with a contingent of adults from in and around the town.

As I reported to Martin what we had been working on, I anxiously informed him of segregationist attacks against local Black activists. Two of our CEP graduates had told me about mounted policemen riding into the church where they were running their classes. "They need support," I insisted. They needed stronger support because nowhere had we had a report of horses being ridden into a church where CEP sessions were being conducted. The use of horses created a major intimidation.

We ended up building one of the South's strongest protest movements in St. Augustine, though the actions here were not viewed around the world, as were the actions in Birmingham, Alabama. Dr. King had addressed a large meeting in May 1964 and his presence had helped to intensify the massive protest marches and demonstrations that followed. St. Augustine became the first city where we staged night marches. These were planned so that Black people who worked during the day could participate. Reverend C. T. Vivian and I led one of the night marches to the old slave market on the corner of St. George and King streets. This site where Africans had been sold into slavery became a place where old men gathered in the evenings to smoke their tobacco and reminisce.

The night C.T. and I led the march, the younger people outnumbered the older people. I was near the front and, as we approached the slave market, I could hear what sounded like chains rattling and a lot of vulgar language aimed at the line of marchers as we approached. I used to say a quick and easy *no* when people asked whether we were ever afraid during protest demonstrations, but this night I was very scared, and I'm sure anyone seeing me close up would have known it. I know that others in the line of marchers were scared as well.

I squeezed C.T.'s hand tighter and tighter as we came closer to the group of segregationists that was gathered to attack us in some way. "C.T., let's pray," I said. C.T. stopped, turned, and faced the long line of marchers. He raised his hand and invoked the name of God. "Our Father God." Instantly, a voice yelled back from the slave market, "Niggers ain't got no God!" My friend and coworker Reverend C. T. Vivian continued his prayer over violent and vulgar language.

We continued slowly into the slave market area. One young White guy tried to trip me with his crutch, which he had purposely stuck out in front of me. I was able to step over the crutch and not fall.

Another night march frightened me even more. A line of marchers, including Edwina Smith (now Mrs. Otis Moss) and me, were walking peacefully and quietly when we were attacked with bricks and bottles. Edwina was working as an assistant to Reverend Walker but came to St. Augustine for some of the protests. I could feel the movement of air as a brick flew within a foot of our faces and then hit and shattered the glass in a store window. The force of the brick could have killed us or at least caused a concussion.

On another night march in May in St. Augustine, I observed Harry Boyte Sr. being beaten. A news reporter (I think it was David Halberstam) attempted to protect Harry, jumping on his back to take the blows. Harry had been brutally attacked in Prince Edward County, Virginia, to the point of being almost castrated. I didn't know this prior to his joining our staff. His son, Harry Boyte (though named after his father, he is not Junior), a longtime professor at the University of Minnesota, shared this with me. Harry is an example of our White allies being attacked, sometimes as viciously as us Black folk. Sometimes there were discussions after we hired Harry as to whether we should have a White man at the front desk of a Black organization. Harry Boyte was very understanding and said, "I'll take any position," because he realized that SCLC might be criticized for giving White people an "up front" position. I believe that we have evolved beyond such questioning now in 2012. Harry was a beautiful Quaker totally committed to the struggle for justice and equality. I still feel a deep and abiding love and appreciation for him.

On June 10, 1964, during one of the night marches, Andy Young suffered a severe beating. He was thrown to the ground, where kicks and blows were heaped upon him by young White men. They did not stop at using their hands and feet. "Someone hit me in the head from the rear with a blackjack," Andy said. Andy, who was quite athletic and a great swimmer, could not even defend himself. The beating was documented by network television reporters who were covering the march. SCLC field organizer Willie Bolden can be seen coming to Andy's rescue. He took blows himself in his effort to shield Andy. Bolden was able to help Andy get up and move away. Much later, Andy revealed that he went behind a nearby building and cried. He also said, "I could have taken that little dude with one hand but there was that long line of marchers walking behind me. If I had fought back physically that long line of marchers could have turned into one big fistfight or worse."

Most of the marchers knew that we needed to stay in order or it would have been even more violent. If there were any who did not know this, there were enough of us marching that night who did, who had committed to take physical blows in an attempt to live the Gandhian and King teaching—"We will take your blows and wear you down with our ability to do so. We lived into the mandate that unarmed suffering is redemptive." Andy, Martin, and I were aware that we were role models, leaders of a throng of suffering Black people who needed to see such commitment to nonviolence in those holding major leadership positions. Andy's strength and commitment to nonviolence were especially tested that night. My time would come later.

AL LINGO, a young White man, checked into the Monson Motor Lodge in St. Augustine and invited J. T. Johnson, a young Black man and one of our best SCLC field staff members, to go swimming with him as his guest despite the rule that the pool was for Whites only. Brock James, the owner of the motor lodge, was furious to see this Black person in his pool. Consequently, Mr. James poured acid in the pool while Al and J.T. were swimming, in an attempt to chase the unwanted swimmers out of his pool. The next day, on June 19, 1964, the Senate passed the Civil Rights Act that would outlaw the motel owner's policy. One would think that J.T. would've received some sort of apology from the motel owner, but Mr. James went to his grave saying that he would never apologize for his actions. His grown daughter, though, did apologize after her father's death.

A group of about twelve or fifteen children and I gathered at what was called our Freedom House in St. Augustine. *Freedom House* was a term used for houses loaned to freedom movement workers for training sessions and demonstration organizing. A group of children had volunteered to go with me on this day, June 20, 1964, to wade in at the beach in an effort to end a for-Whites-only rule. We planned to all go into the water together, but I took one carload of children to the beach, dropped them off, and returned to pick up more before we actually would get into the water. As I returned with the second carload, the first group was running back toward me down the path from the beach, shouting, "Ms. Cotton, Ms. Cotton, some White men back there at the beach said if we come into that water they would beat us up." I grabbed the hands of two of the children and all of us headed back toward the water.

As I approached the water with the children the atmosphere was tense. Policemen were congregated there, and five or six feet away a group of White ruffians started to yell obscenities at us, but we continued walking. I remember holding the hands of two children and walking with great resolve toward the water. When we first stood at the edge of the water an awful kind of quiet descended. I encouraged the girls and said, "Come on, let's go in." As soon as we touched the water they charged us. The lick I suffered from the attack to this day still affects my hearing on the left side. One little girl got her nose broken. This little girl was Cynthia Mitchell, now Cynthia Mitchell Clark, Ph.D., a retired schoolteacher who continues to do work in her community, including developing leadership programs for youth. I am in touch with her now and I have been sent a copy of the report of the doctor who treated her for the nose injury.

After this attack on the beach I have reflected on stories I've read or heard about how there are moments when an individual can use strength that he or she had not known they had. Since I never once considered turning back from our attempt to wade in the water, I think that's what I experienced en route to the water's edge. I felt no fear, only great resolve. Also, because of the children with me, it did not occur to me to turn back. Unconsciously, I'm sure I would not have wanted to have the children see me as afraid or weak, but most important, I was determined to go forward toward our goal. I knew the children would have been impressed negatively or positively by the way I responded to the violence. Perhaps foolishly, my only thought was our mission to break down the policy of White-only.

A strong connection developed between me and some of the people with whom I spent time. This includes some young children who I'm sure were caught up in the energy being generated by our work. I remember a little boy about eight or nine years old who would not let go of my hand for anything. I'll never forget him. He clung to me the rest of the day and anytime he saw me.

I think I learned something through this event: when one is determined, one does not always analyze or assess possible danger. Certainly for me that day I felt only determination. At some level I understand total commitment, and that total commitment is not an intellectual experience; such commitment borders on being motivated by spiritual strength. Why do I tear up as I write this all these years later? We could have been killed. That day at the St. Augustine beach I was moving as if by some kind of special focus and energy. What *could have* happened to us was not in my thoughts. If I had to make that decision today, being conscious of what could possibly happen—for example, children being hurt—I expect my decision would be different. At the time, the overriding goal was to fulfill our mission.

There was a White fellow on the beach at the time, challenging the policemen, shouting, "You're supposed to protect these people. Why don't you protect them?" So it was obvious that the police weren't there to protect us, but rather those there to attack us. I would later learn that the White fellow was the same Al Lingo who had invited

J. T. Johnson to swim with him in Brock James's pool. I'm not sure how we all got back, but we did return to Freedom House, where we had a rather painful debriefing.

I was invited back to St. Augustine from July 1 through July 3, 2011, when I was honored for the Fifth Annual ACCORD Freedom Trail Luncheon. My colleague Andy Young has also recently been honored there by having an area renamed the Andrew Young Crossing. Being back in this, the oldest city in the country, was an emotional experience as I was driven to some of the historic areas where we'd had big protest actions. These included not only the beach where I and the children were beaten and where a historic marker was placed, but also the old slave market, a focal point for some of our protest activity.

AT THE mass meeting in a little wooden church the night after our beating, the floorboards creaked as people sang, clapped their hands, and stomped their feet. I turned around and looked into the face of an elderly Black woman singing very energetically, "Ain't gonna let nobody turn me round." And I heard someone remark, "Imagine! One group of people declaring that they own God's ocean."

June and July 1964 in St. Augustine was the occasion for forty-five straight nights of beatings and intimidation. This was about the roughest experience we'd had in any city. We marched regularly at night, though we were advised not to march, because it was so dangerous and the police had advised us that they could not protect us. As we'd sing and pray and head out of our churches, the Klan—Hoss Manucy and his gang—and other ruffians would wait for us. They would attack us, but we'd nonetheless always come back to the church and hear an analysis of the day's and evening's activity. Always there would be lots of communal singing—songs of hope and of determination. On many nights as we gathered in the churches, we could see some of the activists wearing bandages.

By July 1964, St. Augustine was desegregated by the Civil Rights Act. We could now eat at lunch counters. We were no longer overtly rejected by the White shopkeepers and waitresses in the city, and we could finally swim at the public beaches.

DR. KING felt that it was a good time to bring SCLC board members together at a retreat, to be held at Airlie House, a wonderful conference center not far from the Washington, D.C., area. This gathering would include, for the first time, the spouses of those on our team who were married. Most of these spouses were stay-at-home mothers who bore the responsibility of maintaining their homes and taking care of their children when their partners were away. This was true even for Coretta Scott King, who played a public role and occasionally participated in the demonstrations and other work we did. She was very much interested in our movement and had special skills that helped it as well. She wanted to be involved in the action. Being trained in music as a vocalist, Coretta did fund-raising concerts for SCLC on special occasions. But Martin did not want her out on the lecture circuit very much. I heard him say more than once, "I don't want Miss Lockhart's mark on my children." Miss Lockhart was their housekeeper, who also served as a caretaker of the children sometimes when both Martin and Coretta needed to be away.

Our purpose for the retreat was to come to an agreement on the question *Where do we, as a movement, go from here?* James Bevel was at his creative best at the retreat. I'll never forget how he held the floor, arguing for us to go back to the South and launch a major campaign for the "right of the franchise": the right to vote, with Alabama as the focal point for this campaign. James had talked about the need for SCLC to put forth a major effort to work on voter registration throughout the South for some time. Now SCLC leadership understood that the Citizenship Education Program training was instrumental and indeed was the basis for enlisting our CEP graduates to go home and put forth a great effort to raise awareness of the importance of claiming their political power.

James Bevel won the day.

We decided to head back south, where we intensified our efforts to remove every hindrance to Black people's exercising the civic right, duty, and responsibility to vote.

Ms. Amelia Boynton of the Dallas County Voters League of Selma, Alabama, came to SCLC to ask for our help. Activism in the form of marches and other means of protest was not new to the people of Selma. So, on January 22, 1965, more than one hundred Black teachers from Selma marched in the streets to the courthouse to protest the abridgement of their voting rights. We were checking into the Hotel Albert in Selma on February 18, 1965, when Jimmy Robinson, a member of the National States Rights Party, a White racist group, hit Dr. King in the face. This attack was caught on camera and I'm seen looking startled in the photograph standing next to Dr. King, his head now down on the counter from the blow. (See the photograph in *King: The Photobiography of Martin Luther King, Jr.,* by Charles Johnson and Bob Adelman.)

Reverend Abernathy and I were standing on either side of Dr. King when his head landed on the check-in counter from the force of the blow. Someone else, I don't remember who, intervened to keep the attacker from hitting him again. There was a photographer in the lobby of the hotel as we were checking in, but we didn't realize it at the time. After the attack, we were ushered down to a lower level of the hotel to assess whether Dr. King required medical attention. He said he did not. When I asked him if he was hurt he said, "That fellow strikes a pretty hard blow." I encouraged him to seek medical help, but he said, "No, I'll be all right." Then someone inquired as to whether he wanted his attacker arrested. Again Dr. King said no.

I remember thinking at the time of how deeply impressed Martin had always been by Mahatma Gandhi's decision to dissuade officials from prosecuting someone who had attacked him on one occasion in South Africa. As I've mentioned before, Martin was an intense student of Gandhi's adherence to nonviolence. I thought it was one thing to study the experience of someone else, and to become strongly influenced by how that person handled something; it is quite another thing to have the same response when one suffers a similar experience. Dr. King early on in his studies accepted that Gandhi's response was the kind that would be much more healing—for ourselves and for the attacker. Thankfully this nonviolent response by Dr. King ultimately contributed to at least a degree of healing, even if we would have to wait awhile. It is impossible to put a deadline on work done via nonviolence. As I have deepened my own study of nonviolence, I can see the healing result of such responses.

Among the victims in the march to Selma were Jimmy Lee Jackson and his mother, whom he was trying to protect. Jimmy Lee was beaten and shot in the stomach, and died on February 26. He was only twenty-six years old. At the memorial service for Jimmy Lee, James Bevel and his wife, Diane, announced the march from Selma to Montgomery.

Hosea Williams and John Lewis led the march, which took place on Sunday, March 7. As the marchers crossed the Edmund Pettus Bridge in Selma, troopers rode in on horses and beat the marchers with clubs, driving them back from the bridge to the neighboring streets as the police threw tear gas canisters into the crowd. Bloodied marchers, frightened, confused, and choking from the tear gas, ran in all directions in an attempt to protect themselves as best they could. Some marchers tried to help those who were injured. No one seemed gravely injured, though John Lewis had a concussion and Amelia Boynton was knocked down; there's videotape footage of someone trying to help her get up. On this particular weekend, Dr. King had decided to preach at his home church, the Ebenezer Baptist Church in Atlanta, and so he wasn't in Birmingham for what came to be known as Bloody Sunday. A federal court injunction was handed down after Bloody Sunday to block any more efforts to demonstrate, but our movement kept on moving. There were some whispers criticizing Dr. King for not being with the marchers that day. More thoughtful movement workers knew that no one could be at every event or program. Besides, Dr. King did not plan or sanction the March 7 march; he was already preaching at his Atlanta church for his father. Many different protests were being simultaneously planned by many different organizations. Dr. King was the guiding light of the freedom movement, but he couldn't be everywhere. Even so, he worked so hard at trying to respond to every call that he sometimes made himself sick. The movement was his total life commitment. There can be no doubt about that. Some of those who question his commitment are speaking from dire ignorance.

We gathered for a meeting in the living room of a local supporter in Selma and discussed whether we would go forward with our initial plans for a public protest, such as a march downtown. One of our lawyers, Chauncey Eskridge, said, "Dr. King, if you conduct a march knowing you are under an injunction not to march, you're going to be in great trouble." Dr. King responded, "Chauncey, it's our job to get in trouble, and your job to get us out of trouble." Case closed! A call went out to civil rights activists and supporters across the nation and another march was planned. This March 9 march was led by Dr. King. We walked onto the Edmund Pettus Bridge, stopped halfway across, and prayed. Dr. King then asked people to return to the church. What many participants and observers did not know was that Dr. King had a promise from President Lyndon Johnson that he, the president, would see that we could have our march.

After renegotiating with the powers that be in Washington, D.C., a call went out from Dr. King and other supporters to come to Selma. When I hear people criticize Dr. King for turning around a march, I feel sad—because Dr. King was a more effective strategist than these critics realize. Dr. King's nonviolence did not require him to lead crowds into sure danger and even death. He knew that we would be getting a different injunction, one enjoining the Alabama state officials from attacking us. In other words, the president of the United States would see to it that *we would be protected*, and by the Alabama National Guard, the very same guard that had attacked us on our earlier attempt to cross the Edmund Pettus Bridge.

In the middle of March 1965 the court injunction against us was lifted and a new one issued prohibiting the state from preventing marches. On March 21, some 3,500 people began marching from Selma to Montgomery.

We organizers and leaders of the march were blessed by the outpouring of support for our mission to go to the seat of power in Alabama to fulfill the First Amendment to the Constitution of the United States, which states that the people have the right "to petition the government for a redress of grievances." On this five-day march we pitched tents at night and camped along the way in open fields where we had gotten permission from a couple of property owners. Three hundred marchers of the original 3,500 people were selected to march fifty-two miles from Selma to Montgomery.

In Montgomery there would be a powerful rally where Dr. King would once again focus our goal and knit us all together with his powerful oratory.

As we proceeded, famous entertainers put on an outdoor program. Harry Belafonte, Sammy Davis Jr., Nina Simone, and Johnny Mathis were among the entertainers who came to lend their support. I recall sitting in a van with Nina Simone. She had heard me singing a song, "Why Was a Darky Born?," which I learned from James Bevel, who was an excellent singer. He had created new lines that spoke to the current situation of Black people in America. I sang these lines for Nina Simone. She requested I do so again so she could really get the words and the melody down. She copied the notes so in the future she could use the song in her repertoire. It was a very special time for me as we sat, just the two of us, in the van provided for some of the entertainers who had made their way to Alabama to help protest against the 1963 version of American-style apartheid.

I get all choked up now, even to trying to hold back tears, as I recall some moments of our revolutionary struggle for justice. But I smile, too, as I remember leaving one of the campsites on the Selma to Montgomery march and going back to the motel where I had a room. There had been a bit of a mishap when the rather makeshift stage set up for the performers on the fourth night collapsed at one of our campsites, perhaps because there were too many people on it. As previously mentioned, an impressive number of notable entertainers had joined this protest march, which was mainly for the right to vote. Surprise, surprise! As I got back to the motel grounds there stood Johnny Mathis on the balcony! How in the world did he get there so quickly? I pondered. I didn't get close enough to ask him but we can take note of the fact that Johnny Mathis was an accomplished athlete. His running and high-jumping skills may have been brought into service after the scare of the collapsed stage. Even though we were tired, this was a festive evening program that invigorated us all.

MARCHING FROM Selma to Montgomery, we sang all the way, even though our feet were getting tired and straggly—that is, not moving in the same rhythmic formation as when we started out. I remember that Len Chandler came up to my section with his guitar and started singing, *"Pick 'em up and lay them down."* Our response was, *"Right, right, all the way from Selma town!"* Then we began adding all kinds of verses—about rain coming down and mud being deep and not getting enough sleep. This was another example of our songs emerging from what was going on at any given moment. So the songs were of many kinds and came out of many moods. We never did anything without singing.

The march, thankfully, was uneventful. We arrived in Montgomery without suffering any violence. There we listened to Dr. King deliver one of his most memorable speeches, although we had heard much of it before. The message was one of freedom and basic rights. The marches and protests that emerged from the Selma campaign were pivotal episodes in the struggle for our right to vote.

President Lyndon Johnson signed the Voting Rights Act on August 6, 1965. In just one year, the number of African Americans who voted exceeded previous years by leaps and bounds; in Alabama, for example, more than twice as many African Americans registered to vote in 1966 as had the year before.

Out of the struggle for the right to vote and for new laws to protect that right grew campaigns by Black people for public office. This even included counties in southern states like Alabama.

This kind of transformation in the way African American people saw themselves and their role in society is exactly why our Citizenship Education Program training was so basic and so important to achieving our purpose for ourselves and for our country. Once people accepted that they did not have to live as victims—the goal of CEP training—they changed how they saw and felt about themselves. This personal transformation was fundamental to realizing the promise of democracy. Our country was changing, and people were changing, even though a price was paid at every turn.

Chapter 14

GROWING CHALLENGES TO OUR APPROACH IN WORKING FOR CHANGE

Too many people dying; too many mothers crying.

— MARVIN GAYE

WHILE DR. KING'S influence grew as the civil rights movement evolved, the voices of his critics rose, particularly those who were unconvinced that nonviolence was the best approach to breaking down racial barriers. Some of the criticism stemmed from other Black groups and leaders who asserted the right of Black people to fight fire with fire. I'm convinced there was also some resentment and jealousy. These were not always opposition groups, but rather included organizations from which I could hear ungrounded criticisms, such as from the Student Nonviolent Coordinating Committee. Even if I could name names, I would not do so, for it would serve no purpose. I know that to some, Martin's receiving the Nobel

Prize in 1963 amounted to him taking credit for what belonged to others—to them; it was almost as if they thought he had chosen himself as the recipient. Not everyone in SNCC felt this way, though. John Lewis, once the head of SNCC, was supportive of Dr. King's work. He was actually one of the key leaders who led the Selma to Montgomery march in March 1965. But when the SNCC elections were held in May 1966, John lost his position in the organization to Stokely Carmichael, who gained national attention in June 1966 after the shooting of James Meredith during Meredith's "March Against Fear" in Mississippi. Meredith, who had been the first Black man to defy the "color line" at the University of Mississippi, was shot by a White attacker but recovered from his wounds. Stokely was leading a protest rally in which he used and popularized the slogan "Black Power," which ushered in a change in SNCC's tone and message.

More and more the movement was being energized by people of Stokely's age group. The resentment of younger activists toward SCLC and Dr. King grew. Some saw us as less than progressive. They began to directly criticize not just Martin's getting "all the glory" but, even more important, SCLC's use of nonviolence as the philosophical underpinnings for the changes we sought. I remember being in a discussion and listening in fascination as Stokely Carmichael and a couple of other SNCC members sat around the kitchen table at Dr. King's house on Sunset Avenue in Georgia discussing the efficacy of nonviolence. Stokely often invoked the name and thinking of Frantz Fanon, who had argued in his book *The Wretched of the Earth* that "to overcome the binary system in which Black is bad and White is good, an entirely new world must come into being." Stokely continued, "To be absolutely free of the past requires total revolution, absolute violence." I am not sure what Stokely's vision was for a new and different world. After "total revolution and absolute violence," then what? I had a chance to put this question to him when he spoke at Cornell University years later. The problem with this, to my mind, was that neither Stokely nor any of the other movement workers on his team had a plan or a vision for how this "take up the gun" strategy would work. (I heard him use that expression on more than one occasion. I even pushed back with "Who would you shoot?")

I understood the cry for Black Power—and the situation from which it flowed—but first should come clear goals and answers to the question *What kind of world do you wish for yourselves and other citizens?* Power can be understood in several different ways. There is power *over,* such as power that can be used to put others down; and there is power *with,* such as power that flows from an immersion in the idea of compassion and love for all creation. The latter is expressed as a feeling that exudes from one's very being, and is an *agape,* or spiritual kind of love.

I found myself comparing the dynamic younger members of the freedom struggle to teenagers who resist their parents' input into their evolving belief systems. This especially applied to their denigration of nonviolence. Once an individual comes to a broader understanding of nonviolence, their acceptance of this way of living and working for change will deepen and grow. Now, these younger people's struggle with ways to win our freedom was healthy because they forced all of us to think in a more focused way about our beliefs. I came out of the argument on the side of Dr. King, who said that he would continue to speak about nonviolence as the way forward— even if his was "the last lone voice." I choose to continue my own study of nonviolence even now. Debating and sharing different views is healthy. If we truly listen to one another we stand a much better chance of finding common ground. But an efficacious sense of love must take into consideration the obvious *result* of what one espouses.

The concept of Black Power as originally espoused was based on color or culture or *supposed* racial superiority. Black Power was heard as a militant concept, not a healing one. I was more and more open to healing as the better choice. Healing the culture, all the people of every stripe and racial or ethnic group, was what some of us envisioned.

Nonviolence is an exciting and effective power available to people of all groups, not just one. Any group having power that emanates from a system that excludes another will not be at peace with itself or others. This militant approach could not bring into existence the peaceful world many of us longed for and worked toward.

IF THE goal is healing individuals and, indeed, the whole populace, begging has no place in the dialogue. Just look at the horror stories coming out of Somalia, for example, where many thousands of people have fled to escape. Thousands walking many miles to get away from incredible suffering because of violence, hatred, and the total disregard of others.

Dr. King and Stokely Carmichael spoke from the same stage at an outdoor event in Mississippi in 1966. Stokely argued for a change in tactics if we did not get what we were demanding using nonviolence. On this and other occasions Stokely was heard passionately challenging the crowd with this refrain, "If this nonviolence does not work, take up the gun." The audience gave him a long, rousing ovation.

Dr. King spoke immediately after Stokely, saying, "Mankind must find other ways to solve its problems without violence if we are to create a world in which we can live as brothers, if we would create the 'beloved community.'" He explained that nonviolence is a unique and different power; it is a power whose weapon is love; it is a power that connects with the inner core of one's being and which is deeply rooted in the teachings of Jesus, the greatest teacher that ever lived. He reiterated that nonviolence can connect with the spark of divinity within every individual, even when that individual may not recognize that it lies within him or her. "The end we seek is preexistent in the method we use," Dr. King said, who *also* received a rousing ovation! This was the same audience who moments before had had the same response to Carmichael's espousal of violent confrontation. So, something besides an either/or dynamic was happening with the crowd. We needed a deeper understanding of what exactly a crowd responds to. Could it be emotion only—not content?

I'm convinced that this crowd was made up of people who were, as my sister would say, "dog-tired of second-class citizenship," of being made to feel less than a human being worthy of respect. When one is feeling this way, *anyone* who spoke with passion, whose words and spirit challenged the status quo, would be applauded. A clearer, more focused response would come from being in *action* and experiencing—feeling—a certain energy and response from one with whom one is interacting. In other words, one has to be open to the truth that at some level we are all the same and want the same things, like a peaceful community in which to live and grow and thrive.

I believe one would have to be "unwell," hard-hearted, not to be affected by a true experience of nonviolence. It takes time. It requires a softening of the heart, an openness—a realization that life can be much more rewarding. I think back to the Ku Klux Klan organizer who showed up at a workshop we were conducting at the Highlander Folk School. I think of the leather-jacketed young men who "invaded" our workshop and threw copies of the U.S. Constitution on the floor. I think of James Bevel asking a near-violent policeman, "Excuse me, sir, have you got a cigarette?"

When Stokely Carmichael and other SNCC people said things like "the SCLC is not working with the people" and referred to us as "this bourgeois organization," Dr. King was pained. So was I. The critics were almost like children attacking the father. But we didn't see ourselves as parents or SNCC as children. They rejected us without having gone through our CEP training, though when we followed our trainees home we found we often worked in the very same communities as SNCC did, but frequently with different members of the community, usually older people. Still, we related in important ways—mass meetings, protest demonstrations, and the same goals.

"TO BE sure, the 125th St. nationalists did not support Dr. King. They attacked nonviolence, mocked his talk of redemptive suffering, and questioned the feasibility and desirability of 'integration' as a goal. They felt Dr. King was 'begging White folks to accept us,' something White folks had never done in three hundred years." This statement from *Ready for Revolution: The Life and Struggles of Stokely Carmichael (Kwame Ture)*, by Stokely Carmichael with Ekwueme Michael Thelwell, shows a misunderstanding of Dr. King's goal and purpose. "Integration" was not the goal set by Dr. King. The denial of basic rights, we insisted, had to change—had to be stopped. This was not "begging White people to accept us."

Stokely never moved away from his position. I heard him again, years later at Cornell, when he addressed a mostly Black student audience. He used the same refrain, "Take up the gun." I worked at the university at the time and had the opportunity to chat with him after his speech. Again, I asked Stokely, "Who should these young Black students to whom you spoke today—who should they shoot?" His response was highly unconvincing as he again responded, "It will become clear." I believe such challenges are titillating—romantic even—when there are not more clear and helpful responses to questions such as mine.

BLACK, AS a name for who we are, was regarded as negative and ugly. The way Stokely Carmichael used the phrase "Black is beautiful" took the ugly out of it. It was no longer like an albatross around our necks. "I'm Black and I'm proud," as popularized by a James Brown song, contributed to the lexicon of movement music and also rejected the notion that Black was ugly and that the White standard of beauty was the norm. Nina Simone intoned rather mournfully, "Black is beautiful, don't you see," in one of her songs.

Projecting "White" as the standard still goes on. I have a recording of an interview by Bill Moyers with a historian who described the partner of a painter as beautiful because she had "white skin and blond hair." Every time a woman was considered beautiful she had long blond flowing hair, at least until Elizabeth Taylor came along, and then it could be black. But beauty never looked like me. Whenever a beautiful woman is shown languishing, she sort of tosses her long flowing hair. *I* never had long flowing hair, so I could never be in the "beautiful" category. I came to realize that I too was beautiful when a very high-powered African American man whispered as I was giving a report at SCLC, loud enough for me to hear, "That's a handsome woman!" There are so many ways that one can be insulted, hurt, feel less-than, and be ignored in terms of who you are. Flesh-colored Band-Aids (whose flesh?) was another example of denigration. There were so many ways we were told we did not meet the beauty standard. We never measured up to somebody else's "White standard" of beauty. The Afro (I used to wear one) became the statement we made to "take back ourselves," and the bigger and the bushier the Afro, the better. Black youngsters even started to learn to swim—no longer afraid our hair would "go back." There is definitely progress today; Black women don't feel as called to be measured by standards set by others, especially as this relates to physical appearance. In other words, African American women no longer accept the assessment that they have to resemble White women to be beautiful. This has often meant being very thin as well as the hair issue. Eleanor

Holmes Norton, a congresswoman in Washington, D.C., wears an Afro. This former standard of beauty is summed up in a popular saying: *If you're Black, get back; if you're Brown, stick around; if you're White, you're all right.*

Going to Chicago

Black Americans were up in arms, and we began to see *some* steps toward progress in racial equality, even in the South. This consciousness may have contributed to our accepting Al Raby's request to come help in the struggle for equality in Chicago in July 1966. Al was the head of the Coordinating Council of Community Organizations. After all, northern Blacks, also because of their race, did not escape abuse. As James Bevel once said, "Black Chicago is Mississippi moved north a few hundred miles."

After struggling over Al Raby's invitation, we finally agreed with Dr. King that we should go to Chicago to help. He had asked us to come to Chicago in order to join them in actions to protest the lack of decent housing, jobs, and economic opportunities. I was asked to join our team on this trip to Chicago, but I knew that I could stay only two or three days because there was a Citizenship Education Program workshop scheduled in a few days. As long as I had major responsibility for designing and facilitating the week's workshop, I had to be present at our training center, the Dorchester Center in McIntosh, Georgia. I knew I could not devote too much time to Chicago, but it was a helpful experience to have a firsthand view of some of the problems there. So I stayed only about three or four days to check out whether I could establish any CEP training venues and to generally assess the situation. It was my impression that our Chicago host group was not ready for the kind of movement we traditionally launched in the South. I would need our whole team there, which would interrupt our necessary work in our southern base.

Andy Young made clear to Martin the risks of taking on a Chicago campaign, but Dr. King responded that we had to deal with the North at *some* time. Andy was concerned that our field staff and CEP trainers were already overstretched, and were probably already working in too many places in the southern and border states.

One of our goals in Chicago was to meet with some gang leaders, who we sensed were not responding well to a nonviolent approach for positive change. We hoped to win them over and to ask for their commitment to work with Al Raby, who was providing leadership to secure better housing options and doing so within the framework of nonviolence. As the plans for offering help continued, I determined that I needed to return to Atlanta to oversee planning the upcoming CEP workshop.

On September 4, 1966, after returning home, I watched in alarm on television as bricks were thrown at Dr. King. He was struck by one of them. This was happening in Cicero, Illinois, just outside Chicago. Dr. King was captured on film expressing, almost with a chuckle, his shock over the violence from Whites in Cicero. "They were as hateful as any we had seen in the Deep South," he observed. I know that when people are deeply shocked or impacted by an experience, the response can be one that borders on humor—when in actuality it really is an alternate way of expressing shock at a situation. His experiences in Cicero highlighted the pervasiveness of conditions we had seen in Appalachia as well as in the Deep South. These included poverty and lack of adequate education. This episode broadened Dr. King's already strong social conscience, and deepened his determination to embrace people in dire circumstances throughout the world. This more and more included even the people of Vietnam.

• • •

BY 1966 Martin had begun to see a relationship between the civil rights struggle and the political struggle relative to the war in Vietnam. He accepted an invitation to speak at the Riverside Church in New York on April 4, 1967. This would become his seminal speech against the Vietnam War. Martin was criticized by many notable people, including the leaders of the NAACP and the Urban League, and even by Lyndon Johnson, the president of the United States. Johnson had assumed that Dr. King would not do anything that would destroy the degree of camaraderie the two of them had developed, but Dr. King's speech deeply upset the president. Martin was surprised and dismayed by the level and intensity of the criticism coming from not only the political establishment but also from the Black press and even from some of his friends and coworkers.

I remember a very heated discussion among the staff as to whether it was helpful to make strong statements against the Vietnam War. In one staff meeting Dr. King grew weary of the debate about the issue; he left the meeting and drove to my house. When he arrived there he was sort of giggly about the fact that he'd just left, not telling the team where he was going or why. But they knew. He was tired of the team's loud argument—mostly advising him what many supporters would say if he spoke out against the war. He did not come to my house to discuss the issue. His manner was almost childish. "They don't know where I am," he laughingly said to me. My sense is that the more his leadership was criticized, the stronger he seemed to hold to his view that war was not the way, and that what one seeks must be reflected in the means used to reach the goal. Violence of any kind brings into the mix a negation of positive goals. Tears and death and bitterness are the fruit of "mothers crying and people dying."

As Dr. King's position—adherence to nonviolence—strengthened, my focus on infusing a study of nonviolence in the CEP training grew.

Most notable, it seems to me, was a letter signed by Marian Logan, a King family friend as well as an SCLC board member. I did not read the letter, but it became common knowledge that the letter was suggested by several board members. It went to Dr. King over Marian Logan's signature. I was told that several SCLC board members (I can't name individuals) had input into this letter criticizing Dr. King for speaking out publicly against the Vietnam War. I know that Dr. King was deeply pained that such a letter could come from his close associates and friends. When I saw his pain I felt so angry at Marian Logan—and I think now I blamed her unfairly for some of the pain Dr. King felt. I wrote to her and told her I was angry. I regret my letter to her now because it laid too much blame on her and it was not her decision alone. I know that the more I was involved in conversations about the war, the more I was convinced that Dr. King was coming from a very strong moral perspective. I agreed with him then and even more today; I know that we must find a way to solve problems without the incredible violence we are seeing now in the twenty-first century. Going to war, carrying out suicide bombings, and denying basic human rights to others are atrocities that must be stopped.

Dr. King felt very much under attack and struggled with what his response should be. He told me during that period that he was feeling overwhelmed and sad and was considering another option. He said, "Maybe I should take a sabbatical." I envision him now, sitting in my living room in a yellow upholstered rocking chair. He seemed very sad, more sad than I had ever seen him. This was about a month before he was killed. This sadness, this experience of being so severely criticized, was very painful for him. I saw tears in his eyes one other time, when J. Edgar Hoover called him the "most notorious liar." We were in Jamaica, four of us, as he wrote one of his books. It was as though his life's work was being criticized. Many people everywhere seemingly resented his leadership even as they at the same time admired him—his honesty, his leadership, his talent, his spirit through it all.

In late 1970, I was asked to go to South Vietnam by the Fellowship of Reconciliation (FOR) because of the work the SCLC and Dr. King had done in the name of nonviolence. Dr. King was a longtime member of FOR. I traveled to Saigon with fifteen people. We interacted with quite a cross-section of Vietnamese people—religious leaders, students, parents, as well as people from the university. We spent time with Buddhist monks who were the designated leaders of the antiwar effort.

We met in the university auditorium with a large group, mostly students, and with the monks led those gathered outside to begin a peace march. We were not one block away from the campus before we were teargassed. I have no idea who was tossing the canisters but I assume it was the police or the military, designated to stop this peace march. As we left the auditorium with this large group, and before I had to run, I bent down and picked up a teargas canister. Words printed on it read MADE IN THE USA. By now we were scurrying about, desperately trying to avoid the gas. It was a horrible experience. Some of the younger people were able to run fast and climb fences, which most houses seemed to have. A Vietnamese woman opened her gate and beckoned me to enter her yard to escape the gas. She turned on the faucet in her yard and helped me splash cool water onto my face—showing me what to do even without language. I've often wished I could locate this woman to thank her.

The Vietnamese people I heard had made it clear that despite twenty-five years of struggle, they were determined to maintain their culture and not to be overrun by foreign powers. In the struggle for domination economically and culturally both France and the United States had destroyed a great deal of what was good and beautiful in Vietnam. While we were in Saigon we spoke with and asked then Deputy Ambassador Samuel D. Berger if he was aware of the suffering of the Vietnamese prisoners being held in Con Son Prison. He said, "Well, we will study the situation." To most of the questions we asked he said, "Ladies and gentlemen, we have to let this process work."

One woman I met, Mrs. Go Bar Tan, had studied at Columbia University and served now as a lawyer; she was passionately interested in peace for her country. She was imprisoned in Vietnam for fourteen months because of her public outcry and for working with grassroots women and students. I felt her strength and the strength of so many other women who came to our meetings with the monks. In fact, one outspoken woman reminded me of Mrs. Fannie Lou Hamer, the powerful grassroots woman and one of our star CEP graduates from the Mississippi Delta.

Chapter 15

THE KING IS DEAD!
WHAT IN THE WORLD
DO I DO NOW?

Sometimes I feel discouraged
And think my work's in vain,
Then the Holy Spirit
Revives my soul again.

—"THERE IS A BALM IN GILEAD"

As usual, we were rushing to get to the airport, this time for a plane to Memphis, Tennessee. Reverend James Lawson and Reverend Samuel "Billy" Kyles had invited us to Memphis for the March 28, 1968, demonstration and show of support for the sanitation workers. In Atlanta we were preparing for the Poor People's Campaign, which was going to take the time and the focused energy of all of us at SCLC. But Dr. King certainly could not say no to Jim Lawson or to Reverend Billy Kyles when they asked him to come help. The horror stories of the plight of sanitation workers com-

255

pelled all of us to respond positively. We had long ago accepted Dr. King's declaration that injustice anywhere is injustice everywhere. We were told that the sanitation workers had very unsafe working conditions, which certainly was an insult to their dignity and a grave injustice to these men. Two workers, Echol Cole and Robert Walker, were killed when the grinders in their garbage trucks malfunctioned. We figured we could indeed help the sanitation workers in their struggle to correct the incredible wrongs they had endured for so long. We had confidence that we could help change the brutal system that showed no respect for them. The placards these workers carried declared, I AM A MAN!

Andy Young, Bernard Lee, Ralph Abernathy, and myself, those of us who usually accompanied Martin to most places, gathered at the SCLC offices in Atlanta to prepare for the trip and show our support. A protest in Memphis the week before had been disrupted by young Black men who only knew how to express themselves against injustice through violence. We would need many of our best organizers to do what we knew how to do very well, that is, organize a peaceful protest demonstration.

In our first attempt we joined the sanitation workers without having our ground crew and training team spend time in the city organizing and doing nonviolence training workshops. We in the CEP were ignoring a basic lesson we had learned in other cities where we had responded to calls for help—that if the SCLC leadership would lead, we would assume responsibility for preparing and training protesters.

There was much hustle and bustle. In the office we needed to make phone calls and give input to other ongoing projects. I in particular had to make plans with Delores Harmon, who provided administrative support for the CEP. My next workshop was scheduled for the very next week. Field staff members working in various places around the South would be joining us. Given the prior week's disruption, we were going back to Memphis to *do it right,* we said. We had a pretty good track record and strong confidence in our ability to plan a nonviolent challenge to an unjust system.

Our movement suffered and we paid a dear price whenever we would respond to calls for help without those of us who did training going in first to work with the local people. Our intention always was to convince local activists of our commitment to organizing, teaching, and motivating people to work from the nonviolent perspective.

Steps in Organizing a Nonviolent Campaign

We had learned early on that we needed to follow the correct pattern, the proper steps, in organizing a nonviolent campaign. We knew, for example, that we had to clearly state the problem and describe it in a way so that anyone listening could understand and relate to it. I learned early on that there is more than one way to express a concern and to describe a problem. Identifying the problem clearly is critical. I have sometimes responded to college students who complain that other students on campus are "so apathetic" by asking, "What concerns you?" I rarely get a clear, focused response. Furthermore, I suggest that it's difficult for someone to work with you, join you, if you can't articulate what you are concerned about. The ability to articulate the problem clearly is important.

Then a CEP session would move to the question, "Who needs to know?" Then "How can you get the word to those identified?" I'm talking about organizing a campaign to right a wrong. Remember, none of the amazing electronic tools we have today existed in the 1960s. Burning the midnight oil at the mimeograph machine was the order of the day. Then flooding the community with the leaflets produced. This is how we would get people to join the action. We called this the *Education Step.*

One of my favorite organizing steps in CEP workshops was the one in which we would help participants understand the process of negotiation—the *Negotiation Step*. This would include how to present oneself (here even dress could be a factor), and though the activists were highly energized, even angry, the anger had to be subdued and one's adherence to the more positive concept of nonviolence visible. We needed staff members who could show that they heard and understood the opponent's point of view.

I continued to meet not only school-age people but also adults who did not yet have a sense of the *process* we had to go through before we would be ready to stage a successful confrontation or demonstration. The process was critically important. In other words, we would create a way to make our goals and our demands known. Yes, *demands* for change. Such planning often required a CEP-type session no matter where we were working.

Next came the *Confrontation Step*. We had learned that we had to physically engage in a public action in order to bring an issue to the attention of the community, the nation, or the world if necessary. When the pushback was violent, broad public attention—local, national, and international—was given to our action. *Reaction to our action* always brought important and necessary attention to our struggle for freedom and real democracy.

Adherence to the nonviolent way required that we did all we could do to ensure that reconciliation resulted from our action. After all, our goal was to establish what Dr. King often referred to as the "beloved community." Anyone left angry is evidence that more reconciliation work needs to be done. We would seek ways to come together and work out any differences or misunderstandings. This can take quite a long time, but it is difficult to set a time limit on nonviolent interaction if it truly arises from the core spirit of nonviolence.

• • •

JIM LAWSON was a longtime friend and colleague in the struggle for justice and an acclaimed teacher of nonviolence. Leaders in the Nashville, Tennessee, student freedom movement attended ongoing workshop sessions on nonviolence with Jim. Some workers who became key leaders in the larger struggle said they attended these sessions at first only out of curiosity, but then got caught up in the message of the possibility of nonviolence. Jim had spent several years in India to absorb much of this philosophy, Mahatma Gandhi's *experiment with truth.* Gandhi's experiment with truth was successful in that the nonviolent way helped us achieve success and his work garnered worldwide attention and ultimately led to a transformation in India's relationship to the British Empire.

From Jim Lawson's workshops the civil rights movement inherited some very effective leaders. These included Bernard Lafayette, James Bevel, and Diane Nash. Diane became the first female leader of the Student Nonviolent Coordinating Committee. Her persistence was impressive when she pressed the mayor of Nashville to answer her question as to whether he agreed that their cause was just, whether they had a right to be treated as other citizens in public places. Diane didn't stop questioning the mayor until he said yes.

James Bevel said that he was skeptical on first hearing that Jim Lawson was conducting sessions on nonviolence but decided he would "check him out to determine if anything relevant was going on in that church basement." Once there, listening and interacting with Jim, James saw that Jim was indeed onto something. There was a time when I came to experience James as one of the great teachers and exemplars of nonviolence. As to Jim Lawson, I heard Dr. King say more than once that *he himself* had learned something of nonviolence from Jim. So we had no hesitation in responding to a request from Jim. We would soon be on our way to Memphis.

The Last Plane Ride

On April 3, 1968, we arrived at the Atlanta airport, checked in, and boarded the plane. I noticed that we sat on the plane for what seemed like an unusually long time without the pilots starting the engines. Soon there was an announcement over the intercom system. The pilot said, "I have to ask everyone to leave the plane. Because Dr. King and some of his staff are on the plane there has been a bomb threat." We scurried off the plane in a strange kind of quiet. I'm embarrassed to say that I stepped on Martin's foot as we did so. He was walking so slowly and deliberately. And I was moving energetically! Back in the terminal, we still didn't speak very much as we waited for what would happen next. Policemen brought out search dogs to sniff for bombs and after about a half hour we were advised that all passengers could reboard the plane. No bomb was found.

I have often been asked if we were afraid or nervous as we continued on our journey. I don't recall being nervous, only quiet. We were now all in a pensive mood. We had become quite used to threats, though not on airplanes. I think I was more concerned about the potential for violence than Dr. King was. I remember the anxiety I felt when a man rushed up to him with an outstretched hand in an airport and Martin slowed and smiled broadly. I thought, *Is this to be a friendly greeting?* I didn't say anything but stood close to observe. The man started exclaiming in a very excited, stuttering way, "My goodness, are you . . . I mean are you . . . You couldn't be . . ." Dr. King said, "I'm Martin King," and extended his hand. I remember a good many moments like this. Sometimes Martin would joke about the fact that many people couldn't seem to pronounce his name: something like "Maphin" or "Marfin Luther" would come out. He would laugh heartily as he reflected with us, "I never realized my name was such a tongue twister for so many people!"

But there was no such friendly greeting awaiting us on this trip to Memphis.

ONCE WE arrived, we settled in our various rooms at the Lorraine Motel. Most of the SCLC staffers had rooms on the same level as Dr. King and many of the rooms opened onto the same balcony. Dr. King's room was number 306, mine was number 307, and Reverend Abernathy's room was number 308. Shortly afterward, we gathered in Martin's room and talked briefly about possibly getting something to eat. Before that question could be settled, six or seven young men whom we had asked to meet with us came in. These people, we were told, were selected from among the guys who had helped to disrupt the protest march the week before. They were called the Invaders. They were the ones we most needed to reach if we were going to begin organizing and training for a nonviolent protest demonstration, which was why we had returned to Memphis.

And they were the reason that I, in my role as education director, was along on this trip. We took it as a challenge to engage these young men in some of the strategies and the philosophy of nonviolence—to share with them something of the concept of "ends and means." We wanted them to understand, as we had, Dr. King's espousal of the notion that the end we seek is preexistent in the means we use. We knew how to do that. We were convinced we could persuade these guys to take note of the goals of the demonstrations and show them how throwing bricks and using violent rhetoric would thwart our efforts for success in moving toward the ends we sought. The question was, What really would help the sanitation workers change their work situation, to get their goals met? We were ready to engage these young men by scheduling a series of training sessions.

We had all gathered in Dr. King's room. Martin was reclining on the bed; two or three others were sitting on one side of his bed. Most of us, after the two or three chairs were taken, sat around on the floor as we began to introduce ourselves. The hope was that the members of the Invaders would feel our spirit—the real spirit of what we wanted to bring forth in our struggle for justice, and that they would no longer have a desire to disrupt our planned peaceful challenge to the existing system of discrimination and brutality. Martin enjoyed being a teacher, especially to younger people who could sometimes be swayed by other dynamic speakers with an opposing philosophy and who often did not readily accept the concept and theory of nonviolence. As I mentioned earlier, this was the case when Stokely Carmichael (who had changed his name to Kwame Ture) and Dr. King spoke from the same stage. It was not unusual to meet people who questioned Dr. King's approach in working for change. He especially seemed to get a charge from teaching, questioning, and talking with younger people who doubted the efficacy of nonviolence. Martin was energized by such dialogue.

NOT HAVING eaten, I asked whether we could get some food sent in from a nearby restaurant. At the same time that we were caucusing in Dr. King's room, there was a large mass meeting going on at the Mason Temple Church. People knew that Dr. King was back in town but he had not planned to attend the mass meeting. Rather, he asked Reverend Abernathy to go to the church and to make the expected speech instead. Dr. King was excited to have the opportunity to meet these young men, the Invaders.

Soon the phone rang. It was Reverend Abernathy. Martin got on the phone and listened as Ralph urged him to get over to the church. Ralph, we later learned, told Martin that the crowd *went wild* as he strolled down the aisle toward the pulpit. As Ralph listened to the cheers he realized that the crowd gathered in the church thought Martin was behind him. Ralph, ever ready to introduce Martin, said, "Martin, you've got to come on over here; this crowd came here tonight to hear you and they thought that you were behind me! You should have heard them!"

Martin was very tired. After all, this had not been the easiest trip. However, he didn't like failure. After listening to Ralph, Martin got off the bed after sharing with those of us gathered for the meeting that he needed to get over to the church. As he got ready to leave he urged us to continue. He also asked us to explore the possibility for more training sessions and how we could work together to build a larger coalition across the city. He would join us, he said, after "making some remarks" to the crowd at the Mason Temple Church.

Martin had not planned to speak at the church that night. However, with no manuscript—he rarely used a manuscript anyway—and without notes, he made one of the most memorable and prophetic speeches he ever made. Something mystical seemed to happen when he would walk before a group of people waiting to hear him bring a message of hope and challenge, inspiring them to "keep on keeping on," a phrase often used regularly in southern Black churches. "I may not get there with you," he intoned, "but my people will get to the Promised Land! I have been to the mountaintop; I have seen the Promised Land. . . . Mine eyes have seen the glory and the coming of the Lord; His truth is marching on!"

We who were close to him, and others as well, have concluded that Martin lived consciously with the knowledge that he could be killed, could be taken away from us—even when he would appear to joke about it. On the morning of April 4, 1968, he saw me having breakfast in the motel coffee shop. He asked someone to tell me he wanted me to come up and talk with him about my plans to help do workshops in Memphis, following up on the discussion from our meeting the night before. I told him I would definitely be coming back, but on this day I needed to return to Atlanta to work with Delores Harmon. Delores was very good at keeping things going, as we were so often needed in the field where projects were evolving, but she needed me to get an overview of the week's plan, to finalize presenters, and to structure sessions. Standing there in his room, as he rather pleadingly said, "You can get a later plane," I told him that I really needed to get back because we had forty or fifty people coming to the Dorchester Center for the next scheduled CEP workshop, which would be in four or five days. There was much lesson planning to do and materials to decide on. I felt responsible for pulling it all together. Still, his last words to me were, "Get a later plane." I got a plane back to Atlanta around one o'clock that afternoon, April 4, 1968.

Hearing the Shocking News

I hadn't realized how tired I was until I arrived at my apartment in Atlanta. I knew I could not go to the office to do any workshop planning that night until I took a nap. We had all been expending a lot of energy. I was awakened from a sound sleep by my doorbell ringing. I stumbled to the door. The message I got was unbelievable. Rita Samuels, who lived in the same apartment complex at the time, had come to tell me that Dr. King had been shot. *"Somebody killed him,"* she said.

In a sleepy stupor I wandered around getting myself dressed — not really letting in the gravity of the message I had just heard. Was Rita right? I continued to get dressed, then made it to my car and headed toward the King home on Sunset Avenue. As I turned onto Sunset I saw that the street was lined with cars. Police car lights were flashing, seemingly for several blocks up and down Sunset Avenue. As I took in this scene, reality sank in. I screamed and screamed as I drove around to locate a parking spot.

Inside the house, I made it to the bedroom where Coretta was talking with two or three people. I don't even remember who they were. I'm not sure I really saw who was there. Stilling myself, I sat there in the bedroom just being with Coretta for a while and then left to be with all the other people congregating in the various rooms in the house.

BACK IN my apartment now, long after midnight, my phone rang. Hearing Andy's voice on the other end caused me to shake with tears again. I said, "I wish I could have been there with him in that last moment, talk with him one more time, showing total support for what we were about." Andy said, "That's all right." He was ever the friend and minister, bringing a calmness and different perspective in times of crisis—even when he was shedding his own tears. I reflected on what Martin had said to me that morning: *Get a later plane.* Andy and I both had an abiding love for Martin. We love him still. We both still cry sometimes as we remember. We also laugh sometimes, remembering his antics and the joy it was to be with him, to work and struggle with him toward our freedom goals. I cry again, now, as I write about that day, April 4, 1968. Massive numbers of people nationwide and in other countries deify Martin Luther King Jr. But I think now of what Andy said in a phone conversation with me recently: "Martin didn't need *us* to do that," to deify him. "He needed us to *help* him." And we did. He needed us to be friends. And we were.

• • •

THE KING is dead! He was our inspiration, our leader, our guide. *What in the world do I do now?* I asked myself.

How was I going to say good-bye to Martin? The nation had lost a great leader, but I had lost a special friend who had created a space that allowed me to transcend to some degree the "traditional" roles for women of that era and ushered me into his inner circle, his cabinet, if you will. Though all of us functioned in special ways with specific areas of work, I know that I lived up to the stereotypical roles for women in one sense. Yet also for eight glorious years, I had been on the front lines of history, which were filled with many powerful and wonderful challenges. As the years have progressed I know now that I experienced something extraordinary—more than many people will experience in a lifetime. I loved him. We all loved Martin and will ever love him. He was an inspiration to us as well as an inspiration to those who knew him only from a distance. And he will always be young to us.

The funeral was a rough experience for all of us. Coretta, Andy, Ralph, Fred, Bernard, Bevel, J.T.—all of us. We were in mourning on many levels. Many staff members, board members, and some very special friends not directly connected to the SCLC were told to gather in a building across the street from the Ebenezer Baptist Church, Dr. King's family church, where his father had been the senior pastor for many years. There were probably fifty or sixty of us. We were the ones who had been with him—by his side—in the midst of nonviolent battles and in the midnight hours, grappling with difficult situations and plotting the next steps. At the appropriate time the escort invited us to begin our walk across Auburn Avenue to the service. With heavy hearts and feet this long line of friends and staff headed across the avenue to the church. We slowly made our way through the crowds.

I was fairly close to the front of the long line. Just as I reached the great doors of Ebenezer Baptist Church, they were slammed shut! The shock was an insult on top of injury. I, one of Martin's closest friends and coworkers, along with two of his visiting friends, could not get into his funeral. Bernita Bennett was managing the doors and closed them in our faces. Bernita and I had no particular friendship, nor was she on the SCLC staff. She did marry Reverend Fred Bennett, who was a good friend and functioned almost as a security person for Dr. King. He was also the first director of SCLC's Operation Bread Basket, a program aimed at ensuring, among other things, that stale food was not transferred from stores in White communities to stores in Black communities. Often people in Black communities had little access to fresh food, only "tired" food from stores in White communities. As with other aspects of racist behavior—for example, outdated books being sent to the schools in African American communities from White schools—the same pattern prevailed in food distribution. My sense was that Bernita Bennett resented my place in Dr. King's inner circle. Again I emphasize that Bernita Bennett was not on the SCLC staff at the time but did work with Coretta later. Bernita felt a great sense of power controlling who got in and who didn't. Had she not felt such power (and even jealousy and resentment?) she would have insisted that we get in even if we had to stand. Bernita knew Martin would never have shut me out. She knew he was my best friend. Much later, I became more aware of what smoldering resentment and jealousy can do—how such feelings can manifest in very odd ways. This is what I felt was happening at Martin's funeral. On top of that, there were many in the line behind me who had been *organized* to march in together. They were board members and staff. But in the end most everything that followed is a blur. I have sometimes fantasized forcing entry for the three of us. Martin's two friends had traveled from New Jersey and were staying with me. So we made our way back to my home where we watched the funeral ceremony on television. On the other side of the church's door lay the body of a guru of a whole race of people, someone who had been the guiding light in a profoundly important struggle for justice.

YOU CAN be lucky when a door closes literally and figuratively, because you then have to take full responsibility for your life and work. That can be a moment to look inward, to make an assessment of what you're all about. Where you go from great tragedy, and how, becomes the question.

ON THE one hand I felt as if those heavy oak doors had closed me off from the rest of my life. Yet I had refused to accept the legacy of my birth and my upbringing—the monotonous certainty of poverty and subjugation—and with friends had created my own life of promise. That promise now seemed as lifeless as the physical body of my friend and leader. The door had shut. What had come before that moment had been wonderful. It had also been a difficult as well as a successful and empowering struggle for positive change. Successful in the sense that powerful seeds had been planted. Milestones had been reached. Important lessons had been and were still being learned. Would it all backslide? Could I continue? What could possibly come after such an exciting, energizing involvement? And without the presence of the one who brought such joy, intensity, prominence, hope, and wisdom to it? Would I wake up in the morning on the same hard mattress that served as the bed of my childhood?

Having internalized Dr. King's messages to the world and in-fused into my very being his observations and challenges, I am more and more conscious of the prophetic accuracy of his observations and how the need for his projections and challenges are more and more in evidence as we begin our move through this, the twenty-first century, another leg of the journey toward freedom and justice for all.

Chapter 16

AFTER THE ASSASSINATION

I DIDN'T HAVE a full conversation with Coretta until the week after Martin's passing. She shared with me some of her plans. I always knew that she too had a dream. There were things she had wanted to begin working on much earlier, even before her husband's assassination. One was to resurrect Dr. King's birth home. But Martin always responded, "That's something you do after people are dead." He would often urge her to wait on such things.

I was not surprised that Coretta Scott King, who grew up in Marian, Alabama, would want to build on what was begun back in Montgomery. Though Martin wanted her to stay at home and focus on raising their children, I felt her energy and sensed her desire to be more in the action. Thus, having a music background, she often did fund-raising concerts for SCLC.

But after Martin's assassination, she founded the King Center for Nonviolent Social Change and I later became her vice president for field operations, a full-time staff position I accepted after three years of working for the city of Atlanta in the Bureau of Human

Services. What an emotional experience it was in 1968 when I stood with Coretta at an opening ceremony for the King Center. This center in Atlanta is the official living memorial to Dr. King, dedicated to advancing his legacy and teachings. I would ultimately be a part of important training sessions held every summer at this quite wonderful conference center. I traveled the country and the world doing this work, sometimes accompanying Coretta.

Coretta and me at the celebration of her seventy-fifth birthday.

• • •

OUR FRIEND and leader was taken away from us in the midst of the challenging and exciting planning for the Poor People's Campaign. Our suffering was deep but we had to continue our work to *Redeem the Soul of America,* as was emblazoned on our stationery. We fanned out across the southern and border states; we made contact with ordinary people as well as other activists who were known to be working for change.

It took some time, actually two or three years, before I would start to realize I had to rebuild my life and consider that what we had worked for had indeed brought about change in our country that was profoundly important. Thousands of simple, unlettered people—not just my friend and inspirational leader Martin Luther King—had rearranged the social order. These were the people who came to our Citizenship Education Program workshops every month for five-day sessions to study, to learn, to realize their power. I like the way Andy stated our goal once. He said, "You know, Dorothy, what we did really was to help people un-brainwash themselves."

People were cleansed of any hesitation to organize and protest in order to right wrongs and correct injustice. They left these sessions empowered, with greater confidence. They became the catalysts, the models for others in their communities who were chomping at the bit to act against abuses in the social and political systems but needed a little push, some guidance, and advice. They needed reinforcement in the knowledge that they were not alone. They needed confidence in the knowledge that there indeed was a structure within which to work—nonviolent principles and procedures.

Though I continued to work as education director at SCLC for three years after Dr. King was taken from us, it was not easy. Some of the staff that Hosea had brought on as field workers, who were just what the movement needed at a particular time, seemed to revert back to some old ways and lifestyles that they had put on hold while beginning work in the freedom movement. With Martin Luther King Jr. at the helm, our field staff learned new and positive ways of living their lives. Most of them made wonderful team members. But some of them definitely lost their way after Dr. King's death. Some others are working still to continue the journey toward freedom and a just society.

As some of the field staff seemed to lose their direction, some senior staff relationships began to fall apart as well. I remember once disagreeing with Hosea in a staff meeting. I don't even remember what the disagreement was about, but I know it was not long after Dr. King's death. As a matter of fact, I remember being very angry because the executive staff group had made a particular decision, but Hosea went off and did what he wanted to do anyway without group consensus or involvement. I recall that Hosea looked over at me at the table and said, "Bitch." I've never forgotten that, and I probably will never forgive him, either, especially since he decided to attach "Reverend" to his name like a number of others. I've often thought that I should have told Hosea how I felt at the time, but I remember not saying anything back to him. What would it have wrought? Just some kind of altercation; I was not the kind of person who would take him on and have that kind of argument in a meeting. Besides, I honored his work then and now.

I remember Hosea challenging me again when I disagreed with him. He said something to the effect that I didn't know or understand how some political situation was unfolding. I remember my response was that perhaps I might not always understand the politics of what was happening, but I do understand how people learn. I remember him yelling and cussing and telling me that this wasn't the way to teach people. He could not have been one of our CEP teachers. When he expressed an opinion, it would be his way or no way.

During the early years, Hosea was key in recruiting a lot of people from his area in Savannah, Georgia, to come to our Citizenship Education Program. When he became head of our field staff, we had staff working in almost every state in the South. Hosea was in charge of that staff, so he was involved in the movement quite broadly, and he apparently loved doing that. He seemed to be just where he belonged, but he was a challenge—and not only to me. It's clear that Hosea had some troubling feelings about the members around the table who had a more polished manner. He would especially challenge them.

It eventually became very difficult to work with Ralph Abernathy, although his work and commitment could never be effectively challenged. While sitting in my SCLC office, which was adjacent to the president's office, I heard Ralph telling someone on the phone, "I don't have anyone to help me!" I felt so upset to hear that from him. However, I've learned that helping someone is a two-way street. For me that means that the one offering help needs to do so from a genuine spirit of helping and the one receiving the help needs to be open to receiving it. It needs to be clear what that person is doing, where he or she is heading. It's difficult if not nearly impossible to help someone if you don't know where they're going.

One time an executive staff member had come in to consult with Ralph, who didn't seem to take the appointment seriously. Ralph jokingly made him wait for no apparent reason. Others of us had similar experiences and responses to that behavior, which made us wonder if Ralph *wanted* the position of president in the first place. In any case, I guess you can't *vote* someone into the role Martin played, not in a social change movement. Such a role is *earned,* not bestowed. Each person on the team, including Ralph, had very special skills. Ralph was a dedicated preacher of the gospel and deeply cared about people with whom he worked. I think again about the time Ralph would not accept passage through a blockade unless the police would also allow his choir to pass. As I said earlier, Dr. King described those of us who ran major program areas as a "team of wild horses." I wonder if Ralph felt intimidated by the other "wild horses." The leadership of SCLC required a unique skill set.

Andy Young could not seem to find a way to be helpful to Ralph, either. Rather than be seen as the spokesman for SCLC, Andy would turn down an invitation to be interviewed because he thought Ralph would feel bad when a reporter specifically sought Andy out. Still, what Ralph Abernathy gave to our freedom struggle can never be taken away or diminished. His gifts to the movement were profound.

I say this even as I remember telling him how upset I was when he was showing a visitor around and brought them to a workshop session I was conducting in the Ebenezer Baptist Church. As they walked around the area talking quite loudly, I felt there was no sense of respect for the fact that I was conducting a session—a key part of my work. Yet I think I should not have been surprised, because during the 1960s, in SCLC and in many African American churches in which I have interacted, the minister reigned supreme. The subjugation of females at many levels was rampant, and often nothing women did received the same respect as the men would receive. Though I sense that much of this pattern still prevails, there has been important positive change.

IN 1973 my very special friend and coworker Andrew Young walked into my office at SCLC and told me that the Head Start program in Jefferson County, Alabama, had lost its director and needed a temporary replacement. Andy asked me if I would be interested in going over there to help them out for a few months. I said I would. Actually, I didn't know very much about the Head Start program at the time, but my sense was that I needed a change of venue, of location, and in the emphasis of my life's work.

I accepted and learned a lot as I settled into my new world, with totally new and different responsibilities. Ultimately I was offered the position on a permanent basis. I said yes. I stayed in Birmingham, Alabama, found an apartment, and dug into this work as Head Start director.

I put in long hours overseeing the operation of ten or twelve Head Start centers around Jefferson County. I learned a great deal and actually enjoyed the job, but my long days ended with me and a plate of food, sitting in the middle of my bed watching *Mission: Impossible* on television. I felt a huge void in my life that I discussed with my friend Sheila Morgan. When I told Sheila how I spent my evenings, she said to me, "Oh, so if you can't have the life you had working with Dr. King and the civil rights team, you won't have any life at all?"

She made me think back to the time when Martin and I had walked among the graves of James Chaney, Andrew Goodman, and Michael Schwerner, who were killed in 1964 in Philadelphia, Mississippi, as a result of their work in the movement. I recalled the blows taken by the children and me as we tried to integrate the beach in St. Augustine, Florida. I remembered the terrible beating that Andy Young took in that same town. Though the Head Start program was and is a great concept, I realized how deeply I missed the team spirit, the camaraderie and perhaps the drama of exciting social change work. I also realized that Dave Singleton, the director of the agency and therefore "the boss," and I were not a team. Additionally, I had just discovered that my dad had developed stomach cancer. I left Birmingham quite suddenly after three years and went back to Atlanta—a place that felt more like my hometown. I took my one and only monthlong vacation and drove up to New York to spend some time with my friend Sheila Morgan and attend her daughter's wedding.

Me with the mayor of Atlanta, Maynard Jackson. Elected in 1973,
he was the first African American to hold that position.

When I returned to Atlanta I stopped at Mayor Maynard Jackson's office. Mayor Jackson said, "Hello! I asked someone recently, 'Where is Dorothy Cotton, the woman with the ready smile?'" He immediately offered me a position in the Bureau of Human Services. My three years as Head Start director had been long enough, so I happily accepted Mayor Jackson's offer and settled back in Atlanta working with Connie Curry, who directed this bureau.

Chapter 17

LEGACY

Revisiting the Dorchester Center

O NE DAY NOT long ago I felt a strong desire to revisit the Dorchester Center, where great, important work happened— work that helped change our country. The work of the unsung heroes who met and studied here was *holy work*. Those who gathered here spending five days—intense days—to be transformed are people whose names may never be known, but they left these grounds, this nearly sacred site, with a strengthened determination to heal the sickness with which the country was born. I was glad to revisit this holy ground.

The Dorchester Center is a grand old historic building about thirty miles south of Savannah in Midway, which used to be McIntosh, Georgia. This white wooden structure is a reminder of school design of much earlier times. The former Dorchester Academy was an ideal place to conduct Citizenship Education Program training workshops. The building was well suited to our needs, with a large kitchen for meal preparation and a large gathering room for when we needed to be together. There were adequate anterooms for small group work. This area is now a National Historic District—a well-deserved status because revolutionary work, great awakenings and transformations, occurred here.

The Dorchester Center, where most of the Citizenship Education Program five-day workshops were held.

As I strolled the grounds I could almost hear voices of the workshop participants happily playing volleyball, Andrew Young leading the games. I sat on the steps of the building and realized I was hesitating to go inside. When I finally did, the tears came, as they do now, as I recall what happened there. The realization of what we did from that space was more than I could bear calmly.

When I stood in the large gathering room it seemed as though I could hear again the rousing freedom song renditions with which we would begin every session. After a few songs sung together, no one could feel like a stranger. Though the ones who had accepted our invitation mostly came from different areas of the southern and border states, we soon felt as one. For our purposes we had become one and the songs were those our ancestors had sung from the cotton fields to the churches. Changing the lyrics to fit the current challenges we were facing in our freedom struggle was easy. People felt free to create new lyrics on the spot and often very creative poetry emerged in the paraphrasing.

I remembered, as I stood in the great room, creating a new stanza in the song "I Want Jesus to Walk with Me." I would raise my hand high, which indicated to the group that I had the next verse. The group waited expectantly as I injected a new stanza:

> *I want Jesus to walk with me,*
> *You walked with Jonah in the belly of the whale*
> *You walked with Martin in the Birmingham jail*
> *You walked with Moses through the Red Sea*
> *So, my Lord, won't you walk with me!*
> *I want Jesus to walk with me!*
> *I want Jesus to walk with me*
> *All along this tedious journey*
> *Oh I want Jesus to walk with me.*

Someone often started—especially after two or three days—"I'm Gonna Do What the Spirit Says Do," and continued injecting what might be required of us in our struggle. There emerged an extensive list of what the Spirit could lead us to do. Eventually we heard *I'll go to jail if the Spirit says jail* and *I'll even die if the Spirit says die.* This verse was sung very slowly. The group knew instinctively to sing it slowly.

What happened in this big gathering room is not broadly known. Even many who were friends and supporters of what we were doing often didn't know. Many board members and even some staff who never spent one of these exciting weeks with us didn't know. Yet what occurred in this space was fundamental to changing the culture of our nation because the fifty or sixty who came each month are the unsung heroes who committed themselves and their energy to undoing the lingering "birth defect" in our country—racial segregation and abuse.

As I stood in the room where we gathered regularly each month for eight years, I saw and felt the energy of those times again. Little were we aware at the time of the impact we now know we actually had. It is clear now, decades down the line, that our actions profoundly changed America and had a powerful influence on other organizations here and around the globe. Even though word traveled much more slowly then, the story of our work for change was heard loud and clear in far-off places. Countries where I have experienced this impact include Vietnam (during the war), China, the former Soviet Union, Japan, and Africa (Kenya, Senegal, and South Africa).

I recalled that I had stored several large boxes of three-by-five cards on which participants had filled out their names, addresses, and phone numbers. These boxes were in a makeshift closet constructed on my back porch and they held what I know now to be precious information, the names of every person who went through our CEP five-day sessions and who created this powerful movement for positive change. When the participants returned to their homes from this transformative experience, their cities and towns would never be the same.

The boxes had been moved from house to house and so now took on that aura of just more junk that needed to be discarded. And so in my ignorance at that time of the incredible importance of what we did, one day I tossed the boxes in the trash. But while the participants' handwritten cards may be lost, the work they did for themselves and the country and for posterity was not and never will be. I was not conscious then of the great importance of our work, that it would be studied and written about for generations to come. We had a fire in our souls and just had to do what we did. I know now that when I took other jobs I was just taking a break from what I was called to do. I was transformed forever, just as our eight thousand participants were also transformed by involvement in a people-changing, country-changing experience.

Standing in the great room at the Dorchester Center caused me to consider some specifics of what we learned there:

- We learned that we could make the road by walking it. We didn't know everything up front. There was no blueprint.
- We learned that we had, and still have, more power than we knew. The more we got involved, acted, and came together, the stronger we felt. We realized a new definition of power.
- We learned that we could change patterns and structures, no matter how deeply entrenched they were.
- We learned that we could use our impatience and anger to empower ourselves to act for change.
- We learned that we could confront the powers that be from an understanding of nonviolence—*satyagraha*, as Mahatma Gandhi called it.
- We learned that we could develop whatever skills we lacked when there was work to be done.
- We learned that we could act from our *capacities*, rather than from some deficit attributed to us by others.
- We learned that we have government "by the people" only if we make it so, giving life to this great concept.
- We learned that one is not alone. If one takes some steps to bring about positive change, others will join in the action.
- We learned that when we are serving, giving our life and energy to something that is important to us as well as to others, life is meaningful. And that we can't be bored giving ourselves to positive, transformative work.

- We learned that our freedom struggle was an idea whose time had come. As Dr. King liked to say, "The zeitgeist was upon us." The spirit of the times unfolded with breathtaking power.
- We learned that when those who are victimized become committed to changing an unjust and brutal system, no longer accepting victim status, *change happens.* Systems that maintain patterns of injustice will *have* to change.

The participants who spent those five days with us organized small learning groups and protest activities. They would target all the places that did not allow Black people even to enter. When we went into public establishments we could use only specified areas. We asked ourselves, What else is required of us now—to live into this new awareness? We will no longer live as victims; we will work to remove that which had been one of the major causes of victimhood.

This is not the whole story, however. In untold numbers of situations, we came to recognize when victimhood played a role in one's sense of self and we were determined to be rid of it. There are impressive examples in the history of social movements in which people rose up and altered cruel systems. Change is not often easy or free. A great price is often paid, but the gain is worth it. The killing of some nonviolent freedom fighters such as Jimmy Lee Jackson, who was killed during the march to Selma, and Mrs. Viola Liuzzo, who helped register African Americans so they could vote; the beating of Harry Boyte Sr.; the little girl who got her nose broken as I took her and others to the beach—and blows to *my* head on that beach; the bombing of Reverend Fred Shuttlesworth's home and Dr. King's home; John Lewis, who was beaten in Selma; Reverend Andrew Young, who I watched take a severe beating in St. Augustine, and Willie Bolden going out to rescue him; Reverend C. T. Vivian in Alabama; Rosa Parks, whose action led her to being taken to jail in Montgomery, Alabama, and sparked the Montgomery Bus Boycott, which lasted for 381 days there—people walked rather than ride those buses in humiliation; Lech Walesa in Poland; Mahatma Gandhi in India and South Africa; and Nelson Mandela in South Africa—all paid enormous prices. The list could fill pages. Lives were enriched, and through a willingness to suffer, we became new people moving forward, which advanced freedom and democracy for untold numbers.

Robert S. Leming, director for the Center for Civic Education's We the People: The Citizen and the Constitution, wrote, "Democracies do not just sustain themselves; they must be nurtured by engaged, knowledgeable citizens. Engaged, knowledgeable citizens are not born, they are developed through citizenship education." As the director of education for SCLC, I encouraged participants to continue to engage, to grow their self-esteem, and to weave their community experiences into a cohesive plan. We moved away from thinking of ourselves as isolated and alone, and instead went out into the wider community with our work. Ultimately we were able to envision "community" as including people very different from ourselves. We ensured we met our responsibilities in order to make this a better world for ourselves and future generations.

I recall President John F. Kennedy's challenge: "Ask not what your country can do for you; ask what you can do for your country." I take that question more seriously and very personally now. I see my life's work as a way of rising to President Kennedy's challenge. I see our freedom movement as a way of serving our country. I want Kennedy's question to come alive for people who do not feel they have any degree of ownership of or obligation toward their country. I envision us living up to our responsibilities to continue the journey toward building the *beloved community*, even though the journey may take a lifetime. Such a journey can be an enriching and a rewarding experience.

*I have traveled to many places to do workshops,
continuing the work of the civil rights movement.*

*I was invited to India to speak with members of a Gandhi organization
about our use of nonviolence in the movement. (I dressed in a sari
because my luggage never arrived at my destination.)*

I spoke about the movement at Free University in Amsterdam in November 1978.

When I am invited to give speeches and workshops about the civil rights movement, I'm often challenged to compare today's issues with situations we confronted in the late 1950s and 1960s. I'm told, "The issues were clear for you all. They are so much more complicated now—more difficult." I think of the title of Dr. King's last book, *Where Do We Go from Here?*, and I answer from this list of reasons why we are not *where we should be.* I see those reasons as areas needing our attention. Community "happens" in the midst of such work.

We are not there yet because:

- Xenophobia is rampant—the fear of those seen as different from ourselves.

- There is too much crime and too much punishment rather than teaching and exposing young people to models of positive values that will help them evolve into their best selves.

- We still need to accept our calling as contributing citizens.

- Our educational system needs overhauling, or else we will leave for our world youngsters who have not been exposed to the joys of a great education. They will be pulled down negative, destructive paths, when what they need is exposure to great dreams and noble values that will indeed help build a better world. Who are their role models today? Is it only Lady Gaga, and whoever said young men are cool if they wear their pants down at their knees?

- We have too many young people on a path to prison rather than to education. For example, when invited to do a session with inmates at the Moravia Prison in upstate New York, I walked into the gathering room and had to do a quick retreat. I quickly left the room because I was overcome with emotion—tears. Tears for seeing this room filled with over a hundred young Black and Hispanic men. Why did they get on a path to jail rather than Yale? These young men looked like they could've been in sessions with me at Cornell University. Could they have taken a different path?

- Women are beaten in some parts of the world because they are out without a male member of the family. I have such a beating recorded and no one stopped these men as they wielded their sticks on the backs of these women. And perhaps these women had no brothers! Could these men have said, "I will walk with you"?

- We too readily think that we can solve our problems by going to war, not allowing ourselves to understand deeply the ways of nonviolent work for change, a teaching that helps us to connect with the spark of divinity present in all of us.

- We have not yet learned to have respectful dialogue with those who have different opinions.

- Too many of us are waiting for "somebody" to do something about what we ourselves see as not working right, not accepting that if we ourselves start with the right spirit, others will join us.

- The continuing silence of good people continues—people who see wrong and continue to feel impotent, helpless, not knowing that they can act, speak up, speak out, and all without projecting violence of spirit.

I traveled in South Africa with a congressional delegation hosted by Congressman John Lewis and Congressman Amo Houghton, a pilgrimage regularly sponsored and coordinated by the Faith and Politics Institute. In South Africa people from different tribes gathered to meet with our delegation.

In front of Dr. King's crypt in Atlanta, April 4, 1981.

We had listened to the singing of our South African host groups in many meetings and various gatherings on our South African trip. Sometimes young children would entertain us with songs; sometimes older people would sing their songs. Everywhere we met with the people, they sang their songs. Having been a song leader in our civil rights movement, I was asked to lead some of the gatherings in song. Occasionally we would sing a medley of our freedom songs.

As our delegation stood together, choir-like, facing a quite large gathering of South Africans who had come to meet, greet, and share with us, I got the idea of how interesting it might be to hear this diverse group of South Africans sing our theme song, now known in so many countries around the world. I asked the gathering for a show of hands if they knew the anthem of our movement, "We Shall Overcome." Most hands went up. On the spot I requested our delegation to hold back and just listen.

Top: A workshop in Japan with IFOR. Center: Me singing with students at the University of New England in the 1990s. Bottom: Singing at Highlander with Guy and Candie Carawan in 1997.

Then I requested the South African group to yell out the name of the most widely spoken language in their home area. I asked each group to sing the theme song of our American freedom struggle in their own language or dialect. I was excited with anticipation as each group began to sing our most popular movement song in their own language. One purpose of the journey was to compare our two freedom struggles to see what we might learn from each other. It was exhilarating to hear our anthem joyfully sung in each language separately and then simultaneously in those varied tongues or dialects.

I invited everyone gathered, including our U.S. congressional delegation, to blend their voices with our host group. I wish we'd had a video camera to capture this moment. It was a moving experience, all of us together in South Africa, expressing the same hopes, dreams, and affirmations as we had done across the American South.

In October 2006, I had the opportunity in Japan to repeat this experience. People from more than thirty countries gathered for the International Fellowship of Reconciliation (IFOR) conference. "We Shall Overcome" was sung in French, Swahili, Italian, German, English, Japanese, and other languages. First the song was sung in each language separately, then all together.

What an effective metaphor, I thought—singing the same song in different languages for a vision of a worldwide "beloved community." It flows beautifully with Dr. King's challenge when he spoke of our "learning to live together as brothers and sisters or perish together as fools." I am reminded of the great actor and singer Paul Robeson, who is noted to have said something like, *"If we learn to sing each other's songs, we will get to know and even like each other."*

I envision a time in which we will once again not be so tied to our to-do list that we will cheat ourselves of the love, joy, bonding, community, and freeing of the spirit that singing can provide. In Alabama, Mississippi, North Carolina, South Carolina, Florida, Virginia, Tennessee, and Georgia we sang because we had to. We discovered that singing together made us feel better and stronger — it was cathartic. Singing together again might give us hope and energize us to get involved in creating communities where we will all feel free to sing and rediscover the wonder-working power of music. We still are challenged by the need to learn how to relate to and accept one another — and the wonderful diversity on the planet.

Singing with Pete Seeger again in 1990 at the Omega Institute in Rhinebeck, New York.

With Dora McDonald, Dr. King's administrative assistant, at a celebration
of Dr. King's life. Me at the same event, teaching a song.

Being a victim, we learned, gets us nowhere; becoming open to discovering our own power moves us forward toward the good. Feeling like a victim tends to bring on a diminished view of one's self. You've probably heard that people treat you according to the way you see yourself, what you project. Think again about the effect my question had on the entire group when I challenged a participant who constantly complained about how the city hall clerk treated her: "Well, why aren't you the clerk?" This participant thought the session was about changing the clerk's behavior, rather than how she could refocus the situation and become the clerk herself. My question turned her thinking around and made a powerful difference for the training group. No one seemed stooped any longer.

So I ask here, *What's next for our country? For the world? The same old questions and the same old answers?* No! That just won't do! A twenty-first-century Citizenship Education Program approach, combining lessons from the historic movement with modern technology and new ways of seeing and understanding our problems and challenges, just might be the answer.

Let's think about it—together. Let's talk!

Tavis Smiley, attorney Clarence Jones, me, Harry Belafonte, and
Cornel West standing on the balcony of the Lorraine Motel on April 4, 2008,
forty years after Dr. King was struck in this same spot. We were looking
in the direction from where the bullet came.

EPILOGUE

Going Forward in the Twenty-first Century

Citizenship Education for the Twenty-first Century

One of the participants in one of our five-day CEP workshops, a man from Atlanta, told me that he was going to go home and run for office. I noticed, though, that in the next elections I didn't see that he had run. I ran into him not too long afterward in the grocery store and I asked him, "What happened?" He said, "I was scared I'd win."

What he needed was a follow-up course to build up his confidence not only to run but to handle the job once he won. I think many people today need CEP training, not exactly like what we conducted in the 1960s, but something appropriate for today's challenges. This would include taking individuals into the halls of government to see the process firsthand and therefore understand it. It would include such things as electronic organizing tools. It would include focused intense description and analysis of twenty-first century problems.

A Black man has now reached the highest office in the land. And it's important to note, I think, that before he became an elected of-ficial and then president, he was an organizer. There are many posi-

297

tions for public servants to fill between running for, let's say, a school board and the presidency. And good people need to pursue them. You might have heard of the young African American man who said, when Senator Barack Obama won the White House, "I used to say 'the Man's got to do right by me or else.'" The "Man" he referred to was the White man, almost any White man. But when Mr. Barack Hussein Obama was elected president of what has come to be seen as the greatest country in the world, the young Black guy said, "Gosh, I can't blame 'the Man' anymore because now *I'm* 'the Man.'" I flash back here to the signs carried by the Memphis sanitation workers when they went on strike. Their signs said in big bold letters, I AM A MAN!

The young African American fellow who said, "Now *I'm* 'the Man'" says it all, in a larger sense. No longer can he wait for "the Man" to fix what's wrong. No longer can he blame "the Man" without blaming himself. Therefore, my vision is that as this newly identified man claims his role, he will begin to prepare himself to embark on the next leg of our freedom journey.

Many hundreds of us in various organizations gave our energy to a particular leg of the journey—tearing down walls that shut us out, unlocking doors that kept us out, erasing tapes that programmed us to think so little of ourselves that we lived as victims in what was not yet a democracy. These various organizations were the NAACP, CORE, SNCC, the Urban League, and my own SCLC, led by Martin Luther King Jr., as well as many other less well-known groups. The people making up these organizations gave much on the leg of the journey that brought us to where we are today—even to the White House, to this officeholder touted as "leader of the free world." Barack Obama knows of the shoulders on which he stands. I honor President Obama and even wrote a song with some friends applauding his decision to run for this high office. I see him as hardworking, with the correct vision and the right spirit for the job. President Obama's election as president brought us to the next leg of an incredible journey.

WHY WAS OBAMA BORN?

Tell me, tell me, why was Obama born?
Tell me, tell me, why was Obama born?
Somebody had to take a stand,
Somebody had to offer a new plan,
Somebody had to say, "Yes we can!"
That's why Obama was born,
My Lordy, that's why Obama was born.

Tell me, tell me, why was Obama born?
Tell me, tell me, why was Obama born?
Somebody had to inspire our youth,
Somebody had to hear every voice,
Somebody had to tell the truth,
That's why Obama was born,
My Lordy, that's why Obama was born.

Tell me, tell me, why was Obama born?
Tell me, tell me, why was Obama born?
Somebody had to say, "Let's stop the crime!"
Somebody had to turn things around,
Somebody had to say, "Now is the time!"
That's why Obama was born,
My Lordy, that's why Obama was born.

Tell me, tell me, why was Obama born?
Tell me, tell me, why was Obama born?

Somebody had to be a new kind of leader,
Somebody had to reach across the water,
And we must do it for our sons and daughters,
That's why Obama was born,
I tell you, that's why Obama was born.

Tell me, tell me, why was Obama born?
Tell me, tell me, why was Obama born?
Somebody had to say, "It's time for change,"
Somebody had to make the message plain,
Somebody had to say, "Let's work together,"
That's why Obama was born,
My Lordy, that's why Obama was born.

Tell me, tell me, why was Obama born?
Tell me, tell me, why was Obama born?
Somebody had to continue the fight,
Somebody had to shine a brighter light,
Somebody must show Martin was right!
That's why Obama was born,
My Lordy, that's why Obama was born.

That's why Obama was born, my Lordy,
That's why Obama was born.

—PARAPHRASE BY DOROTHY COTTON,
    WITH HELP FROM SOME FRIENDS,
    OF "WHY WAS A DARKIE BORN?,"
    A SONG HEARD IN MISSISSIPPI IN 1961

I wrote these lyrics with some friends during his campaign. I feel gratitude and pride in what he brought to the campaign and the confidence and wisdom he shows in conducting the business of the office, including the selection of various members of his team. My prayer is that vestiges and paradigms from a prior time will not allow those who are still shocked that an African American man won the White House to win their negative struggle to bring him down.

Human beings have from the beginning of time sensed that there is something larger than ourselves. And if we open up to this larger aspect of our being, we are empowered in a very special way. This sense of knowing is a major reason why we activists in our civil rights struggle continue to give ourselves to the movement. We were transformed in our knowledge and commitment from being victims to claiming our power.

I think back now and wish my dad could have caught the spark of the movement and realized that change in his circumstance, his consciousness, could indeed happen. Massive numbers of people, ordinary people, did catch a spark, creating this powerful movement for change that rearranged the social order in our country. I know we would be even more motivated now. In the CEP training sessions, the most powerful lesson was *Change is possible.*

Former farmworkers, cotton pickers, sharecroppers, and domestic workers, many of whom had felt locked into their social and economic lot in life, began to envision a new life, a life of civic engagement, of possibilities. That's why we can hear Fannie Lou Hamer, an eighth-grade graduate, at the Democratic National Convention asking with great power and confidence, "Is this America?" This sharecropper's voice was heard by people from every educational and social stratum of society, not only in the Mississippi Delta but throughout the country. Many flocked to follow her lead, including college students, teachers, businessmen and businesswomen, preachers, nuns, and priests. Hollywood actors and popular singers like Harry Belafonte took note of activists like Mrs. Hamer and Bernice Johnson Reagon of the Freedom Singers and provided material and moral support, as well as special opportunities such as international travel. Initiators and innovators such as these and many hundreds more in all the southern and border states were our CEP graduates.

I recently asked Andy Young to share his sense of the long-range impact of this grassroots training program that we conducted together with a small team. The CEP was so basic to the preparation, motivation, participation, and commitment of civil rights movement activists. Andy says that he often encounters children of our CEP graduates. Their offspring have a deep curiosity and ask good and useful questions. This is not surprising, because the adults who spent time in the five-day sessions with us were clearly changed people— changed in a way that would affect their children. Yet there are the offspring of others who say, "I couldn't have done what my parents did. No way!"

I say, however, that if they had lived at the same time as we did, our world would have been their world and they would have done what the time and the situation commanded. If they had been a part of our world, they would have done what we had to do. Yes, *had to do,* or else live as victims all our lives. This line from a popular and very useful song fit the moment, expressed the determination *we* felt. As was always the case, we had a song to answer every question, to summarize every mood and challenge any situation. Whether spoken or simply activated, this title and first line captures the experience referred to: *"I'm gonna do what the spirit says do!"* I'm convinced young people today would have done what we did. They would have been caught up in the spirit of the time. There were untold numbers of changed lives. The changes pointed the way to a new and different future. Toward today's world.

Any modern-day freedom struggle, I believe, could well be initiated by a younger generation, with seasoned activists sharing their experiences with those open to it. We could bring our knowledge to generations who are coming after us here and abroad. Younger activists will not have to tear down the walls and doors that shut out my generation from basic human rights, but this does not mean that vestiges of the old paradigms do not still exist. They do, even if they are not as blatant. It's like raking leaves and having to go over the area again to clear out stragglers that resisted being caught up in the rake. I see our movement as a continuing journey toward the goal of freedom and true democracy. Younger generations may not know our song "How We Got Over," which was sung so powerfully by Mahalia Jackson, but this statement expresses the way many of my generation feel and think of our freedom struggle. It is a song of my generation. We have the responsibility of sharing the reservoir of knowledge and experience that we carry and that made us who we are.

So, as this younger generation moves forward, they can learn from what we did and how we did it, but they will also need to create their own models for engagement. I don't believe there is a point at which we can truly say, "It is done." Perhaps we also have an awareness that we are an evolving species on the planet, and that when one is giving energy in a movement for positive change, as needed today, it will require a very special faith that *a change is gonna come*, as Sam Cooke sang so powerfully.

Moreover, we can no longer live isolated from people in other countries. The horrible event of 9/11 should have taught us that.

A SENSE of Spirit prevailed in the era of the civil rights movement. I'm often asked, so long after the main events, what that was like.

This Spirit was and still is an energizing force that held us together and propelled us forward. This force still exists today, even forty-five years since our coming together. When I see or hear from Lula, J.T., Andy, Vincent, C.T., and so many others, what held us together looms large in my consciousness and theirs.

Whether our respective beliefs are rooted in religious faith or not, the Spirit, as I conceive it, is a God Force. And that is what bonded us as a team. The Deity is expressed in different ways by different faith traditions: God by the Christians, Allah by the Muslims, and so on. But the animating principle and energy that flows from our commonly shared values is healing, positive, and caring.

THE PRESIDENT AND MRS. OBAMA

cordially invite you to

THE WHITE HOUSE

for a reception in honor of

DR. MARTIN LUTHER KING, JR.

AND THE

KING FAMILY

on Sunday, October 16, 2011

at two-thirty o'clock

Southeast Entrance

Please respond to
The Office of Public Engagement
The White House
at your earliest convenience
giving full name (first, middle, last),
gender, date of birth, social security number,
city and state of residence, and country of birth

africanamericans@who.eop.gov

ACKNOWLEDGMENTS

IT IS QUITE a challenge to recall and do justice to the friends and colleagues who provided important help to me in completing this book, but I shall try. First, Dr. Clay Carson, director of the King Papers Project at Stanford University, helped make concrete the idea that I shared about getting a book done about the role I played working with Dr. Martin Luther King Jr. in our great civil rights struggle in the 1960s. Clay invited me to spend a couple of months at Stanford University, where he began some basic interviews. It took me a year to gain enough confidence to commit to writing this book. It was at this time that Margo Hittleman worked with me to help get a book proposal completed. A special friend, Dr. Locksley Edmondson, saw the proposal and said it was "riveting." Good friend Joan Bokaer saw the proposal and voluntarily—without my knowledge—got it to an agent. The agent was Ellen Geiger of Frances Goldin Literary Agency. Ellen introduced me around, sharing my book proposal at several publishing houses, including Simon & Schuster. Stewart Burns, whom I had met at Stanford University, actually drove to Ithaca and spent three days working with me, which got me out of the stop-and-start mode. His encouragement continued.

Before any of this happened, Peg Michels of Civic Organizing Inc. in Minnesota regularly encouraged me to write my memoirs. She not only encouraged me but consistently reminded me that my work was an important contribution to our history. She even sought financial support for me, which resulted in a small grant from the Kellogg Foundation, and for which I'm very grateful. That grant provided the income that I needed to free me up to focus on the manuscript. I am deeply grateful for having a perceptive and encouraging friend in Peg Michels, and for the generosity of the Kellogg Foundation, to whom she introduced me.

A major reason this book exists is the major editing job done by Susan Carson and Joan Reid, movement scholars that they are. Not only did they spend an enormous amount of time editing the manuscript, but they regularly suggested important areas that I had overlooked. When Clay Carson, who is Susan's husband, had time to look at Joan's and Susan's editing work, his input at that point again was invaluable. The feedback and editing help on individual chapters provided by three other members of the King Papers Project—Tenisha Armstrong, Madolyn Orr, and Sarah Overton—was also a much-needed contribution.

This book could not have been completed without the support, encouragement, and hands-on help of several friends in my hometown. Some of the team make up the steering committee of the Dorothy Cotton Institute: Anke Wessels, Kirby Edmonds, and Margo Hittleman, all of whom provided important support at many levels. It was Anke who in 2007 brought to me the idea of establishing a Dorothy Cotton Fellowship to support individuals engaged in nonviolent social change work. Anke also introduced me to her daughter, Rachel Bayer, who brought important organizing and computer skills to the project. Very special thanks are due to Kirby Edmonds, who identified my need for continuing hands-on computer help. Kirby's sensitivity to this need resulted in my having the full-time help of Clariluz "Lucy" Tapia, whose competency with the computer was a special gift. Lucy also brought to the task special, much-needed editing and organizing skills, and saw the project almost to the end, at which time she left to work on an advanced degree.

I am deeply grateful to my editor, Malaika Adero, at Atria Books. Malaika, very early on, saw the value in my story, accepted my project, and provided very specific ideas and suggestions for what would make the message of this book more clear and readable. Her manuscript editing skills are first-class. My confidence grew as she provided the help I needed to tell my story. Her skill and close work with me to the end showed a deep commitment to this project. Malaika's belief that this book would be a worthy contribution to the history of the civil rights movement was crucial. I am indebted to her both for her skill and commitment—even once when I disagreed with a suggestion.

There are many whose regular words of encouragement kept me encouraged and energized on this long writing project. For all such people whose names are not found in these pages, I owe deep gratitude. The book could not have been brought to closure without your help.

LETTER TO MARTIN

Dear Martin,

How we miss you! We think about you every day and often wonder how you would feel about how we're doing—we, your team, your close friends and coworkers. I know you must be curious as to whether we are moving closer to "the Promised Land" that you spoke of on your last night with us. So I thought I'd write a letter to you providing a brief report. Anyway, I know you always wanted to know what we were doing and how we were doing in our part of the work. Actually, I always enjoyed it when I had the opportunity to give a Citizenship Education report, especially at an SCLC board meeting. I think about how you used to listen quietly and intently to us discuss our projects—what we were currently doing and how various work projects were progressing. I remember how you would listen to all of us around the conference table vigorously debate how our various projects were going, as well as ideas and suggestions as to what our organization should be responding to—what we should do next. This would always seem to include assessing which part of the region—especially in the southern and border states—most needed you and your team. As you know, there were always—simultaneously—several "hot spots" in our freedom struggle—people wanting us to come to their area to help them. As you will remember, we used to sing a song that spoke to this: "The movement is a-movin' all over this land."

I remember how our debates were sometimes intense because although some of us were already working in areas with the local freedom fighters, there were other places that were still pleading for us to come, and we had to actually get them ready for you to come in. Every area wanted you! They wanted you as their local struggle intensified. Our Citizenship Education work intensified the locals' desire to have you there with us. I remember you saying once that you couldn't be everywhere at the same time. We all knew that when an area was ready, it would be obvious to us—your team—when it was time to bring you in. I still remember how you would listen to us debate where you should go next. We saw you listen respectfully to all of our views before you would decide to which area you would respond. After all, every area wanted you! Not to flatter you, but you had your own way of synthesizing the various aspects of an expressed need for *you* to go into an area. You always knew when it was time for you to go. You would listen to our reports of what we were facing as we worked in various communities across the South; for me, I could make my determination based on the energy people brought to a CEP session. I noticed, too, how you responded to direct invitations from the locals. I smile even now, all these years later, when I reflect on how intensely you would listen to all the views and on your skill in bringing us all together around a unified decision when you decided to speak. I learned much from your leadership style.

Well, what are we seeing since you left us? Actually, your presence, your "spirit," is so strongly felt—not only here in our own country but in many countries around the world. As I have had the opportunity to travel in many countries, I'm confident that people everywhere know of your work; I see roads, buildings, and massive numbers of programs named after you. Though I know you would never seek praise and honor for your work, it is happening. I hope you can take some comfort in this. I am convinced that people need leadership; people need a voice that makes clear the goal of a movement and that can bring insight and clarity to help them articulate problems and situations that need correction. Everywhere people are inspired by your presence, your work. You brought the much-needed voice that helped the people feel confident their cause—our cause—was just.

Your birthday has become a national holiday! And I traveled around the country with Coretta as she led the commission to bring her dream for you and our powerful movement into reality. I remember a conversation between you and Coretta when she wanted to make your birth home a special visitor's center and you responded to her, "Corey"—as you affectionately called her sometimes—"that's something you do after someone dies." Well, guess what?! Not only is your birthday a national holiday, there is a thirty-foot statue of your likeness installed on the National Mall in our nation's capital. How about that?! I cried as I had my picture taken in front of your likeness. I felt your energy as I stood there; I felt your spirit and your dedication to our cause—a great cause demanding justice for everyone. Many of the wise and perceptive things you said when you were here are carved around the very large pavilion and I watched people writing them down. Much of what you said when we worked together is written on my heart, so I did not write as I noted what was carved in stone. But I'm convinced that families, classes from schools and universities, as well as tourists from many other countries will have a rich experience when they come to our capital to visit you there.

Since I get asked to give speeches about you, your legacy, and our freedom struggle, I came up with some specific reasons as to why you are so honored. I'd like you to know that I have written many pages relative to these reasons. I love to share with audiences why our country and other countries, as well, celebrate your life and legacy. I've discovered that people are truly inspired by what you brought to the world. Once when I was traveling with Coretta to a city where she was scheduled to give a speech, she spoke of your commitment and your leadership. Since I was slated to introduce her, I decided to say some things about you and your work as well. I especially wanted to focus on why we celebrate you and your work. I'll mention briefly here several of the points I made in this regard. Actually, a tall blond man said before Coretta spoke that "we don't need another holiday." I was compelled to mention a few of the reasons we did indeed need a holiday—a reminder of the gifts you brought that helped us achieve our goal of tearing down the walls of segregation and the institutionalized abuse that went with it. Our nation has honored many who brought military skills to the scene. To have someone like you, who brought another way to bring peace and justice to the country and the world, was a much-needed contribution.

I'll share a few of the points I made before Coretta spoke. I'm energized as I summarize why your life and work are indeed worth celebrating. And I've shared these thoughts several times before putting them in this letter to you.

1. You were able to put into words what massive numbers of people were feeling—especially African Americans, who had been relegated to a status of less than citizens. Your skill in articulating our problems, our situation, our maltreatment, touched the young and the not so young, White Americans as well as African Ameri-

cans. You were poetic in the way you could challenge people to claim their rights as citizens.

2. You showed us a tool with which we could struggle for our freedom. This tool, of course, was nonviolence. Massive numbers of people—the old, the young, even the infirm—could use this tool and participate in our movement "to advance democracy." In your introducing such a tool, such a method for fighting for our rights, we found great excitement. You said to one of my CEP graduating classes, "Nobody can ride your back if your back's not bent." This was a powerful expression, a wonderful way to help people bring to consciousness that they did not have to live as victims. I took from your closing send-off speech to our graduates the title for my book, *If Your Back's Not Bent.* I saw a powerful transformation in the forty to sometimes sixty people who came to our Citizenship Education Program workshops—I saw the transformation that took place in them, and I know that what you said when you could be with us in our closing session helped further clear away any possible vestige of their being less than other citizens.

3. You pointed us in the direction we needed to go—building toward the "Beloved Community."

4. You helped make clear the relationship between ends and means. You said, "The ends you seek are preexistent in the means you use," an important aspect of nonviolence.

5. You showed us how this tool, this method of nonviolence, was indeed a "force more powerful."

As you know, our Citizenship Education Program was basic to ensuring we were indeed a movement knit together by a very special philosophy, a very special approach to working for change. Actually, we also know that the zeitgeist was upon our land and "we the people" had to play our role—you providing the necessary leadership and ordinary "grassroots" people by the thousands claiming their rights as citizens in this governing system called a democracy.

I wish I could ask you your thoughts on one wonderful manifestation of the success of our movement, but only a part of the success. That is that our country—birth defect notwithstanding—elected an African American as president of the United States! I'm convinced that the election of President Barack Hussein Obama is a direct result of the success of a major aspect of our freedom struggle. Though I know very well that we still have "miles to go before we sleep," it is important to realize and accept that the election of an African American as president of the United States of America is a major result and manifestation of the fact that change is possible—even in the most intransigent of situations, from not being allowed the right to vote to one of us being elected as "leader of the free world." There was a young African American man who said he can't blame "the Man" anymore for his situation because "now *I'm* 'the Man.'" I find this is just another way of realizing that even citizens who have been excluded from the mainstream of life in our country but who take note of this 2008 presidential election surely can undergo a powerful transformation in their thinking. Though our situations were different, I was also affected by a statement made by Mahatma Gandhi as he worked to energize the Indian people, challenging them to join the struggle to free themselves. Gandhi said, "The Brits did not take India from us; we gave it to them." Just as the oppressed people had to work to free themselves, so did we, African Americans here in the United States of America. I repeat what you said at one of my Citizenship Education closing programs: "Nobody can ride your back if your back's not bent."

Well, you taught us all to become smart enough to understand and internalize that "force more powerful"—nonviolence. Your teaching, preaching, and modeling a leadership that many try to emulate today will be a gift to the world always.

There's more, but I want to close this letter by referring to something that's going on now in our country and in other countries around the world. There is much anger in our midst right now. How I wish I could have a dialogue with you. An economic downturn is weighing heavily upon many thousands of families. Massive numbers of people are out of work and their houses are being foreclosed. There are many gatherings around the country and many participants in the Occupy Wall Street movement. Many are comparing it to the civil rights movement protests. People are camping in downtown areas and setting up tents in public spaces. Thousands are out of work and huge numbers of families cannot afford to pay for their children to go to college. Even high school costs are difficult for many families who cannot afford books and other supplies. But as I notice their actions, I've become conscious of the fact that no "program" is being put forth by the "occupiers." I know from what you brought to our movement that a program must be very clearly articulated to garner the kind of support needed for success. Just being angry is not enough. So I have become even more convinced that a voice or voices are needed to make clear the goals of their movement. You did this for our movement and did it so clearly and powerfully that people all over our country—all over the world—understood our goals. At that time we needed what you brought to our movement: your voice, your modeling, your teaching, your inspiration, your wisdom. Otherwise we might have appeared to be just a group of angry people. Some of us are finding ways to provide, we hope, some helpful input to the occupiers. I quoted in a speech recently at a program designed to celebrate your birthday something our team member James Bevel said to a participant in one of my workshops. When the man stood up to declare how he "jumped angry" when he was denied use of a gentlemen's restroom, James responded, "Don't jump angry, jump smart!"

Well, rest easy, my friend. You are a gift to the world. You enriched our lives. You are in the hearts of all of us who walked with you every day. We cry for missing you. Andy and I speak of you every time we are together. You are so present with us in a very deep way.

Your legacy is a gift to the world.

We love you, we miss you.

Your friend and team member,

Dorothy

THE DOROTHY COTTON INSTITUTE

THE JOURNEY CONTINUES. I often ponder Dr. King's question, "Where do we go from here?" I take that question literally and most seriously. Clearly we set some goals—a destination toward which we would aim. Some years ago I may have thought that after breaking down obvious barriers to freedom and justice, we might rest awhile. Rest we might, as long as we are aware that "we have miles to go before we sleep." Another way of saying or sharing what seems very clear to me now is that we have been on a journey and it started long before the leg on which I played a key role. My own section of this journey helped take us, Black and White, from an American-style apartheid to loosening the obvious shackles that bound us—that held us back from the doors of freedom. The shackles are broken and we can walk through many doors that were closed to us—mostly African Americans. But I also think of the White man who, observing our work, said, "If I had known Dr. King—and all of you working for change—if I had known you would succeed, I would have married the woman I loved." You get the point.

I have listed some challenges facing us today both here and abroad and I want to share with you a specific creation that colleagues and I are developing, based in Ithaca, New York—the Dorothy Cotton Institute (DCI). The story of our work for social and political transformation did not end in the 1960s.

In 2007, Anke Wessels, the executive director of the Center for Transformative Action (CTA) in Ithaca, began talking to me about the possibility of establishing a Dorothy Cotton Fellowship to support individuals engaged in nonviolent social change work. I invited a number of friends (Anke, Kirby Edmonds, Jack Roscoe, Cal Walker, Laura Branca, and Margo Hittleman) to my home to explore the idea. By the end of our very first meeting, the possibility of a fellowship in my name had blossomed into a vision for an institute. My friends and associates committed to becoming a steering committee and together we have become a project under CTA with an inspiring vision, a serious mission, and exciting programming.

We see ourselves

- Building and making visible the global movement for human rights.
- Fostering personal and collective transformation by increasing our knowledge of our rights, and by rethinking and redefining our relationship to our life situations and circumstances in ever more powerful, nonviolent ways.

Our global problems are serious, urgent, and life-threatening. We can turn on one another with self-interest, fear, and violence and wait for time to run out and for life systems to collapse, or we can work together. The human rights framework embraces all people and gives us an inspiring and compelling foundation for creating ethical relationships in all levels of community.

As education director of the SCLC, the cornerstone of my work was the Citizenship Education Program. The CEP was a powerful grassroots leadership strategy, focused on ordinary people living in the violent, untenable American-style apartheid, as I've often described it, of the segregated southern United States. In the CEP's intensive, potent, loving, life-affirming gatherings, people learned of their rights and uncovered and reclaimed their power. Participants left prepared to claim those rights, bring tools of liberation back to their communities, and ask their neighbors to join the movement seeking all of our rights. The DCI is bringing the wisdom and key principles of the CEP forward to the contemporary struggle for human rights.

Through peer learning communities, and through the experience of institute gatherings, people are already being invited to articulate problems, share stories and aspirations for a just and loving future, recognize that we are not alone, and find answers to questions such as *What do I want to see happen? How can I get that to happen? With whom can I join? How can I help and what can I offer?*

Thus far, the DCI has made education, leadership, and youth development high priorities. We offer fellowships to individuals who are working to find viable strategies for personal and collective transformation and empowerment, and, as Gandhi said, to *"be the change we want to see."* We have already been successful in bringing a K–12 human rights curriculum and framework into the Ithaca City School District, promoting the transformative principles of the CEP as a useful methodology to accompany the lesson plans, and to support building a culture of human rights in classrooms, schools, agencies, and communities. We offer opportunities to become familiar with the human rights framework and the practical strategies of the CEP to activists, educators, youth, and anyone organizing to create just, sustainable ways of living and solving problems.

Anyone who has spent time with me knows that I use songs and stories to help people connect on a heart level to the spirit that motivates and lifts us in our work together. We recognize the transformative power of storytelling and its place in the journey toward a beloved community and the realization of full human rights. In the future, the Dorothy Cotton Institute will have the capacity to celebrate, preserve, and transmit the personal testimonies of social change and liberation, one story at a time. We are working toward creating a multiuse facility that can house permanent and changing exhibits, and performance, gathering, and meeting spaces. We also hope to provide fellows and small groups with retreat space for reflection, nurture, study, writing, and planning in peaceful, wholesome, and uplifting environments.

The human rights framework is more effective for understanding pressing social problems than others because it encompasses civil, economic, cultural, political, and environmental rights—the universal rights of all people. A sense of our common humanity emerges in this framework, something larger than self, in which we all belong and are interconnected. We have inalienable rights by virtue of simply being human, regardless of who we are or where we live. We are all diminished when the rights of any are violated. We will thrive as individuals and as a collective when all our rights are protected and respected. The movement for human rights is a story about all of us, opening up a space for beloved community.

Our Vision

The Dorothy Cotton Institute envisions the full realization of a just and peaceful beloved community, in which all people understand, respect, protect, and exercise full human rights. We believe that with a global community of human rights leadership, and a well-informed, inspired, and motivated population, in the United States and elsewhere, the goal of human rights for all can be achieved.

To achieve this vision, we are adopting a multistrategy, multilevel, multigenerational approach to inspire, inform, and support change efforts, promote transformative practices, and foster a beloved community of global civil and human rights leadership. Our work derives from a theory of change that is based on the principles that enabled the Citizenship Education Program to serve as the educational infrastructure that made the civil rights movement as successful as it was.

Our Mission

- To develop, nurture, and train leaders for a global human rights movement.
- To build a network and community of civil and human rights leadership.
- To explore, share, and promote practices that transform individuals and communities, opening new pathways to peace, justice, and healing.

For more information about the DCI, visit www.dorothycotton institute.org.